K. C. K. Junior College Library
824 State Avenue

JOHN DEWEY

Makers of the American Tradition Series

General Editors

HIRAM HAYDN

DONALD BIGELOW

Volumes Ready:

Volumes in Preparation:

Volumes Planned:

JOHN DEWEY

His Contribution to the
American Tradition

IRWIN EDMAN

Makers of
the American
Tradition

THE BOBBS-MERRILL COMPANY, INC.
Publishers
INDIANAPOLIS   NEW YORK

To
JOHN HERMAN RANDALL, JR.,
DEWEYAN AND ARISTOTELIAN

GENERAL INTRODUCTION
FOR THE
Makers of the American Tradition Series

THE PURPOSE of this series is to present in a fresh and challenging way the great figures of the American tradition—those individuals who have been most influential throughout the history of the American people in forging that strong and yet complex phenomenon that constitutes what we call the American tradition or the American way of life.

Countless books have been written about these men; a good many books containing their writings and speeches have been published; many biographies of them have appeared. But the *Makers of the American Tradition* Series is a genuinely new approach to the story of our heritage. These books are not biographies; they are not anthologies. They are a combination of original text and interpretation. They embody a new and fresh approach because they combine the best and most characteristic of the original written and recorded spoken words of outstanding American figures with thoughtful and incisive interpretations by the distinguished scholars chosen to put these books together.

In each volume the focus is upon those elements in the contributions of these Americans—whether in terms of original thought or articulate and decisive leadership—which best characterize the *particular* quality, in each case, of the contribution. All other aspects of, say, Benjamin Franklin or Andrew Jackson or Roger Williams are in these books subordinated to what each had most peculiarly to contribute to the shaping of the American tradition.

When we speak of the American tradition, we are, of course, referring to a complex of various and sometimes opposing traditions, but if there is any single outstanding American principle, I suppose that it is that of the finding of unity through multiplicity and diversity. The American tradition, a composite in itself, is analogous to the United States and the American people, each being a complex of many simples.

Similarly, when we speak of the *makers* of this tradition, we are, of course, aware that no ten or twenty or fifty men, however talented, however able, really *made* this tradition. Nevertheless, the individuals we have chosen as the subjects for these books seem to us to have been outstandingly important in shaping the way of life that is our heritage today. Hence, just as we welcome in the American tradition its superficially strange mixture of radical idealism and plain horse sense, of a general love of liberty and a sober sense of social responsibility, of honest conservatism and honest dissidence, so we welcome in this series such conflicting disparate figures as Thomas Jefferson and Alexander Hamilton, Roger Williams and John C. Calhoun, Cotton Mather and John Dewey.

For whom is this series intended? It is our hope and belief that it is intended for every literate American of whatever age and description. For we are firmly convinced that the books in this series will leave their readers with a far more concise and exact idea of what the great leaders of the American people have thought, said and stood for, than they have ever had before.

Much has been made and is being made of the confusion and anxiety under which all of us labor today. Much has been said in various ways of the extent to which all people, and among them notably Americans, are searching for their souls. Much has been said about both the external and internal threats to our American way of life—threats that many Americans, with whatever different interpretations, feel surround us on all sides. We are faced unquestionably with the challenge of building a free and confident America, for ourselves and for the free world in our time.

In a time of crisis, how may we find that strength and that confidence? The editors feel that it is a constant in human nature at such times to turn inward, to return to one's roots, one's origins, to find such resources. They believe this to be as true for peoples as for individuals. The ideal of self-knowledge as a source of strength and confidence does not imply a selfish or extravagant preoccupation with self. Rather, a time of crisis calls for an examination and appraisal of one's own resources in order to turn one's attention outward again, freshened and fortified by a new inner sureness. As Americans, we can best effect this self-examination, we can best find our true origins, by returning to the words and thoughts of those individuals who have contributed most mightily to our enduring strength. And since most of us lack the special training that would enable us to move unaided with ease in the social and intellectual context of another time, we solicit the help of such people as those who are making the books in this series—individual author-editors whom we have chosen for breadth and depth of knowledge and for generosity of mind and spirit—that they may the better guide us, through these books, in our self-examination.

HIRAM HAYDN
DONALD BIGELOW

FOREWORD

IT SHOULD BE MADE clear that the contents of this volume of writings selected from the works of John Dewey, though extensive in one sense at least, are not intended to be comprehensive. As editor I have tried to keep in mind the context of the series in which this book appears. I have taken most seriously the phrase "Makers of the American Tradition" and believe deeply that John Dewey will, in the long future, be regarded as one of the makers of that tradition. The criteria for selection of material in this book have relevance to this sovereign theme. In order to understand the contributions that John Dewey has made to the remaking of American ideas and institutions it is necessary, of course, to understand his general philosophical position, his conception of method and of the relation of philosophy to civilization. There is much in Dewey of special concern to technical students in the various fields of philosophy, logic, theory of knowledge, and ethics, in which Dewey made considerable contributions. Some technical analysis must be studied in Dewey in order to understand his general position, and such basic materials are included in this book, but only such as are needed for the intention of this volume.

It should be added also that, though it has not been a controlling consideration, readability has been taken into account. John Dewey's style—or lack of it—has often, and not without justice, been adversely criticized. But on occasion he did write with edge, eloquence and razor sharpness, as some of the pages in this book will attest. For the most part, the passages are not fragments or snippets, but complete chapters.

Whatever the criteria of selection, the choice of passages from the enormous body of Dewey's writings, prolifically produced in a life of ninety-two years, is not easy. It would have been impossible for me without the great erudition and helpful and industrious counsel of my friend Professor H. S. Thayer, now assistant professor of philosophy at Barnard College, Columbia University. I cannot adequately express my appreciation for his extraordinary helpfulness. I should like simply to say here that Dr. Thayer ought properly to be regarded as a full-fledged partner in this enterprise.

Acknowledgment is herewith made, with thanks, to the following publishers for permission to quote from the following works by John Dewey: Yale University Press, *A Common Faith;* G. P. Putnam's Sons, "Freedom and Culture" and "Creative Democracy" in *The Philosophy of the Common Man;* Henry Holt & Company, *Human Nature and Conduct* and *Logic: the Theory of Inquiry;* The Beacon Press, *Reconstruction in Philosophy;* The Macmillan Company, *Democracy and Education.*

IRWIN EDMAN

Columbia University
June 21, 1954

CONTENTS

CHRONOLOGY
AND SELECTED BIBLIOGRAPHY

1859—Born, Burlington, Vermont, October 20.

1879—Graduated from University of Vermont.

1882—Dewey's first publication: "The Metaphysical Assumptions of Materialism," *Journal of Speculative Philosophy*, April 1882.

1882-1884—Graduate studies at Johns Hopkins University. Ph.D. 1884.

1884-1888—Instructor in Philosophy, University of Michigan.

1888-1889—Teaching philosophy at the University of Minnesota.

1889-1894—Professor and Head of the Department of Philosophy, University of Michigan.

1894-1904—Professor of Philosophy and Pedagogy, University of Chicago.

1897—*My Pedagogic Creed*, E. L. Kellog & Co., New York.

1899—*Psychology and Philosophic Method*, University of California Press, Berkeley.

1900—*The School and Society*, University of Chicago Press (Revised edition, 1915), Chicago.

1902-1904—Director of School of Education, University of Chicago. Development of The Laboratory School. Association with Hull House.

1903—*Studies in Logical Theory*, University of Chicago Press, Chicago.
Logical Conditions of a Scientific Treatment of Morality, University of Chicago Press, Chicago.

1904-1931—Professor of Philosophy, Columbia University. Also teaching at Teachers College, Columbia University.

1908—*Ethics* (with James H. Tufts), Henry Holt & Co. (Revised edition, 1932), New York.

1910—*The Influence of Darwin on Philosophy and Other Essays in Contemporary Thought*, Henry Holt & Co., New York.

How We Think, Heath & Co. (Revised edition, 1933), New York.

1916—*Democracy and Education*, The Macmillan Co., New York.

Essays in Experimental Logic, University of Chicago Press, Chicago.

1917—*Creative Intelligence* (Dewey and others), Henry Holt & Co., New York.

1919—Lectures at Tokyo Imperial University, Japan; National Universities of Peking and Nanking, China.

1920—*Reconstruction in Philosophy*, Henry Holt & Co., New York. (Revised edition, Beacon Press, Boston, 1949.)

1922—*Human Nature and Conduct*, Henry Holt & Co., New York.

1925—*Experience and Nature*, Open Court Publishing Co., Chicago.

1927—*The Public and Its Problems*, Henry Holt & Co., New York.

1928—Trip to Russia.

1929—*The Quest for Certainty*, Minton, Balch & Co., New York.

1930-1939—Professor Emeritus of Philosophy in Residence, Columbia University.

1931—*Philosophy and Civilization*, Minton, Balch & Co., New York.

1934—*Art as Experience*, Minton, Balch & Co., New York. *A Common Faith*, Yale University Press, New Haven.

1935—*Liberalism and Social Action*, G. P. Putnam's Sons, New York.

1937—Chairman of the Commission of Inquiry into the charges against Leon Trotsky at the Moscow trials.

1938—*Experience and Education,* The Macmillan Co., New York.

1939—*Freedom and Culture,* G. P. Putnam's Sons, New York.
Theory of Valuation, International Encyclopedia of Unified Science, University of Chicago Press, Chicago.
Intelligence in the Modern World (edited by Joseph Ratner), The Modern Library, New York.

1946—*Problems of Men,* Philosophical Library, New York.

1949—*Knowing and the Known* (with Arthur F. Bentley), The Beacon Press, Boston.

1952—Died, June 1.

JOHN DEWEY

I ✦ Introduction

THIS volume appears in a series called "Makers of the American Tradition." One uses that term securely when one refers to Thomas Jefferson or Benjamin Franklin. It seems hasty, perhaps, or overconfident to apply the epithet to a philosopher who died only a few years ago, though at the age of ninety-two. But for a half century now, both those who have agreed and those who have disagreed with the major views of John Dewey have recognized in him a force to be dealt with, a leader to follow or to counter, a thinker to affirm or rebut. For better (as many thousands have believed), for worse (as some articulate critics have insisted), Dewey is being recognized now as one of the fashioners or refashioners of contemporary thinking, not simply among professional circles of philosophers but in law, education and art.

John Dewey was born in 1859, the year of the publication of *The Origin of Species* by Charles Darwin, by whom Dewey was later to be much influenced in his philosophic thinking. This child of rural Vermont was to become in this country the voice of scientific method, of disciplined inquiry as the chief agency and instrument of freedom in the complex industrial society of our time.

To describe Dewey as a maker of twentieth-century America, or a remaker of it, implies, of course, certain general assumptions as to the influences of ideas on history. It might be said that, if Dewey is recognized as a peculiarly American philosopher, it is because he caught the voice, accent and temper of the American tradition and the nature of the special contingencies and choices before it in his own era. He did not, it may be argued, make the tradition, or, for that matter, remake it. The expanding forces of technology, the intervolvement of public and private affairs, the rising tides of the labor movement, the revolt against authoritarianism in religion and in education—all of these play a large part in and color his social philosophy—were, it may be argued, themes he translated into general terms of philosophical analysis; they were *not* consequences of his published ideas.

Dewey would be the first to admit—more than that, to insist—that philosophers in their generalized thinking are expressing the deep conflicts and uncertainties within their native civilization. Apart from what those who knew him personally were constantly impressed with—his extraordinary personal modesty—he would in any case have questioned whether one man's ideas could have anything like a decisive effect on the direction of a culture or a nation. Yet the arresting fact is that not only the friends of his thinking but some of its severest critics attest to the extraordinary influence that John Dewey had on our time in America, most directly on education but also indirectly on the whole liberal tradition in politics, in jurisprudence, in the practice even of writers and artists, and most especially through his effect on education.

It is John Dewey himself, incidentally, who, in his central work, *Democracy and Education*, assures us that philosophical differences matter only where they make a difference in educational practice. On that basis alone, again for better or worse, John Dewey's philosophy has had phenomenal influence on America, for everything that is associated with the transformation of education from mere passive learning of the three Rs to education as shared living, everything that is associated with the modern trend in education, the emphasis on education as social and as an experience of shared life (including that virtual parody of Dewey's ideas, the extreme forms of progressive education), is directly or obliquely the consequence of Dewey's ideas. Moreover, to Dewey's inspiration may be credited the whole tendency of modern legal thinking to turn from abstract principles to the estimation of law in terms of the consequences of law on human lives. And, latterly, the more surprising in the light of the fact that Dewey is so often labeled as a pragmatist and instrumentalist is his influence on aesthetics and criticism, which he has done much to take out of the hands of the formalists and semantic and scholastic pedants and reclaim for the exploratory imagination.

It is one of the paradoxes of American culture that this philosopher's philosopher—for his effect on technical philosophy was widespread and his reformulating of philosophical issues impressive to his professional colleagues—should have had so extraordinary a repercussion on American affairs, so that his influence should have been testified to by no less eminent a legal thinker than Justice Oliver Wendell Holmes, so celebrated a labor leader as Walter Reuther, and by practicing teachers all over the world. John Dewey's prose was not easy to read, even by other philosophers habituated to abstract discourse. He lacked the pungency and picturesqueness of William James, the elegance and imagery of Santayana. His language was—for all his emphasis on fact, experience and experiment—full of abstractions. Though he seldom used esoteric words, to the general reader the effect was often esoteric, and the style often lumbering and bumbling.

Yet on occasion, it must be added, he could write an edged and pointed aphorism—"The saint sits in his ivory tower while the burly sinners run the world"—or make even a technical point of logic poetic. The subject in a logical proposition is "the theme of an intellectual gesture, the object of a cognitive regard." His prose, however, as these selections will attest, gives the sovereign effect of a mind genuinely exploring, a spirit inquiring without prejudice

and generous without tears. Nor could John Dewey's influence be ascribed without qualification to his effect on students later to become his propagandizing disciples. He had
pupils who in turn became well-known intellectual leaders,
but the mystery lies in *how* he affected these men. About his
writings, about his speech, there was nothing electrically
contagious nor, at first, freshly enlightening. To someone
who had complained, in a group containing several of his
promising young pupils, that his philosophy dedicated to
democracy was written in a jargon unintelligible to many
literate people, he said, "Let some of these young men explain me: it will make a career for some of them." It did.

This is not the first time in intellectual history that a great
and original thinker has influenced many who could not be
expected to read him at firsthand. But future leaders in the
legal and teaching professions, in social work and government, who were John Dewey's pupils were certainly not influenced, if they heard him first in lecture courses, by any
strikingly revealing utterances, any immediate patency of
sharp analysis, any contagion of rhetoric or, except on rare
occasions, any special felicity of phrase. It remains indeed
one of the sociological paradoxes of American culture why
and how a technician among philosophers should have influenced thought so much more widely than in philosophical circles and why a man, by the usual outward, visible
signs not a good—and indeed by all conventional criteria
a poor—teacher, should have so deeply inspired and
remade the thinking of crucial individuals in all the professions, teaching above all.

The answer to this apparent enigma is not too hard to
find. The fact is that Dewey, as those of us who were his
pupils remember very vividly, in his very hesitations, his
very ignoring of the demands of an audience—that they be
entertained, kept in suspense—these very things emphasized what his discourse positively displayed: the phenomenon of a man patiently thinking, exploring, suggesting,

developing and testing ideas. In a seminar this was even more striking, and of one of these seminars I can speak at firsthand. Its members were, many of them, destined to be variously eminent—like Brand Blanshard, the Yale philosopher, and Albert C. Barnes, already widely known but destined to be even more widely known for his book *The Art in Painting* (a work in aesthetics which on every page betrays Dewey's influence), and Brand Blanshard's brother Paul, long active in liberal politics. The individuals in this seminar felt in Dewey the mark of the true teacher, one who did not lay down dogmas but co-operatively helped to elicit from his students fresh hypotheses and also helped them both to develop and discipline these. He was a master of initiating independent thinking in his pupils.

Who was this man whose central "theory of thinking as inquiry" was to do so much to reshape American ideas and to sharpen issues even for men like Robert Hutchins, who disagreed with him? He was the first decadent, he once jokingly put it, in seven generations of Vermont farmers. He was born in Burlington, Vermont, in 1859 and grew up there to attend the University of Vermont in his native town. He studied further at Johns Hopkins, where he took his doctor's degree. He taught briefly at Michigan, and then, before he came to Columbia University in 1904, for several years at the University of Chicago. It was at the latter institution that he and Mrs. Alice Freeman Dewey, his first wife, founded their experimental school, in which they tried out and found verification for some of Dewey's central ideas: of the relation of theory to practice, of life to society, of means to ends.

Dewey all his life retained something of the simplicity of the nineteenth-century world of individuality and of fair play, of firsthand respect for firsthand experience that was characteristic of the nineteenth-century Vermonters among whom he grew up. For all his recognition of the complex changes science and industry and international commerce

were making in the twentieth century, he retained a paramount sense of the individual, and the private dignity of
the individual, that had been the themes of Thoreau and
Emerson in the nineteenth century. He had the slowness
of speech and the sharpness of perception of the weathered
Vermonter. Nearly all his life he spent in universities; yet he
early had become aware that schools are a function of society, and he spent not a small part of his own life becoming
acquainted with that society outside of schools, in adult
education, in labor movements, in what was happening in
science and government and industry, among plain people
and artists.

His fame became world-wide. He was invited to China,
where he spent two years following World War I teaching
at the University of Peking, and at the Imperial University
of Tokyo, where he gave a series of lectures of which his
book entitled *Reconstruction in Philosophy* was a consequence. He visited Russia, with which, long before a great
many other liberals, he became drastically disillusioned. In
France a generation ago Dewey's philosophical rather than
his educational works were very widely known. But he remained to the end of his life, in his ninety-second year,
characterized by both a shrewd simplicity and an acute
awareness of the complicated new problems of men and
women in the twentieth century. He always "saw around"
the academy and felt that philosophy had its obligations to
that society in which it emerged and which it expressed,
and which it could help intelligently to transform itself,
to grow and change in the light of disciplined guiding
hypotheses, of which for him philosophy essentially consisted.

Yet it was a central idea that animated and controlled
Dewey's thinking. This was a conception of ideas themselves, their origin (in conflict), their development, their
effects. This crucial notion Dewey himself called "the pattern of inquiry": the unique activity of the human animal,

the activity of thinking. Pursued in a speculative direction as it ultimately was in *Experience and Nature* (1929), Dewey's theory of thinking led him into a generalized theory of experience itself, whose traits of security and precariousness, of stability and change, characterized that nature which was simply experience in its most generic form. In another direction Dewey traced the consequences of the critical activity of thought on all other activities, the exploration of new ways of life, the testing and critique of old ones. The whole of experience and of society is given meaning for Dewey just to the degree that individuals freely participate in the operations of inquiry, of imaginative hypothesis, of enlightened critical perception.

It was, one may say, a historical accident that Dewey became widely known as an educator long before he became equally widely influential as a professional philosopher. That accident, though it was an accident that conformed to Dewey's essential intent, was the turning of Dewey's attention to the testing of his philosophical ideas—as he later (in *Democracy and Education*) pointed out that such ideas always are tested—in education. Dewey's school became famous and so did a small book called *School and Society*, written by himself and his daughter Evelyn. So did a small volume written for and very widely used in normal schools and teacher-training colleges—*How We Think*, a handbook in thinking conceived of not as abstract dialectic in a vacuum but as the living process originating in human perplexities. It was a guide for teachers in that thinking which helps to solve human conflicts brought about by new situations colliding with old habits.

In the second decade of the twentieth century, Dewey's influence on education was epidemic. All forms of "progressive" education came to be associated with Dewey's name, including both the healthy reform of educational practice and the faddist excesses by which any new movement in any department of life is soon distorted. Dewey's revolt against authoritarian discipline came in certain quarters to be thought of as a plea for anarchy; the discovery that education was concerned with liberating the capacities and interests of the whole personality of the child was often thought to be—in some cultist followers of Dewey's ideas *was*—indeed a plea for an abandonment of respect for facts, discipline of method and rigorous study. Despite all this distortion by many of his critics and the exaggerations by some of his supposed followers, Dewey brought into the questions raised by both teaching and learning, first at the school and later at the college level, a reviving approach to education as a function of society, learning as an experience in growth and experience—like the acquiring of one's native speech—a mutual communication, a co-operation. At the school levels this view helped transform the rigidities of the old-fashioned martinet type of discipline and the tradition of learning by rote. At a more advanced level it was the source of that wide dissemination of the conception of "general education" and the new social studies which have so extensively affected the colleges and universities of this country. The breakdown of the isolation of school from society, of book learning from vital experience, of the individual from his environment—the extent to which schools and colleges have removed these separations is a measure of the direct impact of refreshing reconstruction of Dewey's thinking.

But if philosophy for Dewey was the most generalized form of a theory of thinking and of education, education, in the narrower sense, was for him merely a special case of philosophy. Dewey has been widely hailed as a prophet (or a corrupter) among teachers, but he was a teacher of philosophers, too, and his theories of teaching themselves were an expression of his more comprehensive philosophical approach. By the date of the publication of *Nature and Experience* in 1926 it was clear to the philosophers that here was a systematic and consistent approach to philosophy itself, below what had seemed episodic forays into the study of the psychology of thinking and the processes of education. But it had been clear to a good many philosophers long before *Experience and Nature* appeared that here were a new voice, a new mode and a new attitude in philosophy. Here were a point of view and a technique of analysis that needed to be reckoned with in the consideration of all the great traditional issues in philosophy, and a reconsideration of the function of philosophy in the future and of the part that it had played in civilizations in the past.

Dewey's theory of the nature of thought itself, that thinking which, simple or complex, entered into the smallest decisions and into the most abstruse metaphysical theorizing, implied a world view as had been clear ever since the publication of Dewey's *Studies in Logical Theory* in 1902. None who had read his *Reconstruction in Philosophy* (1917) could mistake his conception of philosophy, its past and its function. In Dewey's early logical studies he had revealed—as he had in an essay entitled *The Influence of Darwin on Philosophy*—that thinking is a kind of *activity,* as natural to the human animal as breathing or eating, as characteristic as any innate impulse or any other acquired habit. But thinking is an activity that profoundly modifies all other activities, those of habit and of impulse. Thinking is in the first instance the upwelling of a suggestion, an imaginative rehearsal, a leap into some envisioned possibility, an enactment—in imagination—of what may be done. In the light of this biological context of thought, Dewey reformulated the traditional elements of logic. Induction is seen by him as the focusing of facts with respect to the difficulties in the light of which thinking arises. What is called dialectic, or the formal development of an idea, is simply a setting forth in order of the elements already internal to a suggestion. What is called verification is really an experimental testing. An act of thought arises in the solution of a difficulty and its truth is tested by its veritable service in solving it.

This theory of thinking always assumed, in Dewey's mind, a conception as to the nature of experience itself, and the nature of those encountered conditions in which relevant inquiry takes place.

Most classical philosophies regard the universe as something fixed and eternal, as a stable order; nature as a static form, or interrelation of forms to be beheld, to be reflected as in a mirror, more or less faithfully and adequately, by the contemplating mind. But Dewey's conception of the nature of thinking implies in its very terms the notion of a universe which is always in process, always changing, in which time is real and in which time makes a constant difference, the difference being specific variations and change. These at the level of human action, within limits, matter of choice, are alternatives for deliberate determination. Thinking is an activity within—nay, a phase of that reality which is itself in constant process.

In many classical philosophies of the past, notably that of Immanuel Kant, the world of time, of change, and of the causes and effects discoverable in this domain, are appearance merely. Reality is composed of things beyond the vicissitudes and the casual relationships of time and space. In Plato, long before Kant, reality consisted of changeless essences, and the world of time and change was one that was mere illusion, mere opinion with respect to knowledge. To Dewey the reality *is* change, the universe is process, and one of the processes that goes on in that complex species known as man is the process of thinking itself, which intervenes in and to a certain extent can modify and control the changes and chances of existence. Man is a biological inhabitant of nature. He is not an alien in it, he is part of it, and Dewey points out that his thinking is native to it, too. The last three centuries of the development of physical science and the mastery of physical forces in the interest of human purposes, themselves natural, are witness to the immense power of thinking—ingenious, inventive and imaginative to the realization in practice of possibilities first imagined, projected, dreamed of, implemented, tested. The story of the empire of man over nature, as Francis Bacon called it, is written in the now routine miracles of transport, communication and medicine.

Dewey (himself illustrating the imaginative projection of ideas to new domains) reminds us that the steam engine and wireless were once possibilities dreamed of and by intelligent inquiry implemented and realized. He time and again reminds us, too, that governments, laws, social institutions, arts both "fine" and "useful" are all complex active processes always in process of change. These changes generate conflicts between old habits and new situations. These conflicts generate suggestions of the needs and of the possibilities of directing changes toward solutions. The key to meaningful life is growth; the constant alertness to, the freshening, the reshaping, the remaking of experience. The enemy of life (and its opposite) is rigidity and blind resistance to change. The function of intelligence is to be alertly critical of outmoded methods in society, in government, in feeling, in thought. This alertness applies also to those tendencies in human institutions and governments and laws and customs which render life more meaningful, more alive, and at once more integrated and more varied.

Among the enemies of life is social isolation, the rigidities that separate classes into stereotypes, races and social castes. The activity of creative intelligence functions best where there is a genuinely free interplay among individuals, a society where the life of each is challenged, varied, fructified by contacts with the lives of others. Now John Dewey was not the first to emphasize the paramount reality of change and process; William James had been stressing the same point somewhat earlier than Dewey. Nor was the recognition of change and process confined to America. Bergson, beginning with his earliest work, had emphasized the reality of movement and time and had pointed out the artificial rigidities, the deadening abstractions of the "geometrizing" intellect. And in ancient Greece, long before any modern prophet, Heraclitus had declared that "all is changing save the law of change." But the distinctive and original aspect of Dewey's philosophy is his relating of the reality of change to the urgencies and opportunities of human experience of change, and, in a special sense, of the American democratic experience.

Change, as was noted above, is an actuality discerned by others than Dewey and long before the American adventure in a free society. It was Darwinism and modern physics that helped Dewey to emphasize and develop his analysis of the ultimate traits in nature: of contingency, of the stable and the precarious, of tension and resolution, of the recurrent oscillation of security and insecurity. But it is not only in the central half-hidden processes of nature that Dewey finds the fact of change important. The history of the American people in a kaleidoscopically self-transforming society is for him a key illustration of his philosophy. Foreign observers who recognized Dewey as a characteristically American philosopher were right. For democracy in America, as Dewey sees it, is a commitment to a free exploration of the possibilities of the future, a sharing of such challenges and opportunities as are made available in a society relatively free from traditional rigidities and happily placed as to natural resources and in the ingenuities bred of a pioneering history.

The democratic faith is that we in America can make the most of what scientific techniques offer for the remaking of a continent and of ways of life upon it. Dewey saw, as De Tocqueville, that comprehending and prophetic French visitor, limned in his *Democracy in America* a century earlier, the wonderful hopes of a free society in a new world.

For Dewey those possibilities reside not simply in technical expertness and in immense natural wealth, but in the resources of intelligence co-operatively marshaled for the common "shared good." That shared good is life in the individual come to its fullness in vividness and in maturity. Democracy had as its instrument conjoint thinking, the conditions of free choice in industry and in education and the spread through education of the habit of critical reflection and exploration. On critical reflection—unhampered by special pressures and special interests—depend the laws, institutions and customs to meet the changing needs of a changing society. Democracy was for Dewey, among other things, an intellectual ideal. It was another name for that shared living in which each member of the group—given the conditions economically and politically for making his own choices, and the education that makes such intelligent choice habitual and effective—is an agent in common decisions. Democracy was also a moral and indeed a religious ideal, that of a shared life, a community and a communion. And it was an aesthetic ideal, the communication of experience through contagion.

They are quite wrong who misread Dewey as believing that reflective inquiry is all of experience or that thinking for the solution of practical problems is the whole of life. The function of thought for Dewey *is* instrumental, but it is a method for resolving the obstacles to the full and rich realization of life. Thinking itself may be a joy and it may help to establish or to re-establish the conditions of joy. But there are other aspects of life—"consummations," Dewey calls them—and these are to be sought where they are found: in love, in friendship and in art.

If one combines the fine traditional use of the word *liberal* in nineteenth-century England with the notion of imagination as the disciplined projection of the possibilities of experience, one can see why Dewey became the voice for a generation (and will be again) of the liberal movement in politics, in education, in art. Freedom of inquiry is for him the condition of freedom in a larger sense: perpetual growth and deepening insight and widening realization of the possible hopes, the varied enjoyments of intelligence and good will—all of which can help to ensure an ever-renewed fruition.

Shortly after Dewey's death, certain criticisms leveled at his thought during his life came to be stated in exaggerated, sometimes exasperated, form. It is a common occurrence for deflation of a reputation to occur—usually briefly—after the death of a great man. The deflation occurs usually because there has been a change of moral climate, of environing circumstance. John Dewey was the voice of liberal intelligence when the prospects of good will and intelligence seemed better than they do at this brutal moment of modern history. Both the right and the left extremes have of late assailed Dewey. The charges against his philosophy are not new. The doctrinaires and authoritarians, correctly, do not find in him fixed dogmas. The romantic pessimists, like the existentialists, find him both too intellectual and too hopeful. The "analytic" philosophers, sedulously scrutinizing the use of words and the structure of sentences, find him too large and vague. The theologians and the panoplied idealists find him too earthbound and secular. But Dewey in a deep sense is the voice of a persistent central hard core of practical sense and humane hope and courage in this country. A belief in intelligence and in individuals fully themselves and freely sharing their lives—this is an old and a deep strain in the American tradition. Dewey restated it in terms of a machine age, an industrial culture, a necessarily internationally involved nation. The advent of the hydrogen bomb, of demagoguery at home, of dictatorship abroad, have not lessened but rather increased the need for disciplined intelligence and free imagination in the making of the future. The race is still between intelligence and catastrophe. The alternatives are fanaticism, nihilism, sentimentalism, triviality or despair. Dewey would have none of these. His was a voice for reasonableness and for imagination. He will be listened to again and long.

And what, if he is thus listened to, does he have to say to a generation more urgently pressed than was the one in which he started to write and think? What tasks are left that follow from his chief hypotheses?

The first is that of specific inquiries in law, in government, in education, on the lines Dewey opened up. The second is what Dewey once a few years ago eloquently urged on an audience of young philosophers when he himself was nearly ninety. Some despair, he declared, because all the old values and old securities are in question, the old landmarks are gone, and the seas are rough. It is a wonderful era, he suggested, to be young and to be a philosopher. Never was there a time that so called for fresh and courageous hypotheses. Dewey needs not only to be studied but to be emulated.

II ♦ Reconstruction in Philosophy

I. Changing Conceptions of Philosophy *

Man differs from the lower animals because he preserves his past experiences. What happened in the past is lived again in memory. About what goes on today hangs a cloud of thoughts concerning similar things undergone in bygone days. With the animals, an experience perishes as it happens, and each new doing or suffering stands alone. But man lives in a world where each occurrence is charged with echoes and reminiscences of what has gone before, where each event is a reminder of other things. Hence he lives not, like the beasts of the field, in a world of merely physical things but in a world of signs and symbols. A stone is not merely hard, a thing into which one bumps; but it is a monument of a deceased ancestor. A flame is not merely something which warms or burns, but is a symbol of the enduring life of the household, of the abiding source of cheer, nourishment and shelter to which man returns from his casual wanderings. Instead of being a quick fork of fire which may sting and hurt, it is the hearth at which one worships and for which one fights. And all this which marks the difference between bestiality and humanity, between culture and merely physical nature, is because man remembers, preserving and recording his experiences.

The revivals of memory are, however, rarely literal. We

* From *Reconstruction in Philosophy*. New York: Henry Holt and Co., 1920. Enlarged edition—Boston: The Beacon Press, 1948; New York: Mentor Books, 1950. By permission of The Beacon Press.

naturally remember what interests us and because it interests us. The past is recalled not because of itself but because of what it adds to the present. Thus the primary life of memory is emotional rather than intellectual and practical. Savage man recalled yesterday's struggle with an animal not in order to study in a scientific way the qualities of the animal or for the sake of calculating how better to fight tomorrow, but to escape from the tedium of today by regaining the thrill of yesterday. The memory has all the excitement of the combat without its danger and anxiety. To revive it and revel in it is to enhance the present moment with a new meaning, a meaning different from that which actually belongs either to it or to the past. Memory is vicarious experience in which there is all the emotional values of actual experience without its strains, vicissitudes and troubles. The triumph of battle is even more poignant in the memorial war dance than at the moment of victory; the conscious and truly human experience of the chase comes when it is talked over and re-enacted by the camp fire. At the time, attention is taken up with practical details and with the strain of uncertainty. Only later do the details compose into a story and fuse into a whole of meaning. At the time of practical experience man exists from moment to moment, preoccupied with the task of the moment. As he re-surveys all the moments in thought, a drama emerges with a beginning, a middle and a movement toward the climax of achievement or defeat.

Since man revives his past experience because of the interest added to what would otherwise be the emptiness of present leisure, the primitive life of memory is one of fancy and imagination, rather than of accurate recollection. After all, it is the story, the drama, which counts. Only those incidents are selected which have a present emotional value, to intensify the present tale as it is rehearsed in imagination or told to an admiring listener. What does not add to the thrill of combat or contribute to the goal of success or failure is dropped. Incidents are rearranged till they fit into the temper of the tale. Thus early man when left to himself, when not actually engaged in the struggle for existence, lived in a world of memories which was a world of suggestions. A suggestion differs from a recollection in that no attempt is made to test its correctness. Its correctness is a matter of relative indifference. The cloud suggests a camel or a man's face. It could not suggest these things unless sometime there had been an actual, literal experience of camel and face. But the real likeness is of no account. The main thing is the emotional interest in tracing the camel or following the fortunes of the face as it forms and dissolves.

Students of the primitive history of mankind tell of the enormous part played by animal tales, myths and cults. Sometimes a mystery is made out of this historical fact, as if it indicated that primitive man was moved by a different psychology from that which now animates humanity. But the explanation is, I think, simple. Until agriculture and the higher industrial arts were developed, long periods of empty leisure alternated with comparatively short periods of energy put forth to secure food or safety from attack. Because of our own habits, we tend to think of people as busy or occupied, if not with doing at least with thinking and planning. But then men were busy only when engaged in the hunt or fishing or fighting expedition. Yet the mind when awake must have some filling; it cannot remain literally vacant because the body is idle. And what thoughts should crowd into the human mind except experiences with animals, experiences transformed under the influence of dramatic interest to make more vivid and coherent the events typical of the chase? As men in fancy dramatically re-lived the interesting parts of their actual lives, animals inevitably became themselves dramatized.

They were true *dramatis personæ* and as such assumed the traits of persons. They too had desires, hopes and fears, a life of affections, loves and hates, triumphs and defeats.

Moreover, since they were essential to the support of the community, their activities and sufferings made them, in the imagination which dramatically revived the past, true sharers in the life of the community. Although they were hunted, yet they permitted themselves after all to be caught, and hence they were friends and allies. They devoted themselves, quite literally, to the sustenance and well-being of the community group to which they belonged. Thus were produced not merely the multitude of tales and legends dwelling affectionately upon the activities and features of animals, but also those elaborate rites and cults which made animals ancestors, heroes, tribal figure-heads and divinities.

I hope that I do not seem to you to have gone too far afield from my topic, the origin of philosophies. For it seems to me that the historic source of philosophies cannot be understood except as we dwell, at even greater length and in more detail, upon such considerations as these. We need to recognize that the ordinary consciousness of the ordinary man left to himself is a creature of desires rather than of intellectual study, inquiry or speculation. Man ceases to be primarily actuated by hopes and fears, loves and hates, only when he is subjected to a discipline which is foreign to human nature, which is, from the standpoint of natural man, artificial. Naturally our books, our scientific and philosophical books, are written by men who have subjected themselves in a superior degree to intellectual discipline and culture. Their thoughts are habitually reasonable. They have learned to check their fancies by facts, and to organize their ideas logically rather than emotionally and dramatically. When they do indulge in reverie and day-dreaming —which is probably more of the time than is conventionally acknowledged—they are aware of what they are doing. They label these excursions, and do not confuse their results with objective experiences. We tend to judge others by ourselves, and because scientific and philosophic books are

composed by men in whom the reasonable, logical and objective habit of mind predominates, a similar rationality has
been attributed by them to the average and ordinary man.
It is then overlooked that both rationality and irrationality
are largely irrelevent and episodical in undisciplined human
nature; that men are governed by memory rather than by
thought, and that memory is not a remembering of actual
facts, but is association, suggestion, dramatic fancy. The
standard used to measure the value of the suggestions that
spring up in the mind is not congruity with fact but emotional congeniality. Do they stimulate and reinforce feeling,
and fit into the dramatic tale? Are they consonant with the
prevailing mood, and can they be rendered into the traditional hopes and fears of the community? If we are willing
to take the word dreams with a certain liberality, it is hardly
too much to say that man, save in his occasional times of
actual work and struggle, lives in a world of dreams, rather
than of facts, and a world of dreams that is organized about
desires whose success and frustration form its stuff.

To treat the early beliefs and traditions of mankind as if
they were attempts at scientific explanation of the world,
only erroneous and absurd attempts, is thus to be guilty
of a great mistake. The material out of which philosophy
finally emerges is irrelevant to science and to explanation.
It is figurative, symbolic of fears and hopes, made of imagi-
nations and suggestions, not significant of a world of objective fact intellectually confronted. It is poetry and drama,
rather than science, and is apart from scientific truth and
falsity, rationality or absurdity of fact in the same way in
which poetry is independent of these things.

This original material has, however, to pass through at
least two stages before it becomes philosophy proper. One
is the stage in which stories and legends and their accompanying dramatizations are consolidated. At first the emotionalized records of experiences are largely casual and
transitory. Events that excite the emotions of an individual

are seized upon and lived over in tale and pantomime. But some experiences are so frequent and recurrent that they concern the group as a whole. They are socially generalized. The piecemeal adventure of the single individual is built out till it becomes representative and typical of the emotional life of the tribe. Certain incidents affect the weal and woe of the group in its entirety and thereby get an exceptional emphasis and elevation. A certain texture of tradition is built up; the story becomes a social heritage and possession; the pantomime develops into the stated rite. Tradition thus formed becomes a kind of norm to which individual fancy and suggestion conform. An abiding framework of imagination is constructed. A communal way of conceiving life grows up into which individuals are inducted by education. Both unconsciously and by definite social requirement individual memories are assimilated to group memory or tradition, and individual fancies are accommodated to the body of beliefs characteristic of a community. Poetry becomes fixated and systematized. The story becomes a social norm. The original drama which re-enacts an emotionally important experience is institutionalized into a cult. Suggestions previously free are hardened into doctrines.

The systematic and obligatory nature of such doctrines is hastened and confirmed through conquests and political consolidation. As the area of a government is extended, there is a definite motive for systematizing and unifying beliefs once free and floating. Aside from natural accommodation and assimilation springing from the fact of intercourse and the needs of common understanding, there is often political necessity which leads the ruler to centralize traditions and beliefs in order to extend and strengthen his prestige and authority. Judea, Greece, Rome, and I presume all other countries having a long history, present records of a continual working over of earlier local rites and doctrines in the interests of a wider social unity and a more extensive political power. I shall ask you to assume with me that in this way the larger cosmogonies and cosmologies of the race as well as the larger ethical traditions have arisen. Whether this is literally so or not, it is not necessary to inquire, much less to demonstrate. It is enough for our purposes that under social influences there took place a fixing and organizing of doctrines and cults which gave general traits to the imagination and general rules to conduct, and that such a consolidation was a necessary antecedent to the formation of any philosophy as we understand that term.

Although a necessary antecedent, this organization and generalization of ideas and principles of belief is not the sole and sufficient generator of philosophy. There is still lacking the motive for logical system and intellectual proof. This we may suppose to be furnished by the need of reconciling the moral rules and ideals embodied in the traditional code with the matter of fact positivistic knowledge which gradually grows up. For man can never be wholly the creature of suggestion and fancy. The requirements of continued existence make indispensable some attention to the actual facts of the world. Although it is surprising how little check the environment actually puts upon the formation of ideas, since no notions are too absurd not to have been accepted by some people, yet the environment does enforce a certain minimum of correctness under penalty of extinction. That certain things are foods, that they are to be found in certain places, that water drowns, fire burns, that sharp points penetrate and cut, that heavy things fall unless supported, that there is a certain regularity in the changes of day and night and the alteration of hot and cold, wet and dry:—such prosaic facts force themselves upon even primitive attention. Some of them are so obvious and so important that they have next to no fanciful context. Auguste Comte says somewhere that he knows of no savage people who had a God of weight although every other natural quality or force may have been deified. Gradually there grows up a body of homely generalizations preserving and trans-

mitting the wisdom of the race about the observed facts and
sequences of nature. This knowledge is especially connected with industries, arts and crafts where observation
of materials and processes is required for successful action,
and where action is so continuous and regular that
spasmodic magic will not suffice. Extravagantly fantastic
notions are eliminated because they are brought into juxtaposition with what actually happens.

The sailor is more likely to be given to what we now term
superstitions than say the weaver, because his activity is
more at the mercy of sudden change and unforeseen occurrence. But even the sailor while he may regard the wind as
the uncontrollable expression of the caprice of a great spirit,
will still have to become acquainted with some purely mechanical principles of adjustment of boat, sails and oar to
the wind. Fire may be conceived as a supernatural dragon
because some time or other a swift, bright and devouring
flame called before the mind's eye the quick-moving and
dangerous serpent. But the housewife who tends the fire
and the pots wherein food cooks will still be compelled to
observe certain mechanical facts of draft and replenishment,
and passage from wood to ash. Still more will the worker in
metals accumulate verifiable details about the conditions
and consequences of the operation of heat. He may retain
for special and ceremonial occasions traditional beliefs, but
everyday familiar use will expel these conceptions for the
greater part of the time, when fire will be to him of uniform
and prosaic behavior, controllable by practical relations of
cause and effect. As the arts and crafts develop and become
more elaborate, the body of positive and tested knowledge
enlarges, and the sequences observed become more complex
and of greater scope. Technologies of this kind give that
common-sense knowledge of nature out of which science
takes its origin. They provide not merely a collection of positive facts, but they give expertness in dealing with materials and tools, and promote the development of the exper-

imental habit of mind, as soon as an art can be taken away
from the rule of sheer custom.

For a long time the imaginative body of beliefs closely
connected with the moral habits of a community group and
with its emotional indulgences and consolations persists
side by side with the growing body of matter of fact knowledge. Wherever possible they are interlaced. At other points,
their inconsistencies forbid their interweaving, but the two
things are kept apart as if in different compartments. Since
one is merely superimposed upon the other their incompatibility is not felt, and there is no need of reconciliation. In
most cases, the two kinds of mental products are kept apart
because they become the possession of separate social
classes. The religious and poetic beliefs having acquired a
definite social and political value and function are in the
keeping of a higher class directly associated with the ruling
elements in the society. The workers and craftsmen who
possess the prosaic matter of fact knowledge are likely to
occupy a low social status, and their kind of knowledge is
affected by the social disesteem entertained for the manual
worker who engages in activities useful to the body. It
doubtless was this fact in Greece which in spite of the keen-
ness of observation, the extraordinary power of logical reasoning and the great freedom of speculation attained by the
Athenian, postponed the general and systematic employment of the experimental method. Since the industrial
craftsman was only just above the slave in social rank, his
type of knowledge and the method upon which it depended
lacked prestige and authority.

Nevertheless, the time came when matter of fact knowledge increased to such bulk and scope that it came into
conflict with not merely the detail but with the spirit and
temper of traditional and imaginative beliefs. Without
going into the vexed question of how and why, there is no
doubt that this is just what happened in what we term the
sophistic movement in Greece, within which originated

philosophy proper in the sense in which the western world understands that term. The fact that the sophists had a bad name given them by Plato and Aristotle, a name they have never been able to shake off, is evidence that with the sophists the strife between the two types of belief was the emphatic thing, and that the conflict had a disconcerting effect upon the traditional system of religious beliefs and the moral code of conduct bound up with it. Although Socrates was doubtless sincerely interested in the reconciliation of the two sides, yet the fact that he approached the matter from the side of matter of fact method, giving its canons and criteria primacy, was enough to bring him to the condemnation of death as a contemner of the gods and a corrupter of youth.

The fate of Socrates and the ill-fame of the sophists may be used to suggest some of the striking contrasts between traditional emotionalized belief on one hand and prosaic matter of fact knowledge on the other:—the purpose of the comparison being to bring out the point that while all the advantages of what we call science were on the side of the latter, the advantages of social esteem and authority, and of intimate contact with what gives life its deeper lying values were on the side of traditional belief. To all appearances, the specific and verified knowledge of the environment had only a limited and technical scope. It had to do with the arts, and the purpose and good of the artisan after all did not extend very far. They were subordinate and almost servile. Who would put the art of the shoemaker on the same plane as the art of ruling the state? Who would put even the higher art of the physician in healing the body, upon the level of the art of the priest in healing the soul? Thus Plato constantly draws the contrast in his dialogues. The shoemaker is a judge of a good pair of shoes, but he is no judge at all of the more important question whether and when it is good to wear shoes; the physician is a good judge of health, but whether it is a good thing or not to be well or better to die, he knows not. While the artisan is expert as long as purely limited technical questions arise, he is helpless when it comes to the only really important questions, the moral questions as to values. Consequently, his type of knowledge is inherently inferior and needs to be controlled by a higher kind of knowledge which will reveal ultimate ends and purposes, and thus put and keep technical and mechanical knowledge in its proper place. Moreover, in Plato's pages we find, because of Plato's adequate dramatic sense, a lively depicting of the impact in particular men of the conflict between tradition and the new claims of purely intellectual knowledge. The conservative is shocked beyond measure at the idea of teaching the military art by abstract rules, by science. One does not just fight, one fights for one's country. Abstract science cannot convey love and loyalty, nor can it be a substitute, even upon the more technical side, for those ways and means of fighting in which devotion to the country has been traditionally embodied.

The way to learn the fighting art is through association with those who have themselves learned to defend the country, by becoming saturated with its ideals and customs; by becoming in short a practical adept in the Greek tradition as to fighting. To attempt to derive abstract rules from a comparison of native ways of fighting with the enemies' ways is to begin to go over to the enemies' traditions and gods: it is to begin to be false to one's own country.

Such a point of view vividly realized enables us to appreciate the antagonism aroused by the positivistic point of view when it came into conflict with the traditional. The latter was deeply rooted in social habits and loyalties; it was surcharged with the moral aims for which men lived and the moral rules by which they lived. Hence it was as basic and as comprehensive as life itself, and palpitated with the warm glowing colors of the community life in which men realized their own being. In contrast, the positivistic knowledge was concerned with merely physical utilities, and lacked the ardent associations of belief hallowed by sacrifices of ancestors and worship of contemporaries. Because of its limited and concrete character it was dry, hard, cold.

Yet the more acute and active minds, like that of Plato himself, could no longer be content to accept, along with the conservative citizen of the time, the old beliefs in the old way. The growth of positive knowledge and of the critical, inquiring spirit undermined these in their old form. The advantages in definiteness, in accuracy, in verifiability were all on the side of the new knowledge. Tradition was noble in aim and scope, but uncertain in foundation. The unquestioned life, said Socrates, was not one fit to be lived by man, who is a questioning being because he is a rational being. Hence he must search out the reason of things, and not accept them from custom and political authority. What was to be done? Develop a method of rational investigation and proof which should place the essential elements of traditional belief upon an unshakable basis; develop a method of thought and knowledge which while purifying tradition should preserve its moral and social values unimpaired; nay, by purifying them, add to their power and authority. To put it in a word, that which had rested upon custom was to be restored, resting no longer upon the habits of the past, but upon the very metaphysics of Being and the Universe. Metaphysics is a substitute for custom as the source and guarantor of higher moral and social values— that is the leading theme of the classic philosophy of Europe, as evolved by Plato and Aristotle—a philosophy, let us always recall, renewed and restated by the Christian philosophy of Medieval Europe.

Out of this situation emerged, if I mistake not, the entire tradition regarding the function and office of philosophy which till very recently has controlled the systematic and constructive philosophies of the western world. If I am right in my main thesis that the origin of philosophy lay in an attempt to reconcile the two different types of mental product,

then the key is in our hands as to the main traits of subsequent philosophy so far as that was not of a negative and
heterodox kind. In the first place, philosophy did not
develop in an unbiased way from an open and unprejudiced origin. It had its task cut out for it from the start. It
had a mission to perform, and it was sworn in advance to
that mission. It had to extract the essential moral kernel out
of the threatened traditional beliefs of the past. So far so
good; the work was critical and in the interests of the only
true conservatism—that which will conserve and not waste
the values wrought out by humanity. But it was also pre-
committed to extracting this moral essence in a spirit congenial to the spirit of past beliefs. The association with
imagination and with social authority was too intimate to be
deeply disturbed. It was not possible to conceive of the content of social institutions in any form radically different
from that in which they had existed in the past. It became
the work of philosophy to justify on rational grounds the
spirit, though not the form, of accepted beliefs and traditional customs.

The resulting philosophy seemed radical enough and
even dangerous to the average Athenian because of the
difference of form and method. In the sense of pruning
away excrescences and eliminating factors which to the
average citizen were all one with the basic beliefs, it was
radical. But looked at in the perspective of history and in
contrast with different types of thought which developed
later in different social environments, it is now easy to see
how profoundly, after all, Plato and Aristotle reflected the
meaning of Greek tradition and habit, so that their writings
remain, with the writings of the great dramatists, the best
introduction of a student into the innermost ideals and aspirations of distinctively Greek life. Without Greek religion,
Greek art, Greek civic life, their philosophy would have
been impossible; while the effect of that science upon which
the philosophers most prided themselves turns out to have

been superficial and negligible. This apologetic spirit of philosophy is even more apparent when Medieval Christianity about the twelfth century sought for a systematic rational presentation of itself and made use of classic philosophy, especially that of Aristotle, to justify itself to reason. A not unsimilar occurrence characterizes the chief philosophic systems of Germany in the early nineteenth century, when Hegel assumed the task of justifying in the name of rational idealism the doctrines and institutions which were menaced by the new spirit of science and popular government. The result has been that the great systems have not been free from party spirit exercised in behalf of preconceived beliefs. Since they have at the same time professed complete intellectual independence and rationality, the result has been too often to impart to philosophy an element of insincerity, all the more insidious because wholly unconscious on the part of those who sustained philosophy.

And this brings us to a second trait of philosophy springing from its origin. Since it aimed at a rational justification of things that had been previously accepted because of their emotional congeniality and social prestige, it had to make much of the apparatus of reason and proof. Because of the lack of intrinsic rationality in the matters with which it dealt, it leaned over backward, so to speak, in parade of logical form. In dealing with matters of fact, simpler and rougher ways of demonstration may be resorted to. It is enough, so to say, to produce the fact in question and point to it—the fundamental form of all demonstration. But when it comes to convincing men of the truth of doctrines which are no longer to be accepted upon the say-so of custom and social authority, but which also are not capable of empirical verification, there is no recourse save to magnify the signs of rigorous thought and rigid demonstration. Thus arises that appearance of abstract definition and ultra-scientific argumentation which repels so many from philosophy but which has been one of its chief attractions to its devotees.

At the worst, this has reduced philosophy to a show of elaborate terminology, a hair-splitting logic, and a fictitious devotion to the mere external forms of comprehensive and minute demonstration. Even at the best, it has tended to produce an overdeveloped attachment to system for its own sake, and an over-pretentious claim to certainty. Bishop Butler declared that probability is the guide of life; but few philosophers have been courageous enough to avow that philosophy can be satisfied with anything that is merely probable. The customs dictated by tradition and desire had claimed finality and immutability. They had claimed to give certain and unvarying laws of conduct. Very early in its history philosophy made pretension to a similar conclusiveness, and something of this temper has clung to classic philosophies ever since. They have insisted that they were more scientific than the sciences—that, indeed, philosophy was necessary because after all the special sciences fail in attaining final and complete truth. There have been a few dissenters who have ventured to assert, as did William James, that "philosophy is vision" and that its chief function is to free men's minds from bias and prejudice and to enlarge their perceptions of the world about them. But in the main philosophy has set up much more ambitious pretensions. To say frankly that philosophy can proffer nothing but hypotheses, and that these hypotheses are of value only as they render men's minds more sensitive to life about them, would seem like a negation of philosophy itself.

In the third place, the body of beliefs dictated by desire and imagination and developed under the influence of communal authority into an authoritative tradition, was pervasive and comprehensive. It was, so to speak, omnipresent in all the details of the group life. Its pressure was unremitting and its influence universal. It was then probably inevitable that the rival principle, reflective thought, should aim at a similar universality and comprehensiveness. It would be as inclusive and far-reaching metaphysically as tradition had been socially. Now there was just one way in which this pretension could be accomplished in conjunction with a claim of complete logical system and certainty.

All philosophies of the classic type have made a fixed and fundamental distinction between two realms of existence. One of these corresponds to the religious and supernatural world of popular tradition, which in its metaphysical rendering became the world of highest and ultimate reality. Since the final source and sanction of all important truths and rules of conduct in community life had been found in superior and unquestioned religious beliefs, so the absolute and supreme reality of philosophy afforded the only sure guaranty of truth about empirical matters, and the sole rational guide to proper social institutions and individual behavior. Over against this absolute and noumenal reality which could be apprehended only by the systematic discipline of philosophy itself stood the ordinary empirical, relatively real, phenomenal world of everyday experience. It was with this world that the practical affairs and utilities of men were connected. It was to this imperfect and perishing world that matter of fact, positivistic science referred.

This is the trait which, in my opinion, has affected most deeply the classic notion about the nature of philosophy. Philosophy has arrogated to itself the office of demonstrating the existence of a transcendent, absolute or inner reality and of revealing to man the nature and features of this ultimate and higher reality. It has therefore claimed that it was in possession of a higher organ of knowledge than is employed by positive science and ordinary practical experience, and that it is marked by a superior dignity and importance—a claim which is undeniable if philosophy leads man to proof and intuition of a Reality beyond that open to day-by-day life and the special sciences.

This claim has, of course, been denied by various philosophers from time to time. But for the most part these denials have been agnostic and sceptical. They have contented themselves with asserting that absolute and ultimate reality is beyond human ken. But they have not ventured to deny that such Reality would be the appropriate sphere for the exercise of philosophic knowledge provided only it were within the reach of human intelligence. Only comparatively recently has another conception of the proper office of philosophy arisen. This course of lectures will be devoted to setting forth this different conception of philosophy in some of its main contrasts to what this lecture has termed the classic conception. At this point, it can be referred to only by anticipation and in cursory fashion. It is implied in the account which has been given of the origin of philosophy out of the background of an authoritative tradition; a tradition originally dictated by man's imagination working under the influence of love and hate and in the interest of emotional excitement and satisfaction. Common frankness requires that it be stated that this account of the origin of philosophies claiming to deal with absolute Being in a systematic way has been given with malice prepense. It seems to me that this genetic method of approach is a more effective way of undermining this type of philosophic theorizing than any attempt at logical refutation could be.

If this lecture succeeds in leaving in your minds as a reasonable hypothesis the idea that philosophy originated not out of intellectual material, but out of social and emotional material, it will also succeed in leaving with you a changed attitude toward traditional philosophies. They will be viewed from a new angle and placed in a new light. New questions about them will be aroused and new standards for judging them will be suggested.

If any one will commence without mental reservations to study the history of philosophy not as an isolated thing but as a chapter in the development of civilization and culture; if one will connect the story of philosophy with a study of anthropology, primitive life, the history of religion, literature and social institutions, it is confidently asserted that he

will reach his own independent judgment as to the worth
of the account which has been presented today. Considered
in this way, the history of philosophy will take on a new significance. What is lost from the standpoint of would-be
science is regained from the standpoint of humanity. Instead of the disputes of rivals about the nature of reality,
we have the scene of human clash of social purpose and aspirations. Instead of impossible attempts to transcend experience, we have the significant record of the efforts of men
to formulate the things of experience to which they are most
deeply and passionately attached. Instead of impersonal
and purely speculative endeavors to contemplate as remote
beholders the nature of absolute things-in-themselves, we
have a living picture of the choice of thoughtful men about
what they would have life to be, and to what ends they
would have men shape their intelligent activities.

Any one of you who arrives at such a view of past philosophy will of necessity be led to entertain a quite definite
conception of the scope and aim of future philosophizing.
He will inevitably be committed to the notion that what
philosophy has been unconsciously, without knowing or in-
tending it, and, so to speak, under cover, it must henceforth
be openly and deliberately. When it is acknowledged that
under disguise of dealing with ultimate reality, philosophy
has been occupied with the precious values embedded in
social traditions, that it has sprung from a clash of social
ends and from a conflict of inherited institutions with incompatible contemporary tendencies, it will be seen that
the task of future philosophy is to clarify men's ideas as to
the social and moral strifes of their own day. Its aim is to
become so far as is humanly possible an organ for dealing
with these conflicts. That which may be pretentiously unreal when it is formulated in metaphysical distinctions becomes intensely significant when connected with the drama
of the struggle of social beliefs and ideals. Philosophy which
surrenders its somewhat barren monopoly of dealings with

Ultimate and Absolute Reality will find a compensation in enlightening the moral forces which move mankind and in contributing to the aspirations of men to attain to a more ordered and intelligent happiness.

II. Changed Conceptions of Experience and Reason

WHAT is experience and what is Reason, Mind? What is the scope of experience and what are its limits? How far is it a sure ground of belief and a safe guide of conduct? Can we trust it in science and in behavior? Or is it a quagmire as soon as we pass beyond a few low material interests? Is it so shaky, shifting, and shallow that instead of affording sure footing, safe paths to fertile fields, it misleads, betrays, and engulfs? Is a Reason outside experience and above it needed to supply assured principles to science and conduct? In one sense, these questions suggest technical problems of abstruse philosophy; in another sense, they contain the deepest possible questionings regarding the career of man. They concern the criteria he is to employ in forming his beliefs; the principles by which he is to direct his life and the ends to which he is to direct it. Must man transcend experience by some organ of unique character that carries him into the super-empirical? Failing this, must he wander sceptical and disillusioned? Or is human experience itself worth while in its purposes and its methods of guidance? Can it organize itself into stable courses or must it be sustained from without?

We know the answers of traditional philosophy. They do not thoroughly agree among themselves, but they agree that experience never rises above the level of the particular, the contingent, and the probable. Only a power transcending in origin and content any and all conceivable experience can attain to universal, necessary and certain authority and direction. The empiricists themselves admitted the correctness of these assertions. They only said that since there is no faculty of Pure Reason in the possession of mankind, we must put up with what we have, experience, and make the most possible out of it. They contented themselves with sceptical attacks upon the transcendentalist, with indications of the ways in which we might best seize the meaning and good of the passing moment; or like Locke, asserted that in spite of the limitation of experience, it affords the light needed to guide men's footsteps modestly in conduct. They affirmed that the alleged authoritative guidance by a higher faculty had practically hampered men.

It is the function of this lecture to show how and why it is now possible to make claims for experience as a guide in science and moral life which the older empiricists did not and could not make for it.

Curiously enough, the key to the matter may be found in the fact that the old notion of experience was itself a product of experience—the only kind of experience which was then open to men. If another conception of experience is now possible, it is precisely because the quality of experience as it may now be lived has undergone a profound social and intellectual change from that of earlier times. The account of experience which we find in Plato and Aristotle is an account of what Greek experience actually was. It agrees very closely with what the modern psychologist knows as the method of learning by trial and error as distinct from the method of learning by ideas. Men tried certain acts, they underwent certain sufferings and affections. Each of these in the time of its occurrence is isolated, particular—its counterpart is transient appetite and transient sensation. But memory preserves and accumulates these separate incidents. As they pile up, irregular variations get cancelled, common features are selected, reinforced and combined. Gradually a habit of action is built up, and corresponding to this habit there forms a certain generalized picture of an object or situation. We come to know or note not merely this particular which as a particular cannot strictly be known at all (for not being classed it cannot be characterized and identified) but to recognize it as man, tree, stone, leather—an individual of a certain kind, marked by a certain universal form characteristic of a whole species of thing. Along with the development of this common-sense knowledge, there grows up a certain regularity of conduct. The particular incidents fuse, and a way of acting which is general, as far as it goes, builds up. The skill develops which is shown by the artisan, the shoemaker, the carpenter, the gymnast, the physician, who have regular ways of handling cases. This regularity signifies, of course, that the particular case is not treated as an isolated particular, but as one of a kind, which therefore demands a *kind* of action. From the multitude of particular illnesses encountered, the physician in learning to class some of them as indigestion learns also to treat the cases of the class in a common or general way. He forms the rule of recommending a certain diet, and prescribing a certain remedy. All this forms what we call experience. It results, as the illustration shows, in a certain general insight and a certain organized ability in action.

But needless to insist, the generality and the organization are restricted and fallible. They hold, as Aristotle was fond of pointing out, usually, in most cases, as a rule, but not universally, of necessity, or as a principle. The physician is bound to make mistakes, because individual cases are bound to vary unaccountably: such is their very nature. The difficulty does not arise in a defective experience which is capable of remedy in some better experience. Experience itself, as such, is defective, and hence default is inevitable and irremediable. The only universality and certainty is in a region above experience, that of the rational and conceptual. As the particular was a stepping-stone to image and habit, so the latter may become a stepping-stone to conceptions and principles. But the latter leave experience behind, untouched; they do not react to rectify it. Such is the notion which still lingers in the contrast of "empirical" and "rational" as when we say that a certain architect or physician is empirical, not scientific in his procedures. But the difference between the classic and the modern notion of experience is revealed in the fact that such a statement is now a charge, a disparaging accusation, brought against a particular architect or physician. With Plato, Aristotle and the Scholastic, it was a charge against the callings, since they were modes of experience. It was an indictment of all practical action in contrast with conceptual contemplation.

The modern philosopher who has professed himself an empiricist has usually had a critical purpose in mind. Like Bacon, Locke, Condillac and Helvetius, he stood face to face with a body of beliefs and a set of institutions in which he profoundly disbelieved. His problem was the problem of attack upon so much dead weight carried uselessly by humanity, crushing and distorting it. His readiest way of undermining and disintegrating was by appealing to experience as a final test and criterion. In every case, active reformers were "empiricists" in the philosophical sense. They made it their business to show that some current belief or institution that claimed the sanction of innate ideas or necessary conceptions, or an origin in an authoritative revelation of reason, had in fact proceeded from a lowly origin in experience, and had been confirmed by accident, by class interest or by biased authority.

The philosophic empiricism initiated by Locke was thus disintegrative in intent. It optimistically took it for granted that when the burden of blind custom, imposed authority, and accidental associations was removed, progress in science and social organization would spontaneously take place. Its part was to help in removing the burden. The best way to liberate men from the burden was through a natural history of the origin and growth in the mind of the ideas connected with objectionable beliefs and customs. Santayana justly calls the psychology of this school a malicious psychology. It tended to identify the history of the formation of certain ideas with an account of the things to which the ideas refer—an identification which naturally had an unfavorable effect on the things. But Mr. Santayana neglects to notice the social zeal and aim latent in the malice. He fails to point out that this "malice" was aimed at institutions and traditions which had lost their usefulness; he fails to point out that to a large extent it was true of them that an account of their psychological origin was equivalent to a destructive account of the things themselves. But after Hume with debonair clarity pointed out that the analysis of beliefs into sensations and associations left "natural" ideas and institutions in the same position in which the reformers had placed "artificial" ones, the situation changed. The rationalists employed the logic of sensationalistic-empiricism to show that experience, giving only a heap of chaotic and isolated particulars, is as fatal to science and to moral laws and obligations as to obnoxious institutions; and concluded that "Reason" must be resorted to if experience was to be furnished with any binding and connecting principles. The new rationalistic idealism of Kant and his successors seemed to be necessitated by the totally destructive results of the new empirical philosophy.

Two things have rendered possible a new conception of experience and a new conception of the relation of reason to experience, or, more accurately, of the place of reason *in* experience. The primary factor is the change that has taken place in the actual nature of experience, its contents and methods, as it is actually lived. The other is the development of a psychology based upon biology which makes possible a new scientific formulation of the nature of experience.

Let us begin with the technical side—the change in psychology. We are only just now commencing to appreciate how completely exploded is the psychology that dominated philosophy throughout the eighteenth and nineteenth centuries. According to this theory, mental life originated in sensations which are separately and passively received, and which are formed, through laws of retention and association, into a mosaic of images, perceptions, and conceptions. The senses were regarded as gateways or avenues of knowledge. Except in combining atomic sensations, the mind was wholly passive and acquiescent in knowing. Volition, action, emotion, and desire follow in the wake of sensations and images. The intellectual or cognitive factor comes first and emotional and volitional life is only a consequent conjunction of ideas with sensations of pleasure and pain.

The effect of the development of biology has been to reverse the picture. Wherever there is life, there is behavior, activity. In order that life may persist, this activity has to be both continuous and adapted to the environment. This adaptive adjustment, moreover, is not wholly passive; is not a mere matter of the moulding of the organism by the environment. Even a clam acts upon the environment and modifies it to some extent. It selects materials for food and for the shell that protects it. It does something to the environment as well as has something done to itself. There is no such thing in a living creature as mere conformity to conditions, though parasitic forms may approach this limit. In the interests of the maintenance of life there is transformation of some elements in the surrounding medium. The higher the form of life, the more important is the active reconstruction of the medium. This increased control may be illustrated by the contrast of savage with civilized man. Suppose the two are living in a wilderness. With the savage there is the maximum of accommodation to given conditions; the minimum of what we may call hitting back. The savage takes things "as they are," and by using caves and roots and occasional pools leads a meagre and precarious existence. The civilized man goes to distant mountains and dams streams. He builds reservoirs, digs channels, and conducts the waters to what had been a desert. He searches the world to find plants and animals that will thrive. He takes native plants and by selection and cross-fertilization improves them. He introduces machinery to till the soil and care for the harvest. By such means he may succeed in making the wilderness blossom like the rose.

Such transformation scenes are so familiar that we overlook their meaning. We forget that the inherent power of life is illustrated in them. Note what a change this point of view entails in the traditional notions of experience. Experience becomes an affair primarily of doing. The organism does not stand about, Micawberlike, waiting for something to turn up. It does not wait passive and inert for something to impress itself upon it from without. The organism acts in accordance with its own structure, simple or complex, upon its surroundings. As a consequence the changes produced in the environment react upon the organism and its activities. The living creature undergoes, suffers, the consequences of its own behavior. This close connection between doing and suffering or undergoing forms what we call experience. Disconnected doing and disconnected suffering are neither of them experiences. Suppose fire encroaches upon a man when he is asleep. Part of his body is burned away. The burn does not perceptibly result from what he has done. There is nothing which in any instructive way can be named experience. Or again there is a series of mere activities, like twitchings of muscles in a spasm. The movements amount to nothing; they have no consequences for life. Or, if they have, these consequences are not connected with prior doing. There is no experience, no learning, no cumulative process. But suppose a busy infant puts his finger in the fire; the doing is random, aimless, without intention or reflection. But something happens in consequence. The child undergoes heat, he suffers pain. The doing and undergoing, the reaching and the burn, are connected. One comes to suggest and mean the other. Then there is experience in a vital and significant sense.

Certain important implications for philosophy follow. In the first place, the interaction of organism and environment, resulting in some adaptation which secures utilization of the latter, is the primary fact, the basic category. Knowledge is relegated to a derived position, secondary in origin, even if its importance, when once it is established, is overshadowing. Knowledge is not something separate and self-sufficing, but is involved in the process by which life is sustained and evolved. The senses lose their place as gateways of knowing to take their rightful place as stimuli to action. To an animal an affection of the eye or ear is not an idle piece of information about something indifferently going on in the world. It is an invitation and inducement to act in a needed way. It is a clue in behavior, a directive factor in adaptation of life in its surroundings. It is urgent not cognitive in quality. The whole controversy between empiricism and rationalism as to the intellectual worth of sensations is rendered strangely obsolete. The discussion of sensations belongs under the head of immediate stimulus and response, not under the head of knowledge.

As a *conscious* element, a sensation marks an interruption in a course of action previously entered upon. Many psychologists since the time of Hobbes have dwelt upon what they call the relativity of sensations. We *feel* or sense cold in transition from warmth rather than absolutely; hardness is sensed upon a background of less resistance; a color, in contrast with pure light or pure dark or in contrast with some other hue. A continuously unchanged tone or color cannot be attended to or sensed. What we take to be such monotonously prolonged sensations are in truth constantly interrupted by incursions of other elements, and represent a series of excursions back and forth. This fact was, however, misconstrued into a doctrine about the nature of knowledge. Rationalists used it to discredit sense as a valid or high mode of knowing things, since according to it we never get hold of anything *in itself* or intrinsically. Sensationalists used it to disparage all pretence at absolute knowledge.

Properly speaking, however, this fact of the relativity of sensation does not in the least belong in the sphere of knowing. Sensations of this sort are emotional and practical rather than cognitive and intellectual. They are shocks of change, due to interruption of a prior adjustment. They are signals to redirections of action. Let me take a trivial illustration. The person who is taking notes has no sensation of the pressure of his pencil on the paper or on his hand as long as it functions properly. It operates merely as stimulus to ready and effective adjustment. The sensory activity incites automatically and unconsciously its proper motor response. There is a preformed physiological connection, acquired from habit but ultimately going back to an original connection in the nervous system. If the pencil-point gets broken or too blunt and the habit of writing does not operate smoothly, there is a conscious shock: —the feeling of something the matter, something gone wrong. This emotional change operates as a stimulus to a needed change in operation. One looks at his pencil, sharpens it or takes another pencil from one's pocket. The sensation operates as a pivot of readjusting behavior. It marks a break in the prior routine of writing and the beginning of some other mode of action. Sensations are "relative" in the sense of marking transitions in habits of behavior from one course to another way of behaving.

The rationalist was thus right in denying that sensations as such are true elements of knowledge. But the reasons he gave for this conclusion and the consequences he drew from it were all wrong. Sensations are not parts of *any* knowledge, good or bad, superior or inferior, imperfect or complete. They are rather provocations, incitements, challenges to an act of inquiry which is to *terminate* in knowledge. They are not ways of knowing things inferior in value to reflective ways, to the ways that require thought and inference, because they are not ways of knowing at all. They are stimuli to reflection and inference. As interruptions, they raise the questions: What does this shock mean? What is happening? What is the matter? How is my relation to the environment disturbed? What should be done about it? How shall I alter my course of action to meet the change that has taken place in the surroundings? How shall I readjust my behavior in response? Sensation is thus, as the sensationalist claimed, the beginning of knowledge, but only in the sense that the experienced shock of change is the necessary stimulus to the investigating and comparing which eventually produce knowledge.

When experience is aligned with the life-process and sensations are seen to be points of readjustment, the alleged atomism of sensations totally disappears. With this disappearance is abolished the need for a synthetic faculty of super-empirical reason to connect them. Philosophy is not any longer confronted with the hopeless problem of finding a way in which separate grains of sand may be woven into a strong and coherent rope—or into the illusion and pretence of one. When the isolated and simple existences of Locke and Hume are seen not to be truly empirical at all but to answer to certain demands of their theory of mind, the necessity ceases for the elaborate Kantian and Post-Kantian machinery of *a priori* concepts and categories to synthesize the alleged stuff of experience. The true "stuff" of experience is recognized to be adaptive courses of action, habits, active functions, connections of doing and undergoing; sensori-motor co-ordinations. Experience carries principles of connection and organization within itself. These principles are none the worse because they are vital and practical rather than epistemological. Some degree of organization is indispensable to even the lowest grade of life. Even an

amoeba must have some continuity in time in its activity
and some adaptation to its environment in space. Its life
and experience cannot possibly consist in momentary,
atomic, and self-enclosed sensations. Its activity has reference to its surroundings and to what goes before and
what comes after. This organization intrinsic to life renders
unnecessary a super-natural and super-empirical synthesis.
It affords the basis and material for a positive evolution of
intelligence as an organizing factor within experience.

Nor is it entirely aside from the subject to point out the
extent in which social as well as biological organization
enters into the formation of human experience. Probably
one thing that strengthened the idea that the mind is passive and receptive in knowing was the observation of the
helplessness of the human infant. But the observation
points in quite another direction. Because of his physical
dependence and impotency, the contacts of the little child
with nature are mediated by other persons. Mother and
nurse, father and older children, determine what experiences the child shall have; they constantly instruct him as
to the meaning of what he does and undergoes. The conceptions that are socially current and important become
the child's principles of interpretation and estimation long
before he attains to personal and deliberate control of conduct. Things come to him clothed in language, not in physical nakedness, and this garb of communication makes him
a sharer in the beliefs of those about him. These beliefs
coming to him as so many facts form his mind; they furnish
the centres about which his own personal expeditions and
perceptions are ordered. Here we have "categories" of connection and unification as important as those of Kant, but
empirical not mythological.

From these elementary, if somewhat technical considerations, we turn to the change which experience itself has
undergone in the passage from ancient and medieval to
modern life. To Plato, experience meant enslavement to the

past, to custom. Experience was almost equivalent to established customs formed not by reason or under intelligent control but by repetition and blind rule of thumb. Only reason can lift us above subjection to the accidents of the past. When we come to Bacon and his successors, we discover a curious reversal. Reason and its bodyguard of general notions is now the conservative, mind-enslaving factor. Experience is the liberating power. Experience means the new, that which calls us away from adherence to the past, that which reveals novel facts and truths. Faith in experience produces not devotion to custom but endeavor for progress. This difference in temper is the more significant because it was so unconsciously taken for granted. Some concrete and vital change must have occurred in actual experience as that is lived. For, after all, the thought of experience follows after and is modelled upon the experience actually undergone.

When mathematics and other rational sciences developed among the Greeks, scientific truths did not react back into daily experience. They remained isolated, apart and super-imposed. Medicine was the art in which perhaps the greatest amount of positive knowledge was obtained, but it did not reach the dignity of science. It remained an art. In practical arts, moreover, there was no conscious invention or purposeful improvement. Workers followed patterns that were handed down to them, while departure from established standards and models usually resulted in degenerate productions. Improvements came either from a slow, gradual, and unacknowledged accumulation of changes or else from some sudden inspiration, which at once set a new standard. Being the result of no conscious method, it was fittingly attributed to the gods. In the social arts, such a radical reformer as Plato felt that existing evils were due to the absence of such fixed patterns as controlled the productions of artisans. The ethical purport of philosophy was to furnish them, and when once they were instituted, they

were to be consecrated by religion, adorned by art, incul-
cated by education and enforced by magistrates so that
alteration of them would be impossible.

It is unnecessary to repeat what has been so often dwelt
upon as to the effect of experimental science in enabling
man to effect a deliberate control of his environment. But
since the impact of this control upon the traditional notion
of experience is often overlooked, we must point out that
when experience ceased to be empirical and became experimental, something of radical importance occurred. Afore-
time man employed the results of his prior experience only
to form customs that henceforth had to be blindly followed
or blindly broken. Now, old experience is used to suggest
aims and methods for developing a new and improved
experience. Consequently experience becomes in so far con-
structively self-regulative. What Shakespeare so pregnantly
said of nature, it is "made better by no mean, but nature
makes that mean," becomes true of experience. We do not
merely have to repeat the past, or wait foɪ accidents to
force change upon us. We *use* our past experiences to construct new and better ones in the future. The very fact of
experience thus includes the process by which it directs
itself in its own betterment.

Science, "reason," is not therefore something laid from
above upon experience. Suggested and tested in experience, it is also employed through inventions in a thousand
ways to expand and enrich experience. Although, as has
been so often repeated, this self-creation and self-regula-
tion of experience is still largely technological rather than
truly artistic or human, yet what has been achieved con-
tains the guaranty of the possibility of an intelligent admin-
istering of experience. The limits are moral and intellectual,
due to defects in our good will and knowledge. They are
not inherent metaphysically in the very nature of experience. "Reason" as a faculty separate from experience, introducing us to a superior region of universal truths begins

now to strike us as remote, uninteresting and unimportant. Reason, as a Kantian faculty that introduces generality and regularity into experience, strikes us more and more as superfluous—the unnecessary creation of men addicted to traditional formalism and to elaborate terminology. Concrete suggestions arising from past experiences, developed and matured in the light of the needs and deficiencies of the present, employed as aims and methods of specific reconstruction, and tested by success or failure in accomplishing this task of readjustment, suffice. To such empirical suggestions used in constructive fashion for new ends the name intelligence is given.

This recognition of the place of active and planning thought within the very processes of experience radically alters the traditional status of the technical problems of particular and universal, sense and reason, perceptual and conceptual. But the alteration is of much more than technical significance. For reason is experimental intelligence, conceived after the pattern of science, and used in the creation of social arts; it has something to do. It liberates man from the bondage of the past, due to ignorance and accident hardened into custom. It projects a better future and assists man in its realization. And its operation is always subject to test in experience. The plans which are formed, the principles which man projects as guides of reconstructive action, are not dogmas. They are hypotheses to be worked out in practice, and to be rejected, corrected and expanded as they fail or succeed in giving our present experience the guidance it requires. We may call them programmes of action, but since they are to be used in making our future acts less blind, more directed, they are flexible. Intelligence is not something possessed once for all. It is in constant process of forming, and its retention requires constant alertness in observing consequences, an open-minded will to learn and courage in readjustment.

In contrast with this experimental and re-adjusting intelligence, it must be said that Reason as employed by historic rationalism has tended to carelessness, conceit, irresponsibility, and rigidity—in short, absolutism. A certain school of contemporary psychology uses the term "rationalization" to denote those mental mechanisms by which we unconsciously put a better face on our conduct or experience than facts justify. We excuse ourselves to ourselves by introducing a purpose and order into that of which we are secretly ashamed. In like fashion, historic rationalism has often tended to use Reason as an agency of justification and apologetics. It has taught that the defects and evils of actual experience disappear in the "rational whole" of things; that things *appear* evil merely because of the partial, incomplete nature of experience. Or, as was noted by Bacon, "reason" assumes a false simplicity, uniformity and universality, and opens for science a path of fictitious ease. This course results in intellectual irresponsibility and neglect:—irresponsibility because rationalism assumes that the concepts of reason are so self-sufficient and so far above experience that they need and can secure no confirmation in experience. Neglect, because this same assumption makes men careless about concrete observations and experiments. Contempt for experience has had a tragic revenge *in* experience; it has cultivated disregard for fact and this disregard has been paid for in failure, sorrow and war.

The dogmatic rigidity of Rationalism is best seen in the consequences of Kant's attempt to buttress an otherwise chaotic experience with pure concepts. He set out with a laudable attempt at restricting the extravagant pretensions of Reason apart from experience. He called his philosophy critical. But because he taught that the understanding employs fixed, *a priori*, concepts, in order to introduce connection into experience and thereby make known *objects* possible (stable, regular relationships of qualities), he developed in German thought a curious contempt for the living variety of experience and a curious overestimate of the value of system, order, regularity for their own sakes. More practical causes were at work in producing the peculiarly German regard for drill, discipline, "order" and docility.

But Kant's philosophy served to provide an intellectual justification or "rationalization" of subordination of individuals to fixed and ready-made universals, "principles," laws. Reason and law were held to be synonyms. And as reason came into experience from without and above, so law had to come into life from some external and superior authority. The practical correlate to absolutism is rigidity, stiffness, inflexibility of disposition. When Kant taught that some conceptions, and these the important ones, are *a priori*, that they do not arise in experience and cannot be verified or tested in experience, that without such ready-made injections into experience the latter is anarchic and chaotic, he fostered the spirit of absolutism, even though technically he denied the possibility of absolutes. His successors were true to his spirit rather than his letter, and so they taught absolutism systematically. That the Germans with all their scientific competency and technological proficiency should have fallen into their tragically rigid and "superior" style of thought and action (tragic because involving them in inability to understand the world in which they lived) is a sufficient lesson of what may be involved in a systematical denial of the experimental character of intelligence and its conceptions.

By common consent, the effect of English empiricism was sceptical where that of German rationalism was apologetic; it undermined where the latter justified. It detected accidental associations formed into customs under the influence of self- or class-interest where German rational-idealism discovered profound meanings due to the necessary evolution of absolute reason. The modern world has suffered because in so many matters philosophy has offered it only an arbitrary choice between hard and fast opposites: Disintegrating analysis or rigid synthesis; complete radicalism neglecting and attacking the historic past as trivial and harmful, *or* complete conservatism idealizing institutions as embodiments of eternal reason; a resolution of experience into atomic elements that afford no support to stable organization or a clamping down of all experience by fixed categories and necessary concepts—these are the alternatives that conflicting schools have presented.

They are the logical consequences of the traditional opposition of Sense and Thought, Experience and Reason. Common sense has refused to follow both theories to their ultimate logic, and has fallen back on faith, intuition or the exigencies of practical compromise. But common sense too often has been confused and hampered instead of enlightened and directed by the philosophies proffered it by professional intellectuals. Men who are thrown back upon "common sense" when they appeal to philosophy for some general guidance are likely to fall back on routine, the force of some personality, strong leadership or on the pressure of momentary circumstances. It would be difficult to estimate the harm that has resulted because the liberal and progressive movement of the eighteenth and earlier nineteenth centuries had no method of intellectual articulation commensurate with its practical aspirations. Its heart was in the right place. It was humane and social in intention. But it had no theoretical instrumentalities of constructive power. Its head was sadly deficient. Too often the logical import of its professed doctrines was almost anti-social in their atomistic individualism, anti-human in devotion to brute sensation. This deficiency played into the hands of the reactionary and obscurantist. The strong point of the appeal to fixed principles transcending experience, to dogmas incapable of experimental verification, the strong point of reliance upon *a priori* canons of truth and standards of morals in opposition to dependence upon fruits and consequences in experience, has been the unimaginative conception of experience which professed philosophic empiricists have entertained and taught.

A philosophic reconstruction which should relieve men of having to choose between an impoverished and truncated experience on one hand and an artificial and impotent reason on the other would relieve human effort from the heaviest intellectual burden it has to carry. It would destroy the division of men of good will into two hostile camps. It would permit the co-operation of those who respect the past and the institutionally established with those who are interested in establishing a freer and happier future. For it would determine the conditions under which the funded experience of the past and the contriving intelligence which looks to the future can effectually interact with each other. It would enable men to glorify the claims of reason without at the same time falling into a paralyzing worship of superempirical authority or into an offensive "rationalization" of things as they are.

III. RECONSTRUCTION AS AFFECTING SOCIAL PHILOSOPHY

How can philosophic change seriously affect social philosophy? As far as fundamentals are concerned, every view and combination appears to have been formulated already. Society is composed of individuals: this obvious and basic fact no philosophy, whatever its pretensions to novelty, can question or alter. Hence these three alternatives: Society must exist for the sake of individuals; or individuals must have their ends and ways of living set for them by society; or else society and individuals are correlative, organic, to one another, society requiring the service and subordination of individuals and at the same time existing to serve them. Beyond these three views, none seems to be logically conceivable. Moreover, while each of the three types includes many subspecies and variations within itself, yet the changes seem to have been so thoroughly rung that at most only minor variations are now possible.

Especially would it seem true that the "organic" conception meets all the objections to the extreme individualistic and extreme socialistic theories, avoiding the errors alike of Plato and Bentham. Just because society is composed of individuals, it would seem that individuals and the associative relations that hold them together must be of coequal importance. Without strong and competent individuals, the bonds and ties that form society have nothing to lay hold on. Apart from associations with one another, individuals are isolated from one another and fade and wither; or are opposed to one another and their conflicts injure individual development. Law, state, church, family, friendship, industrial association, these and other institutions and arrangements are necessary in order that individuals may grow and find their specific capacities and functions. Without their aid and support human life is, as Hobbes said, brutish, solitary, nasty.

We plunge into the heart of the matter, by asserting that these various theories suffer from a common defect. They are all committed to the logic of general notions under which specific situations are to be brought. What we want light upon is this or that group of individuals, this or that concrete human being, this or that special institution or social arrangement. For such a logic of inquiry, the traditionally accepted logic substitutes discussion of the meaning of concepts and their dialectical relationship to one another. The discussion goes on in terms of *the* state, *the* individual; the nature of institutions as such, society in general.

We need guidance in dealing with particular perplexities in domestic life, and are met by dissertations on the Family or by assertions of the sacredness of individual Personality.

We want to know about the worth of the institution of private property as it operates under given conditions of definite time and place. We meet with the reply of Proudhon that property generally is theft, or with that of Hegel that the realization of will is the end of all institutions, and that private ownership as the expression of mastery of personality over physical nature is a necessary element in such realization. Both answers may have a certain suggestiveness in connection with specific situations. But the conceptions are not proffered for what they may be worth in connection with special historic phenomena. They are general answers supposed to have a universal meaning that covers and dominates all particulars. Hence they do not assist inquiry. They close it. They are not instrumentalities to be employed and tested in clarifying concrete social difficulties. They are ready-made principles to be imposed upon particulars in order to determine their nature. They tell us about *the* state when we want to know about *some* state. But the implication is that what is said about *the* state applies to any state that we happen to wish to know about.

In transferring the issue from concrete situations to definitions and conceptual deductions, the effect, especially of the organic theory, is to supply the apparatus for intellectual justification of the established order. Those most interested in practical social progress and the emancipation of groups from oppression have turned a cold shoulder to the organic theory. The effect, if not the intention, of German idealism as applied in social philosophy was to provide a bulwark for the maintenance of the political *status quo* against the tide of radical ideas coming from revolutionary France. Although Hegel asserted in explicit form that the end of states and institutions is to further the realization of the freedom of all, his effect was to consecrate the Prussian State and to enshrine bureaucratic absolutism. Was this apologetic tendency accidental, or did it spring from something in the logic of the notions that were employed?

Surely the latter. If we talk about *the* state and *the* individual, rather than about this or that political organization and this or that group of needy and suffering human beings, the tendency is to throw the glamor and prestige, the meaning and value attached to the general notion, over the concrete situation and thereby to cover up the defects of the latter and disguise the need of serious reforms. The meanings which are found in the general notions are injected into the particulars that come under them. Quite properly so if we once grant the logic of rigid universals under which the concrete cases have to be subsumed in order to be understood and explained.

Again, the tendency of the organic point of view is to minimize the significance of specific conflicts. Since the individual and the state or social institution are but two sides of the same reality, since they are already reconciled in principle and conception, the conflict in any particular case can be but apparent. Since in theory the individual and the state are reciprocally necessary and helpful to one another, why pay much attention to the fact that in *this* state a whole group of individuals are suffering from oppressive conditions? In "reality" their interests cannot be in conflict with those of the state to which they belong; the opposition is only superficial and casual. Capital and labor cannot "really" conflict because each is an organic necessity to the other, and both to the organized community as a whole. There cannot "really" be any sex-problem because men and women are indispensable both to one another and to the state. In his day, Aristotle could easily employ the logic of general concepts superior to individuals to show that the institution of slavery was in the interests both of the state and of the slave class. Even if the intention is not to justify the existing order the effect is to divert attention from special situations. Rationalistic logic formerly made men careless in observation of the concrete in physical philosophy. It now operates to depress and retard observation in specific social phenomena. The social philosopher, dwelling in the region of his concepts, "solves" problems by showing the relationship of ideas, instead of helping men solve problems in the concrete by supplying them hypotheses to be used and tested in projects of reform.

Meanwhile, of course, the concrete troubles and evils remain. They are not magically waived out of existence because in theory society is organic. The region of concrete difficulties, where the assistance of intelligent method for tentative plans for experimentation is urgently needed, is precisely where intelligence fails to operate. In this region of the specific and concrete, men are thrown back upon the crudest empiricism, upon short-sighted opportunism and the matching of brute forces. In theory, the particulars are all neatly disposed of; they come under their appropriate heading and category; they are labelled and go into an orderly pigeon-hole in a systematic filing cabinet, labelled political science or sociology. But in empirical fact they remain as perplexing, confused and unorganized as they were before. So they are dealt with not by even an endeavor at scientific method but by blind rule of thumb, citation of precedents, considerations of immediate advantage, smoothing things over, use of coercive force and the clash of personal ambitions. The world still survives; it has therefore got on somehow:—so much cannot be denied. The method of trial and error and competition of selfishness has somehow wrought out many improvements. But social theory nevertheless exists as an idle luxury rather than as a guiding method of inquiry and planning. In the question of methods concerned with reconstruction of special situations rather than in any refinements in the general concepts of institution, individuality, state, freedom, law, order, progress, etc., lies the true impact of philosophical reconstruction.

Consider the conception of the individual self. The individualistic school of England and France in the eighteenth and nineteenth centuries was empirical in intent. It based its individualism, philosophically speaking, upon the belief that individuals are alone real, that classes and organizations are secondary and derived. They are artificial, while individuals are natural. In what way then can individualism be said to come under the animadversions that have been passed? To say the defect was that this school overlooked those connections with other persons which are a part of the constitution of every individual is true as far as it goes; but unfortunately it rarely goes beyond the point of just that wholesale justification of institutions which has been criticized.

The real difficulty is that the individual is regarded as something *given,* something already there. Consequently, he can only be something to be catered to, something whose pleasures are to be magnified and possessions multiplied. When the individual is taken as something given already, anything that can be done to him or for him it can only be by way of external impressions and belongings: sensations of pleasure and pain, comforts, securities. Now it is true that social arrangements, laws, institutions are made for man, rather than that man is made for them; that they are means and agencies of human welfare and progress. But they are not means for obtaining something for individuals, not even happiness. They are means of *creating* individuals. Only in the physical sense of physical bodies that to the senses are separate is individuality an original datum. Individuality in a social and moral sense is something to be wrought out. It means initiative, inventiveness, varied resourcefulness, assumption of responsibility in choice of belief and conduct. These are not gifts, but achievements. As achievements, they are not absolute but relative to the use that is to be made of them. And this use varies with the environment.

The import of this conception comes out in considering the fortunes of the idea of self-interest. All members of the empirical school emphasized this idea. It was the sole motive of mankind. Virtue was to be attained by making benevolent action profitable to the individual; social arrangements were to be reformed so that egoism and altruistic consideration of others would be identified. Moralists of the opposite school were not backward in pointing out the evils of any theory that reduced both morals and political science to means of calculating self-interest. Consequently they threw the whole idea of interest overboard as obnoxious to morals. The effect of this reaction was to strengthen the cause of authority and political obscurantism. When the play of interest is eliminated, what remains? What concrete moving forces can be found? Those who identified the self with something ready-made and its interest with acquisition of pleasure and profit took the most effective means possible to reinstate the logic of abstract conceptions of law, justice, sovereignty, freedom, etc.—all of those vague general ideas that for all their seeming rigidity can be manipulated by any clever politician to cover up his designs and to make the worse seem the better cause. Interests are specific and dynamic; they are the natural terms of any concrete social thinking. But they are damned beyond recovery when they are identified with the things of a petty selfishness. They can be employed as vital terms only when the self is seen to be in process, and interest to be a name for whatever is concerned in furthering its movement.

The same logic applies to the old dispute of whether reform should start with the individual or with institutions. When the self is regarded as something complete within itself, then it is readily argued that only internal moralistic changes are of importance in general reform. Institutional changes are said to be merely external. They may add conveniences and comforts to life, but they cannot effect moral improvements. The result is to throw the burden for social improvement upon free-will in its most impossible form.

Moreover, social and economic passivity are encouraged. Individuals are led to concentrate in moral introspection upon their own vices and virtues, and to neglect the character of the environment. Morals withdraw from active concern with detailed economic and political conditions. Let us perfect ourselves within, and in due season changes in society will come of themselves is the teaching. And while saints are engaged in introspection, burly sinners run the world. But when self-hood is perceived to be an active process it is also seen that social modifications are the only means of the creation of changed personalities. Institutions are viewed in their educative effect:—with reference to the types of individuals they foster. The interest in individual moral improvement and the social interest in objective reform of economic and political conditions are identified. And inquiry into the meaning of social arrangements gets definite point and direction. We are led to ask what the spesific stimulating, fostering and nurturing power of each specific social arrangement may be. The old-time separation between politics and morals is abolished at its roots.

Consequently we cannot be satisfied with the general statement that society and the state is organic to the individual. The question is one of specific causations. Just what response does *this* social arrangement, political or economic, evoke, and what effect does it have upon the disposition of those who engage in it? Does it release capacity? If so, how widely? Among a few, with a corresponding depression in others, or in an extensive and equitable way? Is the capacity which is set free also directed in some coherent way, so that it becomes a power, or its manifestation spasmodic and capricious? Since responses are of an indefinite diversity of kind, these inquiries have to be detailed and specific. Are men's senses rendered more delicately sensitive and appreciative, or are they blunted and dulled by this and that form of social organization? Are their minds trained so that the hands are more deft and cunning? Is curiosity awakened or blunted? What is its quality: is it merely esthetic, dwelling on the forms and surfaces of things or is it also an intellectual searching into their meaning? Such questions as these (as well as the more obvious ones about the qualities conventionally labelled moral), become the starting-points of inquiries about every institution of the community when it is recognized that individuality is not originally given but is created under the influences of associated life. Like utilitarianism, the theory subjects every form of organization to continual scrutiny and criticism. But instead of leading us to ask what it does in the way of causing pains and pleasures to individuals already in existence, it inquires what is done to release specific capacities and co-ordinate them into working powers. What sort of individuals are created?

The waste of mental energy due to conducting discussion of social affairs in terms of conceptual generalities is astonishing. How far would the biologist and the physician progress if when the subject of respiration is under consideration, discussion confined itself to bandying back and forth the concepts of organ and organism:—If for example one school thought respiration could be known and understood by insisting upon the fact that it occurs in an individual body and therefore is an "individual" phenomenon, while an opposite school insisted that it is simply one function in organic interaction with others and can be known or understood therefore only by reference to other functions taken in an equally general or wholesale way? Each proposition is equally true and equally futile. What is needed is specific inquiries into a multitude of specific structures and interactions. Not only does the solemn reiteration of categories of individual and organic or social whole not further these definite and detailed inquiries, but it checks them. It detains thought within pompous and sonorous generalities wherein controversy is as inevitable as it is incapable of solution. It is true enough that if cells were not in vital interaction with one another, they could neither conflict nor co-operate. But the fact of the existence of an "organic" social group, instead of answering any questions merely marks the fact that questions exist: Just what conflicts and what co-operations occur, and what are their specific causes and consequences? But because of the persistence within social philosophy of the order of ideas that has been expelled from natural philosophy, even sociologists take conflict or co-operation as general categories upon which to base their science, and condescend to empirical facts only for illustrations. As a rule, their chief "problem" is a purely dialectical one, covered up by a thick quilt of empirical anthropological and historical citations: How do individuals unite to form society? How are individuals socially controlled? And the problem is justly called dialectical because it springs from antecedent conceptions of "individual" and "social."

Just as "individual" is not one thing, but is a blanket term for the immense variety of specific reactions, habits, dispositions and powers of human nature that are evoked, and confirmed under the influences of associated life, so with the term "social." Society is one word, but infinitely many things. It covers all the ways in which by associating together men share their experiences, and build up common interests and aims; street gangs, schools for burglary, clans, social cliques, trades unions, joint stock corporations, villages and international alliances. The new method takes effect in substituting inquiry into these specific, changing and relative facts (relative to problems and purposes, not metaphysically relative) for solemn manipulation of general notions.

Strangely enough, the current conception of the state is a case in point. For one direct influence of the classic order of fixed species arranged in hierarchical order is the attempt of German political philosophy in the nineteenth century to enumerate a definite number of institutions, each having its own essential and immutable meaning; to arrange them in an order of "evolution" which corresponds with the dignity and rank of the respective meanings. The National State was placed at the top as the consummation and culmination, and also the basis of all other institutions.

Hegel is a striking example of this industry, but he is far from the only one. Many who have bitterly quarrelled with him, have ony differed as to the details of the "evolution" or as to the particular meaning to be attributed as essential *Begriff* to some one of the enumerated institutions. The quarrel has been bitter only because the underlying premises were the same. Particularly have many schools of thought, varying even more widely in respect to method and conclusion, agreed upon the final consummating position of the state. They may not go as far as Hegel in making the sole meaning of history to be the evolution of National Territorial States, each of which embodies more than the prior form of the essential meaning or conception of *the* State and consequently displaces it, until we arrive at that triumph of historical evolution, the Prussian State. But they do not question the unique and supreme position of the State in the social hierarchy. Indeed that conception has hardened into unquestionable dogma under the title of sovereignty.

There can be no doubt of the tremendously important rôle played by the modern territorial national state. The formation of these states has been the centre of modern political history. France, Great Britain, Spain were the first peoples to attain nationalistic organization, but in the nineteenth century their example was followed by Japan, Germany and Italy, to say nothing of a large number of smaller states, Greece, Servia, Bulgaria, etc. As everybody knows, one of the most important phases of the recent world war was the struggle to complete the nationalistic movement, resulting in the erection of Bohemia, Poland, etc., into independent states, and the accession of Armenia, Palestine, etc., to the rank of candidates.

The struggle for the supremacy of the State over other forms of organization was directed against the power of minor districts, provinces, principalities, against the dispersion of power among feudal lords as well as, in some countries, against the pretensions of an ecclesiastic potentate. The "State" represents the conspicuous culmination of the great movement of social integration and consolidation taking place in the last few centuries, tremendously accelerated by the concentrating and combining forces of steam and electricity. Naturally, inevitably, the students of political science have been preoccupied with this great historic phenomenon, and their intellectual activities have been directed to its systematic formulation. Because the contemporary progressive movement was to establish the unified state against the inertia of minor social units and against the ambitions of rivals for power, political theory developed the dogma of the sovereignty of the national state, internally and externally.

As the work of integration and consolidation reaches its climax, the question arises, however, whether the national state, once it is firmly established and no longer struggling against strong foes, is not just an instrumentality for promoting and protecting other and more voluntary forms of association, rather than a supreme end in itself. Two actual phenomena may be pointed to in support of an affirmative answer. Along with the development of the larger, more inclusive and more unified organization of the state has gone the emancipation of individuals from restrictions and servitudes previously imposed by custom and class status. But the individuals freed from external and coercive bonds have not remained isolated. Social molecules have at once recombined in new associations and organizations. Compulsory associations have been replaced by voluntary ones; rigid organizations by those more amenable to human choice and purposes—more directly changeable at will. What upon one side looks like a movement toward indivi-

dualism, turns out to be really a movement toward multiplying all kinds and varieties of associations: Political
parties, industrial corporations, scientific and artistic organizations, trade unions, churches, schools, clubs and societies
without number, for the cultivation of every conceivable
interest that men have in common. As they develop in number and importance, the state tends to become more and
more a regulator and adjuster among them; defining the
limits of their actions, preventing and settling conflicts.

Its "supremacy" approximates that of the conductor of an
orchestra, who makes no music himself but who harmonizes
the activities of those who in producing it are doing
the thing intrinsically worth while. The state remains highly
important—but its importance consists more and more in
its power to foster and co-ordinate the activities of voluntary groupings. Only nominally is it in any modern community the end for the sake of which all the other societies and
organizations exist. Groupings for promoting the diversity
of goods that men share have become the real social units.
They occupy the place which traditional theory has
claimed either for mere isolated individuals or for the supreme and single political organization. Pluralism is well
ordained in present political practice and demands a modification of hierarchical and monistic theory. Every combination of human forces that adds its own contribution of value
to life has for that reason its own unique and ultimate worth.
It cannot be degraded into a means to glorify the State.
One reason for the increased demoralization of war is that
it forces the State into an abnormally supreme position.

The other concrete fact is the opposition between the
claim of independent sovereignty in behalf of the territorial
national state and the growth of international and what
have well been called trans-national interests. The weal and
woe of any modern state is bound up with that of others.
Weakness, disorder, false principles on the part of any state
are not confined within its boundaries. They spread and

infect other states. The same is true of economic, artistic and scientific advances. Moreover the voluntary associations just spoken of do not coincide with political boundaries. Associations of mathematicians, chemists, astronomers; business corporations, labor organizations, churches are transnational because the interests they represent are worldwide. In such ways as these, internationalism is not an aspiration but a fact, not a sentimental ideal but a force. Yet these interests are cut across and thrown out of gear by the traditional doctrine of exclusive national sovereignty. It is the vogue of this doctrine, or dogma, that presents the strongest barrier to the effective formation of an international mind which alone agrees with the moving forces of present-day labor, commerce, science, art and religion.

Society, as was said, is many associations not a single organization. Society means association; coming together in joint intercourse and action for the better realization of any form of experience which is augmented and confirmed by being shared. Hence there are as many associations as there are goods which are enhanced by being mutually communicated and participated in. And these are literally indefinite in number. Indeed, capacity to endure publicity and communication is the test by which it is decided whether a pretended good is genuine or spurious. Moralists have always insisted upon the fact that good is universal, objective, not just private, particular. But too often, like Plato, they have been content with a metaphysical universality or, like Kant, with a logical universality. Communication, sharing, joint participation are the only actual ways of universalizing the moral law and end. We insisted at the last hour upon the unique character of every intrinsic good. But the counterpart of this proposition is that the situation in which a good is consciously realized is not one of transient sensations or private appetites but one of sharing and communication—public, social. Even the hermit communes with gods or spirits; even misery loves company; and the most extreme selfishness includes a band of followers or some partner to share in the attained good. Universalization means socialization, the extension of the area and range of those who share in a good.

The increasing acknowledgment that goods exist and endure only through being communicated and that association is the means of conjoint sharing lies back of the modern sense of humanity and democracy. It is the saving salt in altruism and philanthropy, which without this factor degenerate into moral condescension and moral interference, taking the form of trying to regulate the affairs of others under the guise of doing them good or of conferring upon them some right as if it were a gift of charity. It follows that organization is never an end in itself. It is a means of promoting *association,* of multiplying effective points of contact between persons, directing their intercourse into the modes of greatest fruitfulness.

The tendency to treat organization as an end in itself is responsible for all the exaggerated theories in which individuals are subordinated to some institution to which is given the noble name of society. Society is the *process* of associating in such ways that experiences, ideas, emotions, values are transmitted and made common. To this active process, both the individual and the institutionally organized may truly be said to be subordinate. The individual is subordinate because except in and through communication of experience from and to others, he remains dumb, merely sentient, a brute animal. Only in association with fellows does he become a conscious centre of experience. Organization, which is what traditional theory has generally meant by the term Society or State, is also subordinate because it becomes static, rigid, institutionalized whenever it is not employed to facilitate and enrich the contacts of human beings with one another.

The long-time controversy between rights and duties, law and freedom is another version of the strife between the

Individual and Society as fixed concepts. Freedom for an individual means growth, ready change when modification is required.

It signifies an active process, that of release of capacity from whatever hems it in. But since society can develop only as new resources are put at its disposal, it is absurd to suppose that freedom has positive significance for individuality but negative meaning for social interests. Society is strong, forceful, stable against accident only when all its members can function to the limit of their capacity. Such functioning cannot be achieved without allowing a leeway of experimentation beyond the limits of established and santioned custom. A certain amount of overt confusion and irregularity is likely to accompany the granting of the margin of liberty without which capacity cannot find itself. But socially as well as scientifically the great thing is not to avoid mistakes but to have them take place under conditions such that they can be utilized to increase intelligence in the future.

If British liberal social philosophy tended, true to the spirit of its atomistic empiricism, to make freedom and the exercise of rights ends in themselves, the remedy is not to be found in recourse to a philosophy of fixed obligations and authoritative law such as characterized German political thinking. The latter, as events have demonstrated, is dangerous because of its implicit menace to the free self-determination of other social groups. But it is also weak internally when put to the final test. In its hostility to the free experimentation and power of choice of the individual in determining social affairs, it limits the capacity of many or most individuals to share effectively in social operations, and thereby deprives society of the full contribution of all its members. The best guarantee of collective efficiency and power is liberation and use of the diversity of individual capacities in initiative, planning, foresight, vigor and endurance. Personality must be educated, and personality cannot be educated by confining its operations to technical and specialized things, or to the less important relationships of life. Full education comes only when there is a responsible share on the part of each person, in proportion to capacity, in shaping the aims and policies of the social groups to which he belongs. This fact fixes the significance of democracy. It cannot be conceived as a sectarian or racial thing nor as a consecration of some form of government which has already attained constitutional sanction. It is but a name for the fact that human nature is developed only when its elements take part in directing things which are common, things for the sake of which men and women form groups— families, industrial companies, governments, churches, scientific associations and so on. The principle holds as much of one form of association, say in industry and commerce, as it does in government. The identification of democracy with political democracy which is responsible for most of its failures is, however, based upon the traditional ideas which make the individual and the state ready-made entities in themselves.

As the new ideas find adequate expression in social life, they will be absorbed into a moral background, and the ideas and beliefs themselves will be deepened and be unconsciously transmitted and sustained. They will color the imagination and temper the desires and affections. They will not form a set of ideas to be expounded, reasoned out and argumentatively supported, but will be a spontaneous way of envisaging life. Then they will take on religious value. The religious spirit will be revivified because it will be in harmony with men's unquestioned scientific beliefs and their ordinary day-by-day social activities. It will not be obliged to lead a timid, half-concealed and half-apologetic life because tied to scientific ideas and social creeds that are continuously eaten into and broken down. But especially will the ideas and beliefs themselves be deepened and intensified because spontaneously fed by emotion and translated into imaginative vision and fine art, while they are now maintained by more or less conscious effort, by deliberate reflection, by taking thought. They are technical and abstract just because they are not as yet carried as a matter of course by imagination and feelings.

We began by pointing out that European philosophy arose when intellectual methods and scientific results moved away from social traditions which had consolidated and embodied the fruits of spontaneous desire and fancy. It was pointed out that philosophy had ever since had the problem of adjusting the dry, thin and meagre scientific standpoint with the obstinately persisting body of warm and abounding imaginative beliefs. Conceptions of possibility, progress, free movement and infinitely diversified opportunity have been suggested by modern science. But until they have displaced from *imagination* the heritage of the immutable and the once-for-all ordered and systematized, the ideas of mechanism and matter will lie like a dead weight upon the emotions, paralyzing religion and distorting art. When the liberation of capacity no longer seems a menace to organization and established institutions, something that cannot be avoided practically and yet something that is a threat to conservation of the most precious values of the past, when the liberating of human capacity operates as a socially creative force, art will not be a luxury, a stranger to the daily occupations of making a living. Making a living economically speaking, will be at one with making a life that is worth living. And when the emotional force, the mystic force one might say, of communication, of the miracle of shared life and shared experience is spontaneously felt, the hardness and crudeness of contemporary life will be bathed in the light that never was on land or sea.

Poetry, art, religion are precious things. They cannot be maintained by lingering in the past and futilely wishing to restore what the movement of events in science, industry and politics has destroyed. They are an out-flowering of thought and desires that unconsciously converge into a disposition of imagination as a result of thousands and thousands of daily episodes and contact. They cannot be willed into existence or coerced into being. The wind of the spirit bloweth where it listeth and the kingdom of God in such things does not come with observation. But while it is impossible to retain and recover by deliberate volition old sources of religion and art that have been discredited, it is possible to expedite the development of the vital sources of a religion and art that are yet to be. Not indeed by action directly aimed at their production, but by substituting faith in the active tendencies of the day for dread and dislike of them, and by the courage of intelligence to follow whither social and scientific changes direct us. We are weak today in ideal matters because intelligence is divorced from aspiration. The bare force of circumstances compels us onwards in the daily detail of our beliefs and acts, but our deeper thoughts and desires turn backwards. When philosophy shall have cooperated with the course of events and made clear and coherent the meaning of the daily detail, science and emotion will interpenetrate, practice and imagination will embrace. Poetry and religious feeling will be the unforced flowers of life. To further this articulation and revelation of the meanings of the current course of events is the task and problem of philosophy in days of transition.

III ✦ Philosophy as Education

I. EDUCATION AS A NECESSITY OF LIFE*

Renewal of Life by Transmission.—The most notable distinction between living and inanimate beings is that the former maintain themselves by renewal. A stone when struck resists. If its resistance is greater than the force of the blow struck, it remains outwardly unchanged. Otherwise, it is shattered into smaller bits. Never does the stone attempt to react in such a way that it may maintain itself against the blow, much less so as to render the blow a contributing factor to its own continued action. While the living thing may easily be crushed by superior force, it none the less tries to turn the energies which act upon it into means of its own further existence. If it cannot do so, it does not just split into smaller pieces (at least in the higher forms of life), but loses its identity as a living thing.

As long as it endures, it struggles to use surrounding energies in its own behalf. It uses light, air, moisture, and the material of soil. To say that it uses them is to say that it turns them into means of its own conservation. As long as it is growing, the energy it expends in thus turning the environment to account is more than compensated for by the return it gets: it grows. Understanding the word "control" in this sense, it may be said that a living being is one that subjugates and controls for its own continued activity the

---

* From John Dewey, *Democracy and Education.* Copyright 1916, 1944, by John Dewey and used with the permission of The Macmillan Co.

energies that would otherwise use it up. Life is a self-renewing process through action upon the environment.

In all the higher forms this process cannot be kept up indefinitely. After a while they succumb; they die. The creature is not equal to the task of indefinite self-renewal. But continuity of the life process is not dependent upon the prolongation of the existence of any one individual. Reproduction of other forms of life goes on in continuous sequence. And though, as the geological record shows, not merely individuals but also species die out, the life process continues in increasingly complex forms. As some species die out, forms better adapted to utilize the obstacles against which they struggled in vain come into being. Continuity of life means continual readaptation of the environment to the needs of living organisms.

We have been speaking of life in its lowest terms—as a physical thing. But we use the word "life" to denote the whole range of experience, individual and racial. When we see a book called the *Life of Lincoln* we do not expect to find within its covers a treatise on physiology. We look for an account of social antecedents; a description of early surroundings, of the conditions and occupation of the family; of the chief episodes in the development of character; of signal struggles and achievements; of the individual's hopes, tastes, joys and sufferings. In precisely similar fashion we speak of the life of a savage tribe, of the Athenian people, of the American nation. "Life" covers customs, institutions, beliefs, victories and defeats, recreations and occupations.

We employ the word "experience" in the same pregnant sense. And to it, as well as to life in the bare physiological sense, the principle of continuity through renewal applies. With the renewal of physical existence goes, in the case of human beings, the re-creation of beliefs, ideals, hopes, happiness, misery, and practices. The continuity of any experience, through renewing of the social group, is a literal fact. Education, in its broadest sense, is the means of this social continuity of life. Every one of the constituent elements of a social group, in a modern city as in a savage tribe, is born immature, helpless, without language, beliefs, ideas, or social standards. Each individual, each unit who is the carrier of the life-experience of his group, in time passes away. Yet the life of the group goes on.

The primary ineluctable facts of the birth and death of each one of the constituent members in a social group determine the necessity of education. On one hand, there is the contrast between the immaturity of the new-born members of the group—its future sole representatives—and the maturity of the adult members who possess the knowledge and customs of the group. On the other hand, there is the necessity that these immature members be not merely physically preserved in adequate numbers, but that they be initiated into the interests, purposes, information, skill, and practices of the mature members: otherwise the group will cease its characteristic life. Even in a savage tribe, the achievements of adults are far beyond what the immature members would be capable of if left to themselves. With the growth of civilization, the gap between the original capacities of the immature and the standards and customs of the elders increases. Mere physical growing up, mere mastery of the bare necessities of subsistence will not suffice to reproduce the life of the group. Deliberate effort and the taking of thoughtful pains are required. Beings who are born not only unaware of, but quite indifferent to, the aims and habits of the social group have to be rendered cognizant of them and actively interested. Education, and education alone, spans the gap.

Society exists through a process of transmission quite as much as biological life. This transmission occurs by means of communication of habits of doing, thinking, and feeling from the older to the younger. Without this communication of ideals, hopes, expectations, standards, opinions, from those members of society who are passing out of the group life to those who are coming into it, social life could not survive. If the members who compose a society lived on continuously, they might educate the new-born members, but it would be a task directed by personal interest rather than social need. Now it is a work of necessity.

If a plague carried off the members of a society all at once, it is obvious that the group would be permanently done for. Yet the death of each of its constituent members is as certain as if an epidemic took them all at once. But the graded difference in age, the fact that some are born as some die, makes possible through transmission of ideas and practices the constant reweaving of the social fabric. Yet this renewal is not automatic. Unless pains are taken to see that genuine and thorough transmission takes place, the most civilized group will relapse into barbarism and then into savagery. In fact, the human young are so immature that if they were left to themselves without the guidance and succor of others, they could not even acquire the rudimentary abilities necessary for physical existence. The young of human beings compare so poorly in original efficiency with the young of many of the lower animals, that even the powers needed for physical sustentation have to be acquired under tuition. How much more, then, is this the case with respect to all the technological, artistic, scientific, and moral achievements of humanity!

Education and Communication.—So obvious, indeed, is the necessity of teaching and learning for the continued existence of a society that we may seem to be dwelling unduly on a truism. But justification is found in the fact that such emphasis is a means of getting us away from an unduly scholastic and formal notion of education. Schools are, indeed, one important method of the transmission which forms the dispositions of the immature; but it is only one means, and, compared with other agencies, a relatively superficial means. Only as we have grasped the necessity of more fundamental and persistent modes of tuition can we make sure of placing the scholastic methods in their true context.

Society not only continues to exist *by* transmission, *by* communication, but it may fairly be said to exist *in* transmission, *in* communication. There is more than a verbal tie between the words common, community, and communication. Men live in a community in virtue of the things which they have in common; and communication is the way in which they come to possess things in common. What they must have in common in order to form a community or society are aims, beliefs, aspirations, knowledge—a common understanding—like-mindedness as the sociologists say. Such things cannot be passed physically from one to another, like bricks; they cannot be shared as persons would share a pie by dividing it into physical pieces. The communication which insures participation in a common understanding is one which secures similar emotional and intellectual dispositions—like ways of responding to expectations and requirements.

Persons do not become a society by living in physical proximity, any more than a man ceases to be socially influenced by being so many feet or miles removed from others. A book or a letter may institute a more intimate association between human beings separated thousands of miles from each other than exists between dwellers under the same roof. Individuals do not even compose a social group because they all work for a common end. The parts of a machine work with a maximum of coöperativeness for a common result, but they do not form a community. If, however, they were all cognizant of the common end and all interested in it so that they regulated their specific activity in view of it, then they would form a community. But this would involve communication. Each would have to know what the other was about and would have to have some way of keeping the other informed as to his own purpose and progress. Consensus demands communication.

We are thus compelled to recognize that within even the

most social group there are many relations which are not as
yet social. A large number of human relationships in any
social group are still upon the machine-like plane. Individuals use one another so as to get desired results, without reference to the emotional and intellectual disposition and consent of those used. Such uses express physical superiority,
or superiority of position, skill, technical ability, and command of tools, mechanical or fiscal. So far as the relations of
parent and child, teacher and pupil, employer and em-
ployee, governor and governed, remain upon this level, they
form no true social group, no matter how closely their respective activities touch one another. Giving and taking of
orders modifies action and results, but does not of itself
effect a sharing of purposes, a communication of interests.

Not only is social life identical with communication, but
all communication (and hence all genuine social life) is
educative. To be a recipient of a communication is to have
an enlarged and changed experience. One shares in what
another has thought and felt and in so far, meagerly or
amply, has his own attitude modified. Nor is the one who
communicates left unaffected. Try the experiment of com-
municating, with fullness and accuracy, some experience to
another, especially if it be somewhat complicated, and you
will find your own attitude toward your experience changing; otherwise you resort to expletives and ejaculations. The
experience has to be formulated in order to be communicated. To formulate requires getting outside of it, seeing it
as another would see it, considering what points of contact
it has with the life of another so that it may be got into such
form that he can appreciate its meaning. Except in dealing
with commonplaces and catch phrases one has to assimilate,
imaginatively, something of another's experience in order to
tell him intelligently of one's own experience. All communication is like art. It may fairly be said, therefore, that any
social arrangement that remains vitally social, or vitally

shared, is educative to those who participate in it. Only
when it becomes cast in a mold and runs in a routine way
does it lose its educative power.

In final account, then, not only does social life demand
teaching and learning for its own permanence, but the very
process of living together educates. It enlarges and enlight-
ens experience; it stimulates and enriches imagination; it
creates responsibility for accuracy and vividness of statement and thought. A man really living alone (alone
mentally as well as physically) would have little or no occasion to reflect upon his past experience to extract its net
meaning. The inequality of achievement between the mature
and the immature not only necessitates teaching the young,
but the necessity of this teaching gives an immense stimulus
to reducing experience to that order and form which will
render it most easily communicable and hence most usable.

The Place of Formal Education.—There is, accordingly,
a marked difference between the education which every one
gets from living with others, as long as he really lives
instead of just continuing to subsist, and the deliberate edu-
cating of the young. In the former case the education is incidental; it is natural and important, but it is not the express
reason of the association. While it may be said, without exaggeration, that the measure of the worth of any social institution, economic, domestic, political, legal, religious, is its
effect in enlarging and improving experience; yet this effect
is not a part of its original motive, which is limited and more
immediately practical. Religious associations began, for example, in the desire to secure the favor of overruling powers
and to ward off evil influences; family life in the desire to
gratify appetites and secure family perpetuity; systematic
labor, for the most part, because of enslavement to others,
etc. Only gradually was the by-product of the institution,
its effect upon the quality and extent of conscious life,
noted, and only more gradually still was this effect considered as a directive factor in the conduct of the institution.

Even to-day, in our industrial life, apart from certain values of industriousness and thrift, the intellectual and emotional reaction of the forms of human association under which the world's work is carried on receives little attention as compared with physical output.

But in dealing with the young, the fact of association itself as an immediate human fact, gains in importance. While it is easy to ignore in our contact with them the effect of our acts upon their disposition, or to subordinate that educative effect to some external and tangible result, it is not so easy as in dealing with adults. The need of training is too evident; the pressure to accomplish a change in their attitude and habits is too urgent to leave these consequences wholly out of account. Since our chief business with them is to enable them to share in a common life we cannot help considering whether or no we are forming the powers which will secure this ability. If humanity has made some headway in realizing that the ultimate value of every institution is its distinctively human effect—its effect upon conscious experience—we may well believe that this lesson has been learned largely through dealings with the young.

We are thus led to distinguish, within the broad educational process which we have been so far considering, a more formal kind of education—that of direct tuition or schooling. In undeveloped social groups, we find very little formal teaching and training. Savage groups mainly rely for instilling needed dispositions into the young upon the same sort of association which keeps adults loyal to their group. They have no special devices, material, or institutions for teaching save in connection with initiation ceremonies by which the youth are inducted into full social membership. For the most part, they depend upon children learning the customs of the adults, acquiring their emotional set and stock of ideas, by sharing in what the elders are doing. In part, this sharing is direct, taking part in the occupations of adults and thus serving an apprenticeship; in part,

it is indirect, through the dramatic plays in which children
reproduce the actions of grown-ups and thus learn to know
what they are like. To savages it would seem preposterous
to seek out a place where nothing but learning was going on
in order that one might learn.

But as civilization advances, the gap between the capacities of the young and the concerns of adults widens. Learning by direct sharing in the pursuits of grown-ups becomes
increasingly difficult except in the case of the less advanced
occupations. Much of what adults do is so remote in space
and in meaning that playful imitation is less and less adequate to reproduce its spirit. Ability to share effectively in
adult activities thus depends upon a prior training given
with this end in view. Intentional agencies—schools—and
explicit material—studies—are devised. The task of teaching certain things is delegated to a special group of persons.

Without such formal education, it is not possible to transmit all the resources and achievements of a complex society.
It also opens a way to a kind of experience which would not
be accessible to the young, if they were left to pick up their
training in informal association with others, since books and
the symbols of knowledge are mastered.

But there are conspicuous dangers attendant upon the
transition from indirect to formal education. Sharing in
actual pursuit, whether directly or vicariously in play, is at
least personal and vital. These qualities compensate, in
some measure, for the narrowness of available opportunities.
Formal instruction, on the contrary, easily becomes remote
and dead—abstract and bookish, to use the ordinary words
of depreciation. What accumulated knowledge exists in low
grade societies is at least put into practice; it is transmuted
into character; it exists with the depth of meaning that at-
taches to its coming within urgent daily interests.

But in an advanced culture much which has to be
learned is stored in symbols. It is far from translation into
familiar acts and objects. Such material is relatively tech-

nical and superficial. Taking the ordinary standard of reality as a measure, it is artificial. For this measure is connection with practical concerns. Such material exists in a world by itself, unassimilated to ordinary customs of thought and expression. There is the standing danger that the material of formal instruction will be merely the subject matter of the schools, isolated from the subject matter of life-experience. The permanent social interests are likely to be lost from view. Those which have not been carried over into the structure of social life, but which remain largely matters of technical information expressed in symbols, are made conspicuous in schools. Thus we reach the ordinary notion of education: the notion which ignores its social necessity and its identity with all human association that affects conscious life, and which identifies it with imparting information about remote matters and the conveying of learning through verbal signs: the acquisition of literacy.

Hence one of the weightiest problems with which the philosophy of education has to cope is the method of keeping a proper balance between the informal and the formal, the incidental and the intentional, modes of education. When the acquiring of information and of technical intellectual skill do not influence the formation of a social disposition, ordinary vital experience fails to gain in meaning, while schooling, in so far, creates only "sharps" in learning —that is, egoistic specialists. To avoid a split between what men consciously know because they are aware of having learned it by a specific job of learning, and what they unconsciously know because they have absorbed it in the formation of their characters by intercourse with others, becomes an increasingly delicate task with every development of special schooling.

Summary.—It is the very nature of life to strive to continue in being. Since this continuance can be secured only by constant renewals, life is a self-renewing process. What nutrition and reproduction are to physiological life, educa-

tion is to social life. This education consists primarily in
transmission through communication. Communication is a
process of sharing experience till it becomes a common possession. It modifies the disposition of both the parties who
partake in it. That the ulterior significance of every mode
of human association lies in the contribution which it makes
to the improvement of the quality of experience is a fact
most easily recognized in dealing with the immature. That
is to say, while every social arrangement is educative in effect,
the educative effect first becomes an important part of the
purpose of the association in connection with the association
of the older with the younger. As societies become more
complex in structure and resources, the need of formal or
intentional teaching and learning increases. As formal
teaching and training grow in extent, there is the danger of
creating an undesirable split between the experience gained
in more direct associations and what is acquired in school.
This danger was never greater than at the present time, on
account of the rapid growth in the last few centuries
of knowledge and technical modes of skill.

II. EDUCATION AS A SOCIAL FUNCTION

The Nature and Meaning of Environment.—
We have seen that a community or social group sustains itself through continuous self-renewal, and that this renewal
takes place by means of the educational growth of the immature members of the group. By various agencies, unin-
tentional and designed, a society transforms uninitiated
and seemingly alien beings into robust trustees of its own
resources and ideals. Education is thus a fostering, a nurturing, a cultivating, process. All of these words mean that
it implies attention to the *conditions of growth*. We also
speak of rearing, raising, bringing up—words which express
the difference of level which education aims to cover. Ety-
mologically, the word education means just a process of

leading or bringing up. When we have the outcome of the process in mind, we speak of education as shaping, forming, molding activity—that is, a shaping into the standard form of social activity. In this chapter we are concerned with the general features of the *way* in which a social group brings up its immature members into its own social form.

Since what is required is a transformation of the quality of experience till it partakes in the interests, purposes, and ideas current in the social group, the problem is evidently not one of mere physical forming. Things can be physically transported in space; they may be bodily conveyed. Beliefs and aspirations cannot be physically extracted and inserted. How then are they communicated? Given the impossibility of direct contagion or literal inculcation, our problem is to discover the method by which the young assimilate the point of view of the old, or the older bring the young into likemindedness with themselves.

The answer, in general formulation, is: By means of the action of the environment in calling out certain responses. The required beliefs cannot be hammered in; the needed attitudes cannot be plastered on. But the particular medium in which an individual exists leads him to see and feel one thing rather than another; it leads him to have certain plans in order that he may act successfully with others; it strengthens some beliefs and weakens others as a condition of winning the approval of others. Thus it gradually produces in him a certain system of behavior, a certain disposition of action. The words "environment," "medium" denote something more than surroundings which encompass an individual. They denote the specific *continuity* of the surroundings with his own active tendencies. An inanimate being is, of course, continuous with its surroundings; but the environing circumstances do not, save metaphorically, constitute an environment. For the inorganic being is not *concerned* in the influences which affect it. On the other hand, some things which are remote in space and time from a living

creature, especially a human creature, may form his
environment even more truly than some of the things close
to him. The things with which a man *varies* are his genuine
environment. Thus the activities of the astronomer vary
with the stars at which he gazes or about which he calcu-
lates. Of his immediate surroundings, his telescope is most
intimately his environment. The environment of an antiquarian, as an antiquarian, consists of the remote epoch of
human life with which he is concerned, and the relics, in-
scriptions, etc., by which he establishes connections with
that period.

In brief, the environment consists of those conditions that
promote or hinder, stimulate or inhibit, the *characteristic*
activities of a living being. Water is the environment of a
fish because it is necessary to the fish's activities—to its life.
The north pole is a significant element in the environment
of an arctic explorer, whether he succeeds in reaching it or
not, because it defines his activities, makes them what they
distinctively are. Just because life signifies not bare passive
existence (supposing there is such a thing), but a way of
acting, environment or medium signifies what enters into
this activity as a sustaining or frustrating condition.

The Social Environment.—A being whose activities are
associated with others has a social environment. What he
does and what he can do depend upon the expectations,
demands, approvals, and condemnations of others. A being
connected with other beings cannot perform his own activities without taking the activities of others into account. For
they are the indispensable conditions of the realization of
his tendencies. When he moves he stirs them and reciprocally. We might as well try to imagine a business man doing
business, buying and selling, all by himself, as to conceive it
possible to define the activities of an individual in terms of
his isolated actions. The manufacturer moreover is as truly
socially guided in his activities when he is laying plans in
the privacy of his own countinghouse as when he is buy-

ing his raw material or selling his finished goods. Thinking and feeling that have to do with action in association with others is as much a social mode of behavior as is the most overt coöperative or hostile act.

What we have more especially to indicate is how the social medium nurtures its immature members. There is no great difficulty in seeing how it shapes the external habits of action. Even dogs and horses have their actions modified by association with human beings; they form different habits because human beings are concerned with what they do. Human beings control animals by controlling the natural stimuli which influence them; by creating a certain environment in other words. Food, bits and bridles, noises, vehicles, are used to direct the ways in which the natural or instinctive responses of horses occur. By operating steadily to call out certain acts, habits are formed which function with the same uniformity as the original stimuli. If a rat is put in a maze and finds food only by making a given number of turns in a given sequence, his activity is gradually modified till he habitually takes that course rather than another when he is hungry.

Human actions are modified in a like fashion. A burnt child dreads the fire; if a parent arranged conditions so that every time a child touched a certain toy he got burned, the child would learn to avoid that toy as automatically as he avoids touching fire. So far, however, we are dealing with what may be called *training* in distinction from educative teaching. The changes considered are in outer action rather than in mental and emotional dispositions of behavior. The distinction is not, however, a sharp one. The child might conceivably generate in time a violent antipathy, not only to that particular toy, but to the class of toys resembling it. The aversion might even persist after he had forgotten about the original burns; later on he might even invent some reason to account for his seemingly irrational antipathy. In some cases, altering the external habit of action by changing the environment to affect the stimuli to action will also alter the mental disposition concerned in the action. Yet this does not always happen; a person trained to dodge a threatening blow, dodges automatically with no corresponding thought or emotion. We have to find, then, some differentia of training from education.

A clew may be found in the fact that the horse does not really share in the social use to which his action is put. Some one else uses the horse to secure a result which is advantageous by making it advantageous to the horse to perform the act—he gets food, etc. But the horse, presumably, does not get any new interest. He remains interested in food, not in the service he is rendering. He is not a partner in a shared activity. Were he to become a copartner, he would, in engaging in the conjoint activity, have the same interest in its accomplishment which others have. He would share their ideas and emotions.

Now in many cases—too many cases—the activity of the immature human being is simply played upon to secure habits which are useful. He is trained like an animal rather than educated like a human being. His instincts remain attached to their original objects of pain or pleasure. But to get happiness or to avoid the pain of failure he has to act in a way agreeable to others. In other cases, he really shares or participates in the common activity. In this case, his original impulse is modified. He not merely acts in a way agreeing with the actions of others, but, in so acting, the same ideas and emotions are aroused in him that animate the others. A tribe, let us say, is warlike. The successes for which it strives, the achievements upon which it sets store, are connected with fighting and victory. The presence of this medium incites bellicose exhibitions in a boy, first in games, then in fact when he is strong enough. As he fights he wins approval and advancement; as he refrains, he is disliked, ridiculed, shut out from favorable recognition. It is not surprising that his original belligerent tendencies and emotions are strengthened at the expense of others, and that his ideas turn to things connected with war. Only in this way can he become fully a recognized member of his group. Thus his mental habitudes are gradually assimilated to those of his group.

If we formulate the principle involved in this illustration, we shall perceive that the social medium neither implants certain desires and ideas directly, nor yet merely establishes certain purely muscular habits of action, like "instinctively" winking or dodging a blow. Setting up conditions which stimulate certain visible and tangible ways of acting is the first step. Making the individual a sharer or partner in the associated activity so that he feels its success as his success, its failure as his failure, is the completing step. As soon as he is possessed by the emotional attitude of the group, he will be alert to recognize the special ends at which it aims and the means employed to secure success. His beliefs and ideas, in other words, will take a form similar to those of others in the group. He will also achieve pretty much the same stock of knowledge since that knowledge is an ingredient of his habitual pursuits.

The importance of language in gaining knowledge is doubtless the chief cause of the common notion that knowledge may be passed directly from one to another. It almost seems as if all we have to do to convey an idea into the mind of another is to convey a sound into his ear. Thus imparting knowledge gets assimilated to a purely physical process. But learning from language will be found, when analyzed, to confirm the principle just laid down. It would probably be admitted with little hesitation that a child gets the idea of, say, a hat by using it as other persons do; by covering the head with it, giving it to others to wear, having it put on by others when going out, etc. But it may be asked how this principle of shared activity applies to getting through speech or reading the idea of, say, a Greek helmet, where no direct use of any kind enters in. What shared activity is there in learning from books about the discovery of America?

Since language tends to become the chief instrument of learning about many things, let us see how it works. The baby begins of course with mere sounds, noises, and tones having no meaning, expressing, that is, no idea. Sounds are just one kind of stimulus to direct response, some having a soothing effect, others tending to make one jump, and so on. The sound h-a-t would remain as meaningless as a sound in Choctaw, a seemingly inarticulate grunt, if it were not uttered in connection with an action which is participated in by a number of people. When the mother is taking the infant out of doors, she says "hat" as she puts something on the baby's head. Being taken out becomes an interest to the child; mother and child not only go out with each other physically, but both are *concerned* in the going out; they enjoy it in common. By conjunction with the other factors in activity the sound "hat" soon gets the same meaning for the child that it has for the parent; it becomes a sign of the activity into which it enters. The bare fact that language consists of sounds which are *mutually intelligible* is enough of itself to show that its meaning depends upon connection with a shared experience.

In short, the sound h-a-t gains meaning in precisely the same way that the thing "hat" gains it, by being used in a given way. And they acquire the same meaning with the child which they have with the adult because they are used in a common experience by both. The guarantee for the same manner of use is found in the fact that the thing and the sound are first employed in a *joint* activity, as a means of setting up an active connection between the child and a grown-up. Similar ideas or meanings spring up because both persons are engaged as partners in an action where what each does depends upon and influences what the other does. If two savages were engaged in a joint hunt for game, and a certain signal meant "move to the right" to the one who uttered it, and "move to the left" to the one who heard it, they obviously could not successfully carry on their hunt together. Understanding one another means that objects, including sounds, have the same value for both with respect to carrying on a common pursuit.

After sounds have got meaning through connection with other things employed in a joint undertaking, they can be used in connection with other like sounds to develop new meanings, precisely as the things for which they stand are combined. Thus the words in which a child learns about, say, the Greek helmet originally got a meaning (or were understood) by use in an action having a common interest and end. They now arouse a new meaning by inciting the one who hears or reads to rehearse imaginatively the activities in which the helmet has its use. For the time being, the one who understands the words "Greek helmet" becomes mentally a partner with those who used the helmet. He engages, through his imagination, in a shared activity. It is not easy to get the *full* meaning of words. Most persons probably stop with the idea that "helmet" denotes a queer kind of headgear a people called the Greeks once wore. We conclude, accordingly, that the use of language to convey and acquire ideas is an extension and refinement of the principle that things gain meaning by being used in a shared experience or joint action; in no sense does it contravene that principle. When words do not enter as factors into a shared situation, either overtly or imaginatively, they operate as pure physical stimuli, not as having a meaning or intellectual value. They set activity running in a given groove, but there is no accompanying conscious purpose or meaning. Thus, for example, the plus sign may be a stimulus to perform the act of writing one number under another and adding the numbers, but the person forming the act will operate much as an automaton would unless he realizes the meaning of what he does.

The Social Medium as Educative.—Our net result thus

far is that social environment forms the mental and emotional disposition of behavior in individuals by engaging
them in activities that arouse and strengthen certain impulses, that have certain purposes and entail certain consequences. A child growing up in a family of musicians will
inevitably have whatever capacities he has in music stimulated, and, relatively, stimulated more than other impulses
which might have been awakened in another environment.
Save as he takes an interest in music and gains a certain
competency in it, he is "out of it"; he is unable to share in
the life of the group to which he belongs. Some kinds of
participation in the life of those with whom the individual
is connected are inevitable; with respect to them, the social
environment exercises an educative or formative influence
unconsciously and apart from any set purpose.

In savage and barbarian communities, such direct participation (constituting the indirect or incidental education of
which we have spoken) furnishes almost the sole influence
for rearing the young into the practices and beliefs of the
group. Even in present-day societies, it furnishes the basic
nurture of even the most insistently schooled youth. In
accord with the interests and occupations of the group, certain things become objects of high esteem; others of aversion. Association does not create impulses of affection and
dislike, but it furnishes the objects to which they attach
themselves. The way our group or class does things tends to
determine the proper objects of attention, and thus to pre-
scribe the directions and limits of observation and memory.
What is strange or foreign (that is to say outside the activities of the groups) tends to be morally forbidden and intellectually suspect. It seems almost incredible to us, for
example, that things which we know very well could have
escaped recognition in past ages. We incline to account for
it by attributing congenital stupidity to our forerunners
and by assuming superior native intelligence on our own
part. But the explanation is that their modes of life did not

call for attention to such facts, but held their minds riveted to other things. Just as the senses require sensible objects to stimulate them, so our powers of observation, recollection, and imagination do not work spontaneously, but are set in motion by the demands set up by current social occupations. The main texture of disposition is formed, independently of schooling, by such influences. What conscious, deliberate teaching can do is at most to free the capacities thus formed for fuller exercise, to purge them of some of their grossness, and to furnish objects which make their activity more productive of meaning.

While this "unconscious influence of the environment" is so subtle and pervasive that it affects every fiber of character and mind, it may be worth while to specify a few directions in which its effect is most marked. First, the habits of language. Fundamental modes of speech, the bulk of the vocabulary, are formed in the ordinary intercourse of life, carried on not as a set means of instruction but as a social necessity. The babe acquires, as we well say, the *mother* tongue. While speech habits thus contracted may be corrected or even displaced by conscious teaching, yet, in times of excitement, intentionally acquired modes of speech often fall away, and individuals relapse into their really native tongue. Secondly, manners. Example is notoriously more potent than precept. Good manners come, as we say, from good breeding or rather are good breeding; and breeding is acquired by habitual action, in response to habitual stimuli, not by conveying information. Despite the never ending play of conscious correction and instruction, the surrounding atmosphere and spirit is in the end the chief agent in forming manners. And manners are but minor morals. Moreover in major morals, conscious instruction is likely to be efficacious only in the degree in which it falls in with the general "walk and conversation" of those who constitute the child's social environment. Thirdly, good taste and æsthetic appreciation. If the eye is constantly greeted by harmonious objects, having elegance of form and color, a standard of taste naturally grows up. The effect of a tawdry, unarranged, and over-decorated environment works for the deterioration of taste, just as meager and barren surroundings starve out the desire for beauty. Against such odds, conscious teaching can hardly do more than convey second-hand information as to what others think. Such taste never becomes spontaneous and personally engrained, but remains a labored reminder of what those think to whom one has been taught to look up. To say that the deeper standards of judgments of value are framed by the situations into which a person habitually enters is not so much to mention a fourth point, as it is to point out a fusion of those already mentioned. We rarely recognize the extent in which our conscious estimates of what is worth while and what is not, are due to standards of which we are not conscious at all. But in general it may be said that the things which we take for granted without inquiry or reflection are just the things which determine our conscious thinking and decide our conclusions. And these habitudes which lie below the level of reflection are just those which have been formed in the constant give and take of relationship with others.

The School as a Special Environment.—The chief importance of this foregoing statement of the educative process which goes on willynilly is to lead us to note that the only way in which adults consciously control the kind of education which the immature get is by controlling the environment in which they act, and hence think and feel. We never educate directly, but indirectly by means of the environment. Whether we permit chance environments to do the work, or whether we design environments for the purpose makes a great difference. And any environment is a chance environment so far as its educative influence is concerned unless it has been deliberately regulated with reference to its educative effect. An intelligent home differs from an unintelligent one chiefly in that the habits of life and intercourse which prevail are chosen, or at least colored, by the thought of their bearing upon the development of children. But schools remain, of course, the typical instance of environments framed with express reference to influencing the mental and moral disposition of their members.

Roughly speaking, they come into existence when social traditions are so complex that a considerable part of the social store is committed to writing and transmitted through written symbols. Written symbols are even more artificial or conventional than spoken; they cannot be picked up in accidental intercourse with others. In addition, the written form tends to select and record matters which are comparatively foreign to everyday life. The achievements accumulated from generation to generation are deposited in it even though some of them have fallen temporarily out of use. Consequently as soon as a community depends to any considerable extent upon what lies beyond its own territory and its own immediate generation, it must rely upon the set agency of schools to insure adequate transmission of all its resources. To take an obvious illustration: The life of the ancient Greeks and Romans has profoundly influenced our own, and yet the ways in which they affect us do not present themselves on the surface of our ordinary experiences. In similar fashion, peoples still existing, but remote in space, British, Germans, Italians, directly concern our own social affairs, but the nature of the interaction cannot be understood without explicit statement and attention. In precisely similar fashion, our daily associations cannot be trusted to make clear to the young the part played in our activities by remote physical energies, and by invisible structures. Hence a special mode of social intercourse is instituted, the school, to care for such matters.

This mode of association has three functions sufficiently specific, as compared with ordinary associations of life, to be noted. First, a complex civilization is too complex to be assimilated *in toto*. It has to be broken up into portions, as it were, and assimilated piecemeal, in a gradual and graded way. The relationships of our present social life are so numerous and so interwoven that a child placed in the most favorable position could not readily share in many of the most important of them. Not sharing in them, their meaning would not be communicated to him, would not become a part of his own mental disposition. There would be no seeing the trees because of the forest. Business, politics, art, science, religion, would make all at once a clamor for attention; confusion would be the outcome. The first office of the social organ we call the school is to provide a *simplified* environment. It selects the features which are fairly fundamental and capable of being responded to by the young. Then it establishes a progressive order, using the factors first acquired as means of gaining insight into what is more complicated.

In the second place, it is the business of the school environment to eliminate, so far as possible, the unworthy features of the existing environment from influence upon mental habitudes. It establishes a purified medium of action. Selection aims not only at simplifying but at weeding out what is undesirable. Every society gets encumbered with what is trivial, with dead wood from the past, and with what is positively perverse. The school has the duty of omitting such things from the environment which it supplies, and thereby doing what it can to counteract their influence in the ordinary social environment. By selecting the best for its exclusive use, it strives to reënforce the power of this best. As a society becomes more enlightened, it realizes that it is responsible *not* to transmit and conserve the whole of its existing achievements, but only such as make for a better future society. The school is its chief agency for the accomplishment of this end.

In the third place, it is the office of the school environment to balance the various elements in the social environment, and to see to it that each individual gets an opportunity to escape from the limitations of the social group in which he was born, and to come into living contact with a broader environment. Such words as "society" and "community" are likely to be misleading, for they have a tendency to make us think there is single thing corresponding to the single word. As a matter of fact, a modern society is many societies more or less loosely connected. Each household with its immediate extension of friends makes a society; the village or street group of playmates is a community; each business group, each club, is another. Passing beyond these more intimate groups, there is in a country like our own a variety of races, religious affiliations, economic divisions. Inside the modern city, in spite of its nominal political unity, there are probably more communities, more differing customs, traditions, aspirations, and forms of government or control, than existed in an entire continent at an earlier epoch.

Each such group exercises a formative influence on the active dispositions of its members. A clique, a club, a gang, a Fagin's household of thieves, the prisoners in a jail, provide educative environments for those who enter into their collective or conjoint activities, as truly as a church, a labor union, a business partnership, or a political party. Each of them is a mode of associated or community life, quite as much as is a family, a town, or a state. There are also communities whose members have little or no direct contact with one another, like the guild of artists, the republic of letters, the members of the professional learned class scattered over the face of the earth. For they have aims in common, and the activity of each member is directly modified by knowledge of what others are doing.

In the olden times, the diversity of groups was largely a geographical matter. There were many societies, but each, within its own territory, was comparatively homogeneous.

But with the development of commerce, transportation, intercommunication, and emigration, countries like the United States are composed of a combination of different groups with different traditional customs. It is this situation which has, perhaps more than any other one cause, forced the demand for an educational institution which shall provide something like a homogeneous and balanced environment for the young. Only in this way can the centrifugal forces set up by juxtaposition of different groups within one and the same political unit be counteracted. The intermingling in the school of youth of different races, differing religions, and unlike customs creates for all a new and broader environment. Common subject matter accustoms all to a unity of outlook upon a broader horizon than is visible to the members of any group while it is isolated. The assimilative force of the American public school is eloquent testimony to the efficacy of the common and balanced appeal.

The school has the function also of coördinating within the disposition of each individual the diverse influences of the various social environments into which he enters. One code prevails in the family; another, on the street; a third, in the workshop or store; a fourth, in the religious association. As a person passes from one of the environments to another, he is subjected to antagonistic pulls, and is in danger of being split into a being having different standards of judgment and emotion for different occasions. This danger imposes upon the school a steadying and integrating office.

Summary.—The development within the young of the attitudes and dispositions necessary to the continuous and progressive life of a society cannot take place by direct conveyance of beliefs, emotions, and knowledge. It takes place through the intermediary of the environment. The environment consists of the sum total of conditions which are concerned in the execution of the activity characteristic of a living being. The social environment consists of all the activities of fellow beings that are bound up in the carrying on of the activities of any one of its members. It is truly educative in its effect in the degree in which an individual shares or participates in some conjoint activity. By doing his share in the associated activity, the individual appropriates the purpose which actuates it, becomes familiar with its methods and subject matters, acquires needed skill, and is saturated with its emotional spirit.

The deeper and more intimate educative formation of disposition comes, without conscious intent, as the young gradually partake of the activities of the various groups to which they may belong. As a society becomes more complex, however, it is found necessary to provide a special social environment which shall especially look after nurturing the capacities of the immature. Three of the more important functions of this special environment are: simplifying and ordering the factors of the disposition it is wished to develop; purifying and idealizing the existing social customs; creating a wider and better balanced environment than that by which the young would be likely, if left to themselves, to be influenced.

III. EDUCATION AS DIRECTION

The Environment as Directive.—We now pass to one of the special forms which the general function of education assumes: namely, that of direction, control, or guidance. Of these three words, direction, control, and guidance, the last best conveys the idea of assisting through coöperation the natural capacities of the individuals guided; control conveys rather the notion of an energy brought to bear from without and meeting some resistance from the one controlled; direction is a more neutral term and suggests the fact that the active tendencies of those directed are led in a certain continuous course, instead of dispersing aimlessly. Direction expresses the basic function, which tends at one extreme to become a guiding assistance and at another, a regulation or ruling. But in any case, we must carefully avoid a meaning sometimes read into the term "control." It is sometimes assumed, explicitly or unconsciously, that an individual's tendencies are naturally purely individualistic or egoistic, and thus antisocial. Control then denotes the process by which he is brought to subordinate his natural impulses to public or common ends. Since, by conception, his own nature is quite alien to this process and opposes it rather than helps it, control has in this view a flavor of coercion or compulsion about it. Systems of government and theories of the state have been built upon this notion, and it has seriously affected educational ideas and practices. But there is no ground for any such view. Individuals are certainly interested, at times, in having their own way, and their own way may go contrary to the ways of others. But they are also interested, and chiefly interested upon the whole, in entering into the activities of others and taking part in conjoint and coöperative doings. Otherwise, no such thing as a community would be possible. And there would not even be any one interested in furnishing the policeman to keep a semblance of harmony unless he thought that thereby he could gain some personal advantage. Control, in truth, means only an emphatic form of direction of powers, and covers the regulation gained by an individual through his own efforts quite as much as that brought about when others take the lead.

In general, every stimulus directs activity. It does not simply excite it or stir it up, but directs it toward an object. Put the other way around, a response is not just a re-action, a protest, as it were, against being disturbed; it is, as the word indicates, an answer. It meets the stimulus, and corresponds with it. There is an adaptation of the stimulus and response to each other. A light is the stimulus to the eye to see something, and the business of the eye is to see. If the eyes are open and there is light, seeing occurs; the stimulus is but a condition of the fulfillment of the proper function of the organ, not an outside interruption. To some extent, then, all direction or control is a guiding of activity to its own end; it is an assistance in doing fully what some organ is already tending to do.

This general statement needs, however, to be qualified in two respects. In the first place, except in the case of a small number of instincts, the stimuli to which an immature human being is subject are not sufficiently definite to call out, in the beginning, specific responses. There is always a great deal of superfluous energy aroused. This energy may be wasted, going aside from the point; it may also go against the successful performance of an act. It does harm by getting in the way. Compare the behavior of a beginner in riding a bicycle with that of the expert. There is little axis of direction in the energies put forth; they are largely dispersive and centrifugal. Direction involves a focusing and fixating of action in order that it may be truly a response, and this requires an elimination of unnecessary and confusing movements. In the second place, although no activity can be produced in which the person does not coöperate to some extent, yet a response may be of a kind which does not fit into the sequence and continuity of action. A person boxing may dodge a particular blow successfully, but in such a way as to expose himself the next instant to a still harder blow. Adequate control means that the successive acts are brought into a continuous order; each act not only meets its immediate stimulus but helps the acts which follow.

In short, direction is both simultaneous and successive. At a given time, it requires that, from all the tendencies that are partially called out, those be selected which center energy upon the point of need. Successively, it requires that each act be balanced with those which precede and come after, so that *order* of activity is achieved. *Focusing and ordering are thus the two aspects of direction, one spatial, the other temporal.* The first insures hitting the mark;

the second keeps the balance required for further action. Obviously, it is not possible to separate them in practice as we have distinguished them in idea. Activity must be centered at a given time *in such a way* as to prepare for what comes next. The problem of the immediate response is complicated by one's having to be on the lookout for future occurrences.

Two conclusions emerge from these general statements. On the one hand, purely external direction is impossible. The environment can at most only supply stimuli to call out responses. These responses proceed from tendencies already possessed by the individual. Even when a person is frightened by threats into doing something, the threats work only because the person has an instinct of fear. If he has not, or if, though having it, it is under his own control, the threat has no more influence upon him than light has in causing a person to see who has no eyes. While the customs and rules of adults furnish stimuli which direct as well as evoke the activities of the young, the young, after all, participate in the direction which their actions finally take. In the strict sense, nothing can be forced upon them or into them. To overlook this fact means to distort and pervert human nature. To take into account the contribution made by the existing instincts and habits of those directed is to direct them economically and wisely. Speaking accurately, all direction is but *re*-direction; it shifts the activities already going on into another channel. Unless one is cognizant of the energies which are already in operation, one's attempts at direction will almost surely go amiss.

On the other hand, the control afforded by the customs and regulations of others may be short-sighted. It may accomplish its immediate effect, but at the expense of throwing the subsequent action of the person out of balance. A threat may, for example, prevent a person from doing something to which he is naturally inclined by arousing fear of disagreeable consequences if he persists. But he may be left in the position which exposes him later on to influences which will lead him to do even worse things. His instincts of cunning and slyness may be aroused, so that things henceforth appeal to him on the side of evasion and trickery more than would otherwise have been the case. Those engaged in directing the actions of others are always in danger of overlooking the importance of the sequential development of those they direct.

Modes of Social Direction.—Adults are naturally most conscious of directing the conduct of others when they are immediately aiming so to do. As a rule, they have such an aim consciously when they find themselves resisted; when others are doing things they do not wish them to do. But the more permanent and influential modes of control are those which operate from moment to moment continuously without such deliberate intention on our part.

1. When others are not doing what we would like them to or are threatening disobedience, we are most conscious of the need of controlling them and of the influences by which they are controlled. In such cases, our control becomes most direct, and at this point we are most likely to make the mistakes just spoken of. We are even likely to take the influence of superior force for control, forgetting that while we may lead a horse to water we cannot make him drink; and that while we can shut a man up in a penitentiary we cannot make him penitent. In all such cases of immediate action upon others, we need to discriminate between physical results and moral results. A person may be in such a condition that forcible feeding or enforced confinement is necessary for his own good. A child may have to be snatched with roughness away from a fire so that he shall not be burnt. But no improvement of disposition, no educative effect, need follow. A harsh and commanding tone may be effectual in keeping a child away from the fire, and the same desirable physical effect will follow as if he had been snatched away. But there may be

no more obedience of a moral sort in one case than in the other. A man can be prevented from breaking into other persons' houses by shutting him up, but shutting him up may not alter his disposition to commit burglary. When we confuse a physical with an educative result, we always lose the chance of enlisting the person's own participating disposition in getting the result desired, and thereby of developing within him an intrinsic and persisting direction in the right way.

In general, the occasion for the more conscious acts of control should be limited to acts which are so instinctive or impulsive that the one performing them has no means of foreseeing their outcome. If a person cannot foresee the consequences of his act, and is not capable of understanding what he is told about its outcome by those with more experience, it is impossible for him to guide his act intelligently. In such a state, every act is alike to him. Whatever moves him does move him, and that is all there is to it. In some cases, it is well to permit him to experiment, and to discover the consequences for himself in order that he may act intelligently next time under similar circumstances. But some courses of action are too discommoding and obnoxious to others to allow of this course being pursued. Direct disapproval is now resorted to. Shaming, ridicule, disfavor, rebuke, and punishment are used. Or contrary tendencies in the child are appealed to to divert him from his troublesome line of behavior. His sensitiveness to approbation, his hope of winning favor by an agreeable act, are made use of to induce action in another direction.

2. These methods of control are so obvious (because so intentionally employed) that it would hardly be worth while to mention them if it were not that notice may now be taken, by way of contrast, of the other more important and permanent mode of control. This other method resides in the ways in which persons, with whom the immature being is associated, *use things;* the instrumentalities with

which they accomplish their own ends. The very existence of the social medium in which an individual lives, moves, and has his being is the standing effective agency of directing his activity.

This fact makes it necessary for us to examine in greater detail what is meant by the social environment. We are given to separating from each other the physical and social environments in which we live. The separation is responsible on one hand for an exaggeration of the moral importance of the more direct or personal modes of control of which we have been speaking; and on the other hand for an exaggeration, in current psychology and philosophy, of the *intellectual* possibilities of contact with a purely physical environment. There is not, in fact, any such thing as the direct influence of one human being on another apart from use of the physical environment as an intermediary. A smile, a frown, a rebuke, a word of warning or encouragement, all involve some physical change. Otherwise, the attitude of one would not get over to alter the attitude of another. Comparatively speaking, such modes of influence may be regarded as personal. The physical medium is reduced to a mere means of personal contact. In contrast with such direct modes of mutual influence, stand associations in common pursuits involving the use of things as means and as measures of results. Even if the mother never told her daughter to help her, or never rebuked her for not helping, the child would be subjected to direction in her activities by the mere fact that she was engaged, along with the parent, in the household life. Imitation, emulation, the need of working together, enforce control.

If the mother hands the child something needed, the latter must reach the thing in order to get it. Where there is giving there must be taking. The way the child handles the thing after it is got, the use to which it is put, is surely influenced by the fact that the child has watched the mother. When the child sees the parent looking for something, it is as natural for it also to look for the object and to give it over when it finds it, as it was, under other circumstances, to receive it. Multiply such an instance by the thousand details of daily intercourse, and one has a picture of the most permanent and enduring method of giving direction to the activities of the young.

In saying this, we are only repeating what was said previously about participating in a joint activity as the chief way of forming disposition. We have explicitly added, however, the recognition of the part played in the joint activity by the *use of things*. The philosophy of learning has been unduly dominated by a false psychology. It is frequently stated that a person learns by merely having the qualities of things impressed upon his mind through the gateway of the senses. Having received a store of sensory impressions, association or some power of mental synthesis is supposed to combine them into ideas—into things with a *meaning*. An object, stone, orange, tree, chair, is supposed to convey different impressions of color, shape, size, hardness, smell, taste, etc., which aggregated together constitute the characteristic meaning of each thing. But as matter of fact, it is the characteristic use to which the thing is put, because of its specific qualities, which supplies the meaning with which it is identified. A chair is a thing which is put to one use; a table, a thing which is employed for another purpose; an orange is a thing which costs so much, which is grown in warm climes, which is eaten, and when eaten has an agreeable odor and refreshing taste, etc.

The difference between an adjustment to a physical stimulus and a *mental* act is that the latter involves response to a thing in its *meaning;* the former does not. A noise may make me jump without my mind being implicated. When I hear a noise and run and get water and put out a blaze, I respond intelligently; the sound meant fire, and fire meant need of being extinguished. I bump into a stone, and kick it one side purely physically. I put it to one side for fear some one will stumble upon it, intelligently; I respond to a meaning which the thing has. I am startled by a thunderclap whether I recognize it or not—more likely, if I do not recognize it. But if I say, either out loud or to myself, that is thunder, I respond to the disturbance as a meaning. My behavior has a mental quality. When things have a meaning for us, we *mean* (intend, propose) what we do: when they do not, we act blindly, unconsciously, unintelligently.

In both kinds of responsive adjustment, our activities are directed or controlled. But in the merely blind response, direction is also blind. There may be training, but there is no education. Repeated responses to recurrent stimuli may fix a habit of acting in a certain way. All of us have many habits of whose import we are quite unaware, since they were formed without our knowing what we were about. Consequently they possess us, rather than we them. They move us; they control us. Unless we become aware of what they accomplish, and pass judgment upon the worth of the result, we do not control them. A child might be made to bow every time he met a certain person by pressure on his neck muscles, and bowing would finally become automatic. It would not, however, be an act of recognition or deference on his part, till he did it with a certain end in view—as having a certain meaning. And not till he knew what he was about and performed the act for the sake of its meaning could he be said to be "brought up" or educated to act in a certain way. To have an *idea* of a thing is thus not just to get certain sensations from it. It is to be able to respond to the thing in view of its place in an inclusive scheme of action; it is to foresee the drift and probable consequence of the action of the thing upon us and of our action upon it.

To have the same ideas about things which others have, to be like-minded with them, and thus to be really members of a social group, is therefore to attach the same meanings to things and to acts which others attach. Otherwise, there is no common understanding, and no community life. But in a shared activity, each person refers what he is doing to what the other is doing and *vice-versa*. That is, the activity of each is placed in the same inclusive situation. To pull at a rope at which others happen to be pulling is not a shared or conjoint activity, unless the pulling is done with knowledge that others are pulling and for the sake of either helping or hindering what they are doing. A pin may pass in the course of its manufacture through the hands of many persons. But each may do his part without knowledge of what others do or without any reference to what they do; each may operate simply for the sake of a separate result—his own pay. There is, in this case, no common consequence to which the several acts are referred, and hence no genuine intercourse or association, in spite of juxtaposition, and in spite of the fact that their respective doings contribute to a single outcome. But if each views the consequences of his own acts as having a bearing upon what others are doing and takes into account the consequences of their behavior upon himself, then there is a common mind; a common intent in behavior. There is an understanding set up between the different contributors; and this common understanding controls the action of each.

Suppose that conditions were so arranged that one person automatically caught a ball and then threw it to another person who caught and automatically returned it; and that each so acted without knowing where the ball came from or went to. Clearly, such action would be without point or meaning. It might be physically controlled, but it would not be socially directed. But suppose that each becomes aware of what the other is doing, and becomes interested in the other's action and thereby interested in what he is doing himself as connected with the action of the other. The behavior of each would then be intelligent; and socially intelligent and guided. Take one more example of a less imaginary kind. An infant is hungry, and cries while food is prepared in his presence. If he does not connect his own state with what others are doing, nor what they are doing with his own satisfaction, he simply reacts with increasing impatience to his own increasing discomfort. He is physically controlled by his own organic state. But when he makes a back and forth reference, his whole attitude changes. He takes an interest, as we say; he takes note and watches what others are doing. He no longer reacts just to his own hunger, but behaves in the light of what others are doing for its prospective satisfaction. In that way, he also no longer just gives way to hunger without knowing it, but he notes, or recognizes, or identifies his own state. It becomes an object for him. His attitude toward it becomes in some degree intelligent. And in such noting of the meaning of the actions of others and of his own state, he is socially directed.

It will be recalled that our main proposition had two sides. One of them has now been dealt with: namely, that physical things do not influence mind (or form ideas and beliefs) except as they are implicated in action for prospective consequences. The other point is persons modify *one another's dispositions* only through the special use they make of physical conditions. Consider first the case of so-called expressive movements to which others are sensitive; blushing, smiling, frowning, clinching of fists, natural gestures of all kinds. In themselves, these are not expressive. They are organic parts of a person's attitude. One does not blush to show modesty or embarrassment to others, but because the capillary circulation alters in response to stimuli. But others *use* the blush, or a slightly perceptible tightening of the muscles of a person with whom they are associated, as a sign of the state in which that person finds himself, and as an indication of what course to pursue. The frown signifies an imminent rebuke for which one must prepare, or an uncertainty and hesitation which one must, if possible, remove by saying or doing something to restore confidence.

A man at some distance is waving his arms wildly. One has only to preserve an attitude of detached indifference, and the motions of the other person will be on the level of any remote physical change which we happen to note. If we have no concern or interest, the waving of the arms is as meaningless to us as the gyrations of the arms of a windmill. But if interest is aroused, we begin to participate. We refer his action to something we are doing ourselves or that we should do. We have to judge the meaning of his act in order to decide what to do. Is he beckoning for help? Is he warning us of an explosion to be set off, against which we should guard ourselves? In one case, his action means to run toward him; in the other case, to run away. In any case, it is the change he effects in the physical environment which is a sign to us of how we should conduct ourselves. Our action is *socially* controlled because we endeavor to refer what we are to do to the same situation in which he is acting.

Language is, as we have already seen (*Ante*, p. 106) a case of this joint reference of our own action and that of another to a common situation. Hence its unrivaled significance as a means of social direction. But language would not be this efficacious instrument were it not that it takes place upon a background of coarser and more tangible use of physical means to accomplish results. A child sees persons with whom he lives using chairs, hats, tables, spades, saws, plows, horses, money, in certain ways. If he has any share at all in what they are doing, he is led thereby to use things in the same way, or to use other things in a way which will fit in. If a chair is drawn up to a table, it is a sign that he is to sit in it; if a person extends his right hand, he is to extend his; and so on in a never ending stream of detail. The prevailing habits of using the products of human art and the raw materials of nature constitute by all odds the deepest and the most pervasive mode of social control. When children go to school, they already have "minds"—

they have knowledge and dispositions of judgment which may be appealed to through the use of language. But these "minds" are the organized habits of intelligent response which they have previously required by putting things to use in connection with the way other persons use things. The control is inescapable; it saturates disposition.

The net outcome of the discussion is that the fundamental means of control is not personal but intellectual. It is not "moral" in the sense that a person is moved by direct personal appeal from others, important as is this method at critical junctures. It consists in the habits of *understanding*, which are set up in using objects in correspondence with others, whether by way of coöperation and assistance or rivalry and competition. *Mind* as a concrete thing is precisely the power to understand things in terms of the use made of them; a socialized mind is the power to understand them in terms of the use to which they are turned in joint or shared situations. *And mind in this sense is the method of social control.*

Imitation and Social Psychology.—We have already noted the defects of a psychology of learning which places the individual mind naked, as it were, in contact with physical objects, and which believes that knowledge, ideas, and beliefs accrue from their interaction. Only comparatively recently has the predominating influence of association with fellow beings in the formation of mental and moral disposition been perceived. Even now it is usually treated as a kind of adjunct to an alleged method of learning by direct contact with things, and as merely supplementing knowledge of the physical world with knowledge of persons. The purport of our discussion is that such a view makes an absurd and impossible separation between persons and things. Interaction with things may form habits of external adjustment. But it leads to activity having a meaning and conscious intent only when things are used to produce a result. And the only way one person can

modify the mind of another is by using physical conditions, crude or artificial, so as to evoke some answering
activity from him. Such are our two main conclusions. It
is desirable to amplify and enforce them by placing them in
contrast with the theory which uses a psychology of supposed *direct* relationships of human beings to one another
as an adjunct to the psychology of the supposed direct relation of an individual to physical objects. In substance, this
so-called social psychology has been built upon the notion
of imitation. Consequently, we shall discuss the nature and
rôle of imitation in the formation of mental disposition.

According to this theory, social control of individuals
rests upon the instinctive tendency of individuals to imitate
or copy the actions of others. The latter serve as models.
The imitative instinct is so strong that the young devote
themselves to conforming to the patterns set by others and
reproducing them in their own scheme of behavior. According to our theory, what is here called imitation is a misleading name for partaking with others in a use of things which
leads to consequences of common interest.

The basic error in the current notion of imitation is that
it puts the cart before the horse. It takes an effect for the
cause of the effect. There can be no doubt that individuals
in forming a social group are like-minded; they understand
one another. They tend to act with the same controlling
ideas, beliefs, and intentions, given similar circumstances.
Looked at from without, they might be said to be engaged
in "imitating" one another. In the sense that they are doing
much the same sort of thing in much the same sort of way,
this would be true enough. But "imitation" throws no light
upon *why* they so act; it repeats the fact as an explanation
of itself. It is an explanation of the same order as the famous saying that opium puts men to sleep because of its
dormitive power.

Objective likeness of acts and the mental satisfaction
found in being in conformity with others are baptized by

the name imitation. This social fact is then taken for a psychological force, which produced the likeness. A considerable portion of what is called imitation is simply the fact that persons being alike in structure respond in the same way to like stimuli. Quite independently of imitation, men on being insulted get angry and attack the insulter. This statement may be met by citing the undoubted fact that response to an insult takes place in different ways in groups having different customs. In one group, it may be met by recourse to fisticuffs, in another by a challenge to a duel, in a third by an exhibition of contemptuous disregard. This happens, so it is said, because the model set for imitation is different. But there is no need to appeal to imitation. The mere fact that customs are different means that the actual stimuli to behavior are different. Conscious instruction plays a part; prior approvals and disapprovals have a large influence. Still more effective is the fact that unless an individual acts in the way current in his group, he is literally out of it. He can associate with others on intimate and equal terms only by behaving in the way in which they behave. The pressure that comes from the fact that one is let into the group action by acting in one way and shut out by acting in another way is unremitting. What is called the effect of imitation is mainly the product of conscious instruction and of the selective influence exercised by the unconscious confirmations and ratifications of those with whom one associates.

Suppose that some one rolls a ball to a child; he catches it and rolls it back, and the game goes on. Here the stimulus is not just the sight of the ball, or the sight of the other rolling it. It is the *situation*—the game which is playing. The response is not merely rolling the ball back; it is rolling it back so that the other one may catch and return it,—that the game may continue. The "pattern" or model is not the action of the other person. The whole situation requires that each should adapt his action in view of what the other person has done and is to do. Imitation may come in but its rôle is subordinate. The child has an interest on his own account; he wants to keep it going. He may then note how the other person catches and holds the ball in order to improve his own acts. He imitates the means of doing, not the end or thing to be done. And he imitates the means because he wishes, on his own behalf, as part of his own initiative, to take an effective part in the game. One has only to consider how completely the child is dependent from his earliest days for successful execution of his purposes upon fitting his acts into those of others to see what a premium is put upon behaving as others behave, and of developing an understanding of them in order that he may so behave. The pressure for likemindedness in action from this source is so great that it is quite superfluous to appeal to imitation.

As matter of fact, imitation of ends, as distinct from imitation of means which help to reach ends, is a superficial and transitory affair which leaves little effect upon disposition. Idiots are especially apt at this kind of imitation; it affects outward acts but not the meaning of their performance. When we find children engaging in this sort of mimicry, instead of encouraging them (as we would do if it were an important means of social control) we are more likely to rebuke them as apes, monkeys, parrots, or copy cats. Imitation of means of accomplishment is, on the other hand, an intelligent act. It involves close observation, and judicious selection of what will enable one to do better something which he already is trying to do. Used for a purpose, the imitative instinct may, like any other instinct, become a factor in the development of effective action.

This excursus should, accordingly, have the effect of reënforcing the conclusion that genuine social control means the formation of a certain mental disposition; a way of *understanding* objects, events, and acts which enables one to participate effectively in associated activities. Only the friction engendered by meeting resistance from others leads to the view that it takes place by forcing a line of action contrary to natural inclinations. Only failure to take account of the situations in which persons are mutually concerned (or interested in acting responsively to one another) leads to treating imitation as the chief agent in promoting social control.

Some Applications to Education.—Why does a savage group perpetuate savagery, and a civilized group civilization? Doubtless the first answer to occur to mind is because savages are savages; beings of low-grade intelligence and perhaps defective moral sense. But careful study has made it doubtful whether their native capacities are appreciably inferior to those of civilized man. It has made it certain that native differences are not sufficient to account for the difference in culture. In a sense the mind of savage peoples is an effect, rather than a cause, of their backward institutions. Their social activities are such as to restrict their objects of attention and interest, and hence to limit the stimuli to mental development. Even as regards the objects that come within the scope of attention, primitive social customs tend to arrest observation and imagination upon qualities which do not fructify in the mind. Lack of control of natural forces means that a scant number of natural objects enter into associated behavior. Only a small number of natural resources are utilized and they are not worked for what they are worth. The advance of civilization means that a larger number of natural forces and objects have been transformed into instrumentalities of action, into means for securing ends. We start not so much with superior capacities as with superior stimuli for evocation and direction of our capacities. The savage deals largely with crude stimuli; we have *weighted* stimuli.

Prior human efforts have made over natural conditions. As they originally existed they were indifferent to human endeavors. Every domesticated plant and animal, every tool, every utensil, every appliance, every manufactured

article, every aesthetic decoration, every work of art means
a transformation of conditions once hostile or indifferent to
characteristic human activities into friendly and favoring
conditions. Because the activities of children to-day are controlled by these selected and charged stimuli, children are
able to traverse in a short lifetime what the race has needed
slow, tortured ages to attain. The dice have been loaded by
all the successes which have preceded.

Stimuli conducive to economical and effective response,
such as our system of roads and means of transportation,
our ready command of heat, light, and electricity, our
readymade machines and apparatus for every purpose, do
not, by themselves or in their aggregate, constitute a civilization. But the uses to which they are put are civilization,
and without the things the uses would be impossible. Time
otherwise necessarily devoted to wresting a livelihood from
a grudging environment and securing a precarious protection against its inclemencies is freed. A body of knowledge
is transmitted, the legitimacy of which is guaranteed by the
fact that the physical equipment in which it is incarnated
leads to results that square with the other facts of nature.
Thus these appliances of art supply a protection, perhaps
our chief protection, against a recrudescence of these super-
stitious beliefs, those fanciful myths and infertile imaginings
about nature in which so much of the best intellectual
power of the past has been spent. If we add one other factor,
namely, that such appliances be not only used, but *used in
the interests of a truly shared or associated life*, then the
appliances become the *positive* resources of civilization. If
Greece, with a scant tithe of our material resources,
achieved a worthy and noble intellectual and artistic
career, it is because Greece operated for social ends such
resources as it had.

But whatever the situation, whether one of barbarism or
civilization, whether one of stinted control of physical
forces, or of partial enslavement to a mechanism not yet

made tributary to a shared experience, things as they enter into action furnish the educative conditions of daily life and direct the formation of mental and moral disposition.

Intentional education signifies, as we have already seen, a specially selected environment, the selection being made on the basis of materials and method specifically promoting growth in the desired direction. Since language represents the physical conditions that have been subjected to the maximum transformation in the interests of social life—physical things which have lost their original quality in becoming social tools—it is appropriate that language should play a large part compared with other appliances. By it we are led to share vicariously in past human experience, thus widening and enriching the experience of the present. We are enabled, symbolically and imaginatively, to anticipate situations. In countless ways, language condenses meanings that record social outcomes and presage social outlooks. So significant is it of a liberal share in what is worth while in life that unlettered and uneducated have become almost synonymous.

The emphasis in school upon this particular tool has, however, its dangers:—dangers which are not theoretical but exhibited in practice. Why is it, in spite of the fact that teaching by pouring in, learning by a passive absorption, are universally condemned, that they are still so intrenched in practice? That education is not an affair of "telling" and being told, but an active and constructive process, is a principle almost as generally violated in practice as conceded in theory. Is not this deplorable situation due to the fact that the doctrine is itself merely told? It is preached; it is lectured; it is written about. But its enactment into practice requires that the school environment be equipped with agencies for doing, with tools and physical materials, to an extent rarely attained. It requires that methods of instruction and administration be modified to allow and to secure direct and continuous occupations with things. Not that the

use of language as an educational resource should lessen;
but that its use should be more vital and fruitful by having
its normal connection with shared activities. "These things
ought ye to have done, and not to have left the others undone." And for the school "these things" mean equipment
with the instrumentalities of coöperative or joint activity.

For when the schools depart from the educational conditions effective in the out-of-school environment, they necessarily substitute a bookish, a pseudo-intellectual spirit for a
social spirit. Children doubtless go to school to learn, but it
has yet to be proved that learning occurs most adequately
when it is made a separate conscious business. When treating it as a business of this sort tends to preclude the social
sense which comes from sharing in an activity of common
concern and value, the effort at isolated intellectual learning contradicts its own aim. We may secure motor activity
and sensory excitation by keeping an individual by himself,
but we cannot thereby get him to understand the meaning
which things have in the life of which he is a part. We may
secure technical specialized ability in algebra, Latin, or bot-
any, but not the kind of intelligence which directs ability to
useful ends. Only by engaging in a joint activity, where one
person's use of material and tools is consciously referred to
the use other persons are making of their capacities and appliances, is a social direction of disposition attained.

Summary.—The natural or native impulses of the young
do not agree with the life-customs of the group into which
they are born. Consequently they have to be directed or
guided. This control is not the same thing as physical compulsion; it consists in centering the impulses acting at any
one time upon some specific end and in introducing an order of continuity into the sequence of acts. The action of
others is always influenced by deciding what stimuli shall
call out their actions. But in some cases as in commands,
prohibitions, approvals, and disapprovals, the stimuli proceed from persons with a direct view to influencing action.

Since in such cases we are most conscious of controlling the action of others, we are likely to exaggerate the importance of this sort of control at the expense of a more permanent and effective method. The basic control resides in the nature of the situations in which the young take part. In social situations the young have to refer their way of acting to what others are doing and make it fit in. This directs their action to a common result, and gives an understanding common to the participants. For all *mean* the same thing, even when performing different acts. This common understanding of the means and ends of action is the essence of social control. It is indirect, or emotional and intellectual, not direct or personal. Moreover it is intrinsic to the disposition of the person, not external and coercive. To achieve this internal control through identity of interest and understanding is the business of education. While books and conversation can do much, these agencies are usually relied upon too exclusively. Schools require for their full efficiency more opportunity for conjoint activities in which those instructed take part, so that they may acquire a *social* sense of their own powers and of the materials and appliances used.

IV. EDUCATION AS GROWTH

The Conditions of Growth.—In directing the activities of the young, society determines its own future in determining that of the young. Since the young at a given time will at some later date compose the society of that period, the latter's nature will largely turn upon the direction children's activities were given at an earlier period. This cumulative movement of action toward a later result is what is meant by growth.

The primary condition of growth is immaturity. This may seem to be a mere truism—saying that a being can develop only in some point in which he is undeveloped. But the prefix "im" of the word immaturity means something positive, not a mere void or lack. It is noteworthy that the terms "capacity" and "potentiality" have a double meaning, one sense being negative, the other positive. Capacity may denote mere receptivity, like the capacity of a quart measure. We may mean by potentiality a merely dormant or quiescent state—a capacity to become something different under external influences. But we also mean by capacity an ability, a power; and by potentiality potency, force. Now when we say that immaturity means the possibility of growth, we are not referring to absence of powers which may exist at a later time; we express a force positively present—the *ability* to develop.

Our tendency to take immaturity as mere lack, and growth as something which fills up the gap between the immature and the mature is due to regarding childhood *comparatively,* instead of intrinsically. We treat it simply as a privation because we are measuring it by adulthood as a fixed standard. This fixes attention upon what the child has not, and will not have till he becomes a man. This comparative standpoint is legitimate enough for some purposes, but if we make it final, the question arises whether we are not guilty of an overweening presumption. Children, if they could express themselves articulately and sincerely, would tell a different tale; and there is excellent adult authority for the conviction that for certain moral and intellectual purposes adults must become as little children.

The seriousness of the assumption of the negative quality of the possibilities of immaturity is apparent when we reflect that it sets up as an ideal and standard a static end. The fulfillment of growing is taken to mean an *accomplished* growth: that is to say, an Ungrowth, something which is no longer growing. The futility of the assumption is seen in the fact that every adult resents the imputation of having no further possibilities of growth; and so far as he finds that they are closed to him mourns the fact as evidence of loss, instead of falling back on the achieved as adequate manifestation of power. Why an unequal measure for child and man?

Taken absolutely, instead of comparatively, immaturity designates a positive force or ability,—the *power* to grow. We do not have to draw out or educe positive activities from a child, as some educational doctrines would have it. Where there is life, there are already eager and impassioned activities. Growth is not something done to them; it is something they do. The positive and constructive aspect of possibility gives the key to understanding the two chief traits of immaturity, dependence and plasticity. (1) It sounds absurd to hear dependence spoken of as something positive, still more absurd as a power. Yet if helplessness were all there were in dependence, no development could ever take place. A merely impotent being has to be carried, forever, by others. The fact that dependence is accompanied by growth in ability, not by an ever increasing lapse into parasitism, suggests that it is already something constructive. Being merely sheltered by others would not promote growth. For (2) it would only build a wall around impotence. With reference to the physical world, the child is helpless. He lacks at birth and for a long time thereafter power to make his way physically, to make his own living. If he had to do that by himself, he would hardly survive an hour. On this side his helplessness is almost complete. The young of the brutes are immeasurably his superiors. He is physically weak and not able to turn the strength which he possesses to coping with the physical environment.

1. The thoroughgoing character of this helplessness suggests, however, some compensating power. The relative ability of the young of brute animals to adapt themselves fairly well to physical conditions from an early period suggests the fact that their life is not intimately bound up with the life of those about them. They are compelled, so to speak, to have physical gifts because they are lacking in social gifts. Human infants, on the other hand, can get along with physi-

cal incapacity just because of their social capacity. We sometimes talk and think as if they simply happened to be *physically* in a social environment; as if social forces exclusively existed in the adults who take care of them, they being passive recipients. If it were said that children are themselves marvelously endowed with *power* to enlist the coöperative attention of others, this would be thought to be a backhanded way of saying that others are marvelously attentive to the needs of children. But observation shows that children are gifted with an equipment of the first order for social intercourse. Few grown-up persons retain all of the flexible and sensitive ability of children to vibrate sympathetically with the attitudes and doings of those about them. Inattention to physical things (going with incapacity to control them) is accompanied by a corresponding intensification of interest and attention as to the doings of people. The native mechanism of the child and his impulses all tend to facile social responsiveness. The statement that children, before adolescence, are egotistically self-centered, even if it were true, would not contradict the truth of this statement. It would simply indicate that their social responsiveness is employed on their own behalf, not that it does not exist. But the statement is not true as matter of fact. The facts which are cited in support of the alleged pure egoism of children really show the intensity and directness with which they go to their mark. If the ends which form the mark seem narrow and selfish to adults, it is only because adults (by means of a similar engrossment in their day) have mastered these ends, which have consequently ceased to interest them. Most of the remainder of children's alleged native egoism is simply an egoism which runs counter to an adult's egoism. To a grown-up person who is too absorbed in his own affairs to take an interest in children's affairs, children doubtless seem unreasonably engrossed in *their* own affairs.

From a social standpoint, dependence denotes a power rather than a weakness; it involves interdependence. There is always a danger that increased personal independence will decrease the social capacity of an individual. In making him more self-reliant, it may make him more self-sufficient; it may lead to aloofness and indifference. It often makes an individual so insensitive in his relations to others as to develop an illusion of being really able to stand and act alone —an unnamed form of insanity which is responsible for a large part of the remediable suffering of the world.

2. The specific adaptability of an immature creature for growth constitutes his *plasticity*. This is something quite different from the plasticity of putty or wax. It is not a capacity to take on change of form in accord with external pressure. It lies near the pliable elasticity by which some persons take on the color of their surroundings while retaining their own bent. But it is something deeper than this. It is essentially the ability to learn from experience; the power to retain from one experience something which is of avail in coping with the difficulties of a later situation. This means power to modify actions on the basis of the results of prior experiences, the power to *develop dispositions*. Without it, the acquisition of habits is impossible.

It is a familiar fact that the young of the higher animals, and especially the human young, have to *learn* to utilize their instinctive reactions. The human being is born with a greater number of instinctive tendencies than other animals. But the instincts of the lower animals perfect themselves for appropriate action at an early period after birth, while most of those of the human infant are of little account just as they stand. An original specialized power of adjustment secures immediate efficiency, but, like a railway ticket, it is good for one route only. A being who, in order to use his eyes, ears, hands, and legs, has to experiment in making varied combinations of their reactions, achieves a control that is flexible and varied. A chick, for example, pecks accurately at a bit of food in a few hours after hatching. This means that definite coördinations of activities of the eyes in

seeing and of the body and head in striking are perfected in
a few trials. An infant requires about six months to be able
to gauge with approximate accuracy the action in reaching
which will coördinate with his visual activities; to be able,
that is, to tell whether he can reach a seen object and just
how to execute the reaching. As a result, the chick is limited by the relative perfection of its original endowment.
The infant has the advantage of the *multitude* of instinctive
tentative reactions and of the experiences that accompany
them, even though he is at a temporary disadvantage because they cross one another. In learning an action, instead
of having it given ready-made, one of necessity learns to
vary its factors, to make varied combinations of them, according to change of circumstances. A possibility of continuing progress is opened up by the fact that in learning
one act, methods are developed good for use in other situations. Still more important is the fact that the human being
acquires a habit of learning. He learns to learn.

The importance for human life of the two facts of dependence and variable control has been summed up in the
doctrine of the significance of prolonged infancy.* This prolongation is significant from the standpoint of the adult
members of the group as well as from that of the young.
The presence of dependent and learning beings is a stimulus to nurture and affection. The need for constant continued care was probably a chief means in transforming
temporary cohabitations into permanent unions. It certainly
was a chief influence in forming habits of affectionate and
sympathetic watchfulness; that constructive interest in the
well-being of others which is essential to associated life.
Intellectually, this moral development meant the introduction of many new objects of attention; it stimulated foresight and planning for the future. Thus there is a reciprocal

---

* Intimations of its significance are found in a number of writers, but
John Fiske, in his *Excursions of an Evolutionist,* is accredited with its first
systematic exposition.

influence. Increasing complexity of social life requires a longer period of infancy in which to acquire the needed powers; this prolongation of dependence means prolongation of plasticity, or power of acquiring variable and novel modes of control. Hence it provides a further push to social progress.

Habits as Expressions of Growth.—We have already noted that plasticity is the capacity to retain and carry over from prior experience factors which modify subsequent activities. This signifies the capacity to acquire habits, or develop definite dispositions. We have now to consider the salient features of habits. In the first place, a habit is a form of executive skill, of efficiency in doing. A habit means an ability to use natural conditions as means to ends. It is an active control of the environment through control of the organs of action. We are perhaps apt to emphasize the control of the body at the expense of control of the environment. We think of walking, talking, playing the piano, the specialized skills characteristic of the etcher, the surgeon, the bridge-builder, as if they were simply ease, deftness, and accuracy on the part of the organism. They are that, of course; but the measure of the value of these qualities lies in the economical and effective control of the environment which they secure. To be able to walk is to have certain properties of nature at our disposal—and so with all other habits.

Education is not infrequently defined as consisting in the acquisition of those habits that effect an adjustment of an individual and his environment. The definition expresses an essential phase of growth. But it is essential that adjustment be understood in its active sense of *control* of means for achieving ends. If we think of a habit simply as a change wrought in the organism, ignoring the fact that this change consists in ability to effect subsequent changes in the environment, we shall be lead to think of "adjustment" as a conformity to environment as wax conforms to the seal which impresses it. The environment is thought of as something fixed, providing in its fixity the end and standard of changes taking place in the organism; adjustment is just fitting ourselves to this fixity of external conditions.* Habit as *habituation* is indeed something *relatively* passive; we get used to our surroundings—to our clothing, our shoes, and gloves; to the atmosphere as long as it is fairly equable; to our daily associates, etc. Conformity to the environment, a change wrought in the organism without reference to ability to modify surroundings, is a marked trait of such habituations. Aside from the fact that we are not entitled to carry over the traits of such adjustments (which might well be called *accommodations*, to mark them off from active adjustments) into habits of active use of our surroundings, two features of habituations are worth notice. In the first place, we get used to things by *first* using them.

Consider getting used to a strange city. At first, there is excessive stimulation and excessive and ill-adapted response. Gradually certain stimuli are selected because of their relevancy, and others are degraded. We can say either that we do not respond to them any longer, or more truly that we have effected a persistent response to them—an equilibrium of adjustment. This means, in the second place, that this enduring adjustment supplies the background upon which are made specific adjustments, as occasion arises. We are never interested in changing the *whole* environment; there is much that we take for granted and accept just as it already is. Upon this background our activities focus at certain points in an endeavor to introduce needed changes. Habituation is thus our adjustment to an environment which at the time we are not concerned with modifying, and which supplies a leverage to our active habits.

-----

* This conception is, of course, a logical correlate of the conceptions of the external relation of stimulus and response, considered in the last chapter, and of the negative conceptions of immaturity and plasticity noted in this chapter.

Adaptation, in fine, is quite as much adaptation *of* the environment to our own activities as of our activities *to* the environment. A savage tribe manages to live on a desert plain. It adapts itself. But its adaptation involves a maximum of accepting, tolerating, putting up with things as they are, a maximum of passive acquiescence, and a minimum of active control, of subjection to use. A civilized people enters upon the scene. It also adapts itself. It introduces irrigation; it searches the world for plants and animals that will flourish under such conditions; it improves, by careful selection, those which are growing there. As a consequence, the wilderness blossoms as a rose. The savage is merely habituated; the civilized man has habits which transform the environment.

The significance of habit is not exhausted, however, in its executive and motor phase. It means formation of intellectual and emotional disposition as well as an increase in ease, economy, and efficiency of action. Any habit marks an *inclination*—an active preference and choice for the conditions involved in its exercise. A habit does not wait, Micawber-like, for a stimulus to turn up so that it may get busy; it actively seeks for occasions to pass into full operation. If its expression is unduly blocked, inclination shows itself in uneasiness and intense craving. A habit also marks an intellectual disposition. Where there is a habit, there is acquaintance with the materials and equipment to which action is applied. There is a definite way of understanding the situations in which the habit operates. Modes of thought, of observation and reflection, enter as forms of skill and of desire into the habits that make a man an engineer, an architect, a physician, or a merchant. In unskilled forms of labor, the intellectual factors are at minimum precisely because the habits involved are not of a high grade. But there are habits of judging and reasoning as truly as of handling a tool, painting a picture, or conducting an experiment.

Such statements are, however, understatements. The habits of mind involved in habits of the eye and hand supply the latter with their significance. Above all, the intellectual element in a habit fixes the relation of the habit to varied and elastic use, and hence to continued growth. We speak of *fixed* habits. Well, the phrase may mean powers so well established that their possessor always has them as resources when needed. But the phrase is also used to mean ruts, routine ways, with loss of freshness, openmindedness, and originality. Fixity of habit may mean that something has a fixed hold upon us, instead of our having a free hold upon things. This fact explains two points in a common notion about habits: their identification with mechanical and external modes of action to the neglect of mental and moral attitudes, and the tendency to give them a bad meaning, an identification with "bad habits." Many a person would feel surprised to have his aptitude in his chosen profession called a habit, and would naturally think of his use of tobacco, liquor, or profane language as typical of the meaning of habit. A habit is to him something which has a hold on him, something not easily thrown off even though judgment condemn it.

Habits reduce themselves to routine ways of acting, or degenerate into ways of action to which we are enslaved just in the degree in which intelligence is disconnected from them. Routine habits are unthinking habits; "bad" habits are habits so severed from reason that they are opposed to the conclusions of conscious deliberation and decision. As we have seen, the acquiring of habits is due to an original plasticity of our natures: to our ability to vary responses till we find an appropriate and efficient way of acting. Routine habits, and habits that possess us instead of our possessing them, are habits which put an end to plasticity. They mark the close of power to vary. There can be no doubt of the tendency of organic plasticity, of the physiological basis, to lessen with growing years. The instinctively mobile and eagerly varying action of childhood, the love of new stimuli and new developments, too easily passes into a "settling down," which means aversion to change and a resting on past achievements. Only an environment which secures the full use of intelligence in the process of forming habits can counteract this tendency. Of course, the same hardening of the organic conditions affects the physiological structures which are involved in thinking. But this fact only indicates the need of persistent care to see to it that the function of intelligence is invoked to its maximum possibility. The short-sighted method which falls back on mechanical routine and repetition to secure external efficiency of habit, motor skill without accompanying thought, marks a deliberate closing in of surroundings upon growth.

The Educational Bearings of the Conception of Development.—We have had so far but little to say in this chapter about education. We have been occupied with the conditions and implications of growth. If our conclusions are justified, they carry with them, however, definite educational consequences. When it is said that education is development, everything depends upon *how* development is conceived. Our net conclusion is that life is development, and that developing, growing, is life. Translated into its educational equivalents, this means (*i*) that the educational process has no end beyond itself; it is its own end; and that (*ii*) the educational process is one of continual reorganizing, reconstructing, transforming.

1. Development when it is interpreted in *comparative* terms, that is, with respect to the special traits of child and adult life, means the direction of power into special channels: the formation of habits involving executive skill, definiteness of interest, and specific objects of observation and thought. But the comparative view is not final. The child has specific powers; to ignore that fact is to stunt or distort the organs upon which his growth depends. The adult uses his powers to transform his environment, thereby

occasioning new stimuli which redirect his powers and keep
them developing. Ignoring this fact means arrested development, a passive accommodation. Normal child and normal
adult alike, in other words, are engaged in growing. The
difference between them is not the difference between
growth and no growth, but between the modes of growth
appropriate to different conditions. With respect to the development of powers devoted to coping with specific scientific and economic problems we may say the child should
be growing in manhood. With respect to sympathetic curiosity, unbiased responsiveness, and openness of mind, we
may say that the adult should be growing in childlikeness.
One statement is as true as the other.

Three ideas which have been criticized, namely, the
merely privative nature of immaturity, static adjustment to
a fixed environment, and rigidity of habit, are all connected
with a false idea of growth or development,—that it is a
movement toward a fixed goal. Growth is regarded as
having an end, instead of *being* an end. The educational
counterparts of the three fallacious ideas are first, failure to
take account of the instinctive or native powers of the
young; secondly, failure to develop initiative in coping with
novel situations; thirdly, an undue emphasis upon drill and
other devices which secure automatic skill at the expense of
personal perception. In all cases, the adult environment is
accepted as a standard for the child. He is to be brought up
to it.

Natural instincts are either disregarded or treated as nui-
sances—as obnoxious traits to be suppressed, or at all events
to be brought into conformity with external standards.
Since conformity is the aim, what is distinctively individual in a young person is brushed aside, or regarded as a
source of mischief or anarchy. Conformity is made equivalent to uniformity. Consequently, there are induced lack
of interest in the novel, aversion to progress, and dread of
the uncertain and the unknown. Since the end of growth is

outside of and beyond the process of growing, external agents have to be resorted to to induce movement towards it. Whenever a method of education is stigmatized as mechanical we may be sure that external pressure is brought to bear to reach an external end.

2. Since in reality there is nothing to which growth is relative save more growth, there is nothing to which education is subordinate save more education. It is a commonplace to say that education should not cease when one leaves school. The point of this commonplace is that the purpose of school education is to insure the continuance of education by organizing the powers that insure growth. The inclination to learn from life itself and to make the conditions of life such that all will learn in the process of living is the finest product of schooling.

When we abandon the attempt to define immaturity by means of fixed comparison with adult accomplishments, we are compelled to give up thinking of it as denoting lack of desired traits. Abandoning this notion, we are also forced to surrender our habit of thinking of instruction as a method of supplying this lack by pouring knowledge into a mental and moral hole which awaits filling. Since life means growth, a living creature lives as truly and positively at one stage as at another, with the same intrinsic fullness and the same absolute claims. Hence education means the enterprise of supplying the conditions which insure growth, or adequacy of life, irrespective of age. We first look with impatience upon immaturity, regarding it as something to be got over as rapidly as possible. Then the adult formed by such educative methods looks back with impatient regret upon childhood and youth as a scene of lost opportunities and wasted powers. This ironical situation will endure till it is recognized that living has its own intrinsic quality and that the business of education is with that quality.

Realization that life is growth protects us from that so-called idealizing of childhood which in effect is nothing but lazy indulgence. Life is not to be identified with every superficial act and interest. Even though it is not always easy to tell whether what appears to be mere surface fooling is a sign of some nascent as yet untrained power, we must remember that manifestations are not to be accepted as ends in themselves. They are signs of possible growth. They are to be turned into means of development, of carrying power forward, not indulged or cultivated for their own sake. Excessive attention to surface phenomena (even in the way of rebuke as well as of encouragement) may lead to their fixation and thus to arrested development. What impulses are moving toward, not what they have been, is the important thing for parent and teacher. The true principle of respect for immaturity cannot be better put than in the words of Emerson: "Respect the child. Be not too much his parent. Trespass not on his solitude. But I hear the outcry which replies to this suggestion: Would you verily throw up the reins of public and private discipline; would you leave the young child to the mad career of his own passions and whimsies, and call this anarchy a respect for the child's nature? I answer,—Respect the child, respect him to the end, but also respect yourself. . . . The two points in a boy's training are, to keep his *naturel* and train off all but that; to keep his *naturel,* but stop off his uproar, fooling, and horseplay; keep his nature *and arm it with knowledge in the very direction in which it points.*" And as Emerson goes on to show this reverence for childhood and youth instead of opening up an easy and easy-going path to the instructors, "involves at once, immense claims on the time, the thought, on the life of the teacher. It requires time, use, insight, event, all the great lessons and assistances of God; and only to think of using it implies character and profoundness."

Summary.—Power to grow depends upon need for others and plasticity. Both of these conditions are at their height in childhood and youth. Plasticity or the power to learn from experience means the formation of habits. Habits give control over the environment, power to utilize it for human purposes. Habits take the form both of habituation, or a general and persistent balance of organic activities with the surroundings, and of active capacities to readjust activity to meet new conditions. The former furnishes the background of growth; the latter constitute growing. Active habits involve thought, invention, and initiative in applying capacities to new aims. They are opposed to routine which marks an arrest of growth. Since growth is the characteristic of life, education is all one with growing; it has no end beyond itself. The criterion of the value of school education is the extent in which it creates a desire for continued growth and supplies means for making the desire effective in fact.

V. EDUCATION AS RECONSTRUCTION

The present . . . generates the problems which lead us to search the past for suggestion, and which supplies meaning to what we find when we search. The past is the past precisely because it does not include what is characteristic in the present. The moving present includes the past on condition that it uses the past to direct its own movement. The past is a great resource for the imagination; it adds a new dimension to life, but on condition that it be seen as the past *of* the present, and not as another and disconnected world. The principle which makes little of the present act of living and operation of growing the only thing *always* present, naturally looks to the past because the future goal which it sets up is remote and empty. But having turned its back upon the present, it has no way of returning to it laden with the spoils of the past. A mind that is adequately sensitive to the needs and occasions of the present actuality will have the liveliest of motives for interest in the background of the present, and will never have to hunt for a way back because it will never have lost connection.

Education as Reconstruction.—In its contrast with the ideas both of unfolding of latent powers from within, and of formation from without, whether by physical nature or by the cultural products of the past, the ideal of growth results in the conception that education is a constant re-organizing or reconstructing of experience. It has all the time an immediate end, and so far as activity is educative, it reaches that end—the direct transformation of the qual-ity of experience. Infancy, youth, adult life,—all stand on the same educative level in the sense that what is really *learned* at any and every stage of experience constitutes the value of that experience, and in the sense that it is the chief business of life at every point to make living thus con-tribute to an enrichment of its own perceptible meaning.

We thus reach a technical definition of education: It is that reconstruction or reorganization of experience which adds to the meaning of experience, and which increases ability to direct the course of subsequent experience. 1. The increment of meaning corresponds to the increased perception of the connections and continuities of the activ-ities in which we are engaged. The activity begins in an impulsive form; that is, it is blind. It does not know what it is about; that is to say, what are its interactions with other activities. An activity which brings education or instruction with it makes one aware of some of the connections which had been imperceptible. To recur to our simple example, a child who reaches for a bright light gets burned. Hence-forth he *knows* that a certain act of touching in connection with a certain act of vision (and *vice-versa*) means heat and pain; or, a certain light means a source of heat. The acts by which a scientific man in his laboratory learns more about flame differ no whit in principle. By doing certain things, he makes perceptible certain connections of heat with other things, which had been previously ignored. Thus his acts in relation to these things get more meaning; he knows better what he is doing or "is about" when he has to do with them; he can *intend* consequences instead of just letting them happen—all synonymous ways of saying the same thing. At the same stroke, the flame has gained in meaning; all that is known about combustion, oxidation, about light and temperature, may become an intrinsic part of its intellectual content.

2. The other side of an educative experience is an added power of subsequent direction or control. To say that one knows what he is about, or can intend certain consequences, is to say, of course, that he can better anticipate what is going to happen; that he can, therefore, get ready or prepare in advance so as to secure beneficial consequences and avert undesirable ones. A genuinely educative experience, then, one in which instruction in conveyed and ability increased, is contradistinguished from a routine activity on one hand, and a capricious activity on the other. (*a*) In the latter one "does not care what happens"; one just lets himself go and avoids connecting the consequences of one's act (the evidences of its connections with other things) with the act. It is customary to frown upon such aimless random activity, treating it as willful mischief or carelessness or lawlessness. But there is a tendency to seek the cause of such aimless activities in the youth's own disposition, isolated from everything else. But in fact such activity is explosive, and due to maladjustment with surroundings. Individuals act capriciously whenever they act under external dictation, or from being told, without having a purpose of their own or perceiving the bearing of the deed upon other acts. One may learn by doing something which he does not understand; even in the most intelligent action, we do much which we do not mean, because the largest portion of the connections of the act we consciously intend are not perceived or anticipated. But we learn only because after the act is performed we note results which we

had not noted before. But much work in school consists in
setting up rules by which pupils are to act of such a sort
that even after pupils have acted, they are not led to see
the connection between the result—say the answer—and
the method pursued. So far as they are concerned, the
whole thing is a trick and a kind of miracle. Such action
is essentially capricious, and leads to capricious habits.
(*b*) Routine action, action which is automatic, may increase skill to do a *particular* thing. In so far, it might be
said to have an educative effect. But it does not lead to new
perceptions of bearings and connections; it limits rather
than widens the meaning-horizon. And since the environment changes and our way of acting has to be modified in
order successfully to keep a balanced connection with
things, an isolated uniform way of acting becomes disas-
trous at some critical moment. The vaunted "skill" turns
out gross ineptitude.

The essential contrast of the idea of education as continuous reconstruction with the other one-sided conceptions
which have been criticized in this and the previous chapter
is that it identifies the end (the result) and the process.
This is verbally self-contradictory, but only verbally. It
means that experience as an active process occupies time
and that its later period completes its earlier portion; it
brings to light connections involved, but hitherto unper-
ceived. The later outcome thus reveals the meaning of the
earlier, while the experience as a whole establishes a bent
or disposition toward the things possessing this meaning.
Every such continuous experience or activity is educative,
and all education resides in having such experiences.

It remains only to point out (what will receive more
ample attention later) that the reconstruction of experience
may be social as well as personal. For purposes of simplification we have spoken in the earlier chapters somewhat as
if the education of the immature which fills them with the
spirit of the social group to which they belong, were a sort

of catching up of the child with the aptitudes and resources of the adult group. In static societies, societies which make the maintenance of established custom their measure of value, this conception applies in the main. But not in progressive communities. They endeavor to shape the experiences of the young so that instead of reproducing current habits, better habits shall be formed, and thus the future adult society be an improvement on their own. Men have long had some intimation of the extent to which education may be consciously used to eliminate obvious social evils through starting the young on paths which shall not produce these ills, and some idea of the extent in which education may be made an instrument of realizing the better hopes of men. But we are doubtless far from realizing the potential efficacy of education as a constructive agency of improving society, from realizing that it represents not only a development of children and youth but also of the future society of which they will be the constituents.

Summary.—Education may be conceived either retrospectively or prospectively. That is to say, it may be treated as a process of accommodating the future to the past, or as an utilization of the past for a resource in a developing future. The former finds its standards and patterns in what has gone before. The mind may be regarded as a group of contents resulting from having certain things presented. In this case, the earlier presentations constitute the material to which the later are to be assimilated. Emphasis upon the value of the early experiences of immature beings is most important, especially because of the tendency to regard them as of little account. But these experiences do not consist of externally presented material, but of interaction of native activities with the environment which progressively modifies both the activities and the environment. The defect of the Herbartian theory of formation through presentations consists in slighting this constant interaction and change.

The same principle of criticism applies to theories which find the primary subject matter of study in the cultural products—especially the literary products—of man's history. Isolated from their connection with the present environment in which individuals have to act, they become a kind of rival and distracting environment. Their value lies in their use to increase the meaning of the things with which we have actively to do at the present time. The idea of education advanced in these chapters is formally summed up in the idea of continuous reconstruction of experience, an idea which is marked off from education as preparation for a remote future, as unfolding, as external formation, and as recapitulation of the past.

VI. THE DEMOCRATIC CONCEPTION IN EDUCATION

For the most part, save incidentally, we have hitherto been concerned with education as it may exist in any social group. We have now to make explicit the differences in the spirit, material, and method of education as it operates in different types of community life. To say that education is a social function, securing direction and development in the immature through their participation in the life of the group to which they belong, is to say in effect that education will vary with the quality of life which prevails in a group. Particularly is it true that a society which not only changes but which has the ideal of such change as will improve it, will have different standards and methods of education from one which aims simply at the perpetuation of its own customs. To make the general ideas set forth applicable to our own educational practice, it is, therefore, necessary to come to closer quarters with the nature of present social life.

The Implications of Human Association.—Society is one word, but many things. Men associate together in all kinds of ways and for all kinds of purposes. One man is concerned in a multitude of diverse groups, in which his associates may be quite different. It often seems as if they had nothing in common except that they are modes of associated life. Within every larger social organization there are numerous minor groups: not only political subdivisions, but industrial, scientific, religious, associations. There are political parties with differing aims, social sets, cliques, gangs, corporations, partnerships, groups bound closely together by ties of blood, and so in endless variety. In many modern states, and in some ancient, there is great diversity of populations, of varying languages, religions, moral codes, and traditions. From this standpoint, many a minor political unit, one of our large cities, for example, is a congeries of loosely associated societies, rather than an inclusive and permeating community of action and thought.*

The terms society, community, are thus ambiguous. They have both a eulogistic or normative sense, and a descriptive sense; a meaning *de jure* and a meaning *de facto*. In social philosophy, the former connotation is almost always uppermost. Society is conceived as one by its very nature. The qualities which accompany this unity, praiseworthy community of purpose and welfare, loyalty to public ends, mutuality of sympathy, are emphasized. But when we look at the facts which the term *denotes* instead of confining our attention to its intrinsic *connotation*, we find not unity, but a plurality of societies, good and bad. Men banded together in a criminal conspiracy, business aggregations that prey upon the public while serving it, political machines held together by the interest of plunder, are included. If it is said that such organizations are not societies because they do not meet the ideal requirements of the notion of society, the answer, in part, is that the conception of society is then made so "ideal" as to be of no use, having no reference to facts; and in part, that each of these organizations,

---

* See *ante*, p. 112.

no matter how opposed to the interests of other groups, has
something of the praiseworthy qualities of "Society" which
hold it together. There is honor among thieves, and a band
of robbers has a common interest as respects its members.
Gangs are marked by fraternal feeling, and narrow cliques
by intense loyalty to their own codes. Family life may be
marked by exclusiveness, suspicion, and jealousy as to those
without, and yet be a model of amity and mutual aid
within. Any education given by a group tends to socialize
its members, but the quality and value of the socialization
depends upon the habits and aims of the group.

Hence, once more, the need of a measure for the worth of
any given mode of social life. In seeking this measure, we
have to avoid two extremes. We cannot set up, out of our
heads, something we regard as an ideal society. We must
base our conception upon societies which actually exist, in
order to have any assurance that our ideal is a practicable
one. But, as we have just seen, the ideal cannot simply
repeat the traits which are actually found. The problem is
to extract the desirable traits of forms of community life
which actually exist, and employ them to criticize undesirable features and suggest improvement. Now in any social
group whatever, even in a gang of thieves, we find some
interest held in common, and we find a certain amount of
interaction and coöperative intercourse with other groups.
From these two traits we derive our standard. How numerous and varied are the interests which are consciously
shared? How full and free is the interplay with other forms
of association? If we apply these considerations to, say, a
criminal band, we find that the ties which consciously hold
the members together are few in number, reducible almost
to a common interest in plunder; and that they are of such
a nature as to isolate the group from other groups with
respect to give and take of the values of life. Hence, the
education such a society gives is partial and distorted. If
we take, on the other hand, the kind of family life which

illustrates the standard, we find that there are material, intellectual, æsthetic interests in which all participate and that the progress of one member has worth for the experience of other members—it is readily communicable—and that the family is not an isolated whole, but enters intimately into relationships with business groups, with schools, with all the agencies of culture, as well as with other similar groups, and that it plays a due part in the political organization and in return receives support from it. In short, there are many interests consciously communicated and shared; and there are varied and free points of contact with other modes of association.

The Democratic Ideal.—The two elements in our criterion both point to democracy. The first signifies not only more numerous and more varied points of shared common interest, but greater reliance upon the recognition of mutual interests as a factor in social control. The second means not only freer interaction between social groups (once isolated so far as intention could keep up a separation) but change in social habit—its continuous readjustment through meeting the new situations produced by varied intercourse. And these two traits are precisely what characterize the democratically constituted society.

Upon the educational side, we note first that the realization of a form of social life in which interests are mutually interpenetrating, and where progress, or readjustment, is an important consideration, makes a democratic community more interested than other communities have cause to be in deliberate and systematic education. The devotion of democracy to education is a familiar fact. The superficial explanation is that a government resting upon popular suffrage cannot be successful unless those who elect and who obey their governors are educated. Since a democratic society repudiates the principle of external authority, it must find a substitute in voluntary disposition and interest; these can be created only by education. But there is a deeper explanation. A democracy is more than a form of government; it is primarily a mode of associated living, of conjoint communicated experience. The extension in space of the number of individuals who participate in an interest so that each has to refer his own action to that of others, and to consider the action of others to give point and direction to his own, is equivalent to the breaking down of those barriers of class, race, and national territory which kept men from perceiving the full import of their activity. These more numerous and more varied points of contact denote a greater diversity of stimuli to which an individual has to respond; they consequently put a premium on variation in his action. They secure a liberation of powers which remain suppressed as long as the incitations to action are partial, as they must be in a group which in its exclusiveness shuts out many interests.

The widening of the area of shared concerns, and the liberation of a greater diversity of personal capacities which characterize a democracy, are not of course the product of deliberation and conscious effort. On the contrary, they were caused by the development of modes of manufacture and commerce, travel, migration, and intercommunication which flowed from the command of science over natural energy. But after greater individualization on one hand, and a broader community of interest on the other have come into existence, it is a matter of deliberate effort to sustain and extend them. Obviously a society to which stratification into separate classes would be fatal, must see to it that intellectual opportunities are accessible to all on equable and easy terms. A society marked off into classes need be specially attentive only to the education of its ruling elements. A society which is mobile, which is full of channels for the distribution of a change occurring anywhere, must see to it that its members are educated to personal initiative and adaptability. Otherwise, they will be overwhelmed by the changes in which they are caught and whose significance or connections they do not perceive. The result will be a confusion in which a few will appropriate to themselves the results of the blind and externally directed activities of others.

VII. Aims in Education

An aim denotes the result of any natural process brought to consciousness and made a factor in determining present observation and choice of ways of acting. It signifies that an activity has become intelligent. Specifically it means foresight of the alternative consequences attendant upon acting in a given situation in different ways, and the use of what is anticipated to direct observation and experiment. A true aim is thus opposed at every point to an aim which is imposed upon a process of action from without. The latter is fixed and rigid; it is not a stimulus to intelligence in the given situation, but is an externally dictated order to do such and such things. Instead of connecting directly with present activities, it is remote, divorced from the means by which it is to be reached. Instead of suggesting a freer and better balanced activity, it is a limit set to activity. In education, the currency of these externally imposed aims is responsible for the emphasis put upon the notion of preparation for a remote future and for rendering the work of both teacher and pupil mechanical and slavish.

Nature as Supplying the Aim.—We have just pointed out the futility of trying to establish *the* aim of education —some one final aim which subordinates all others to itself. We have indicated that since general aims are but prospective points of view from which to survey the existing conditions and estimate their possibilities, we might have any number of them, all consistent with one another. As matter of fact, a large number have been stated at different times, all having great local value. For the *statement* of aim

is a matter of emphasis at a given time. And we do not
emphasize things which do not require emphasis—that is,
such things as are taking care of themselves fairly well. We
tend rather to frame our statement on the basis of the defects and needs of the contemporary situation; we take for
granted, without explicit statement which would be of no
use, whatever is right or approximately so. We frame our
explicit aims in terms of some alteration to be brought
about. It is, then, no paradox requiring explanation that a
given epoch or generation tends to emphasize in its conscious projections just the things which it has least of in
actual fact. A time of domination by authority will call out
as response the desirability of great individual freedom; one
of disorganized individual activities the need of social control as an educational aim.

Culture as Aim.—Whether or not social efficiency is an
aim which is consistent with culture turns upon these considerations. Culture means at least something cultivated,
something ripened; it is opposed to the raw and crude.
When the "natural" is identified with this rawness, culture
is opposed to what is called natural development. Culture
is also something personal; it is cultivation with respect to
appreciation of ideas and art and broad human interests.
When efficiency is identified with a narrow range of *acts*,
instead of with the spirit and meaning of *activity*, culture
is opposed to efficiency. Whether called culture or complete
development of personality, the outcome is identical with
the true meaning of social efficiency whenever attention is
given to what is unique in an individual—and he would
not be an individual if there were not something incommen-
surable about him. Its opposite is the mediocre, the average.
Whenever distinctive quality is developed, distinction of
personality results, and with it greater promise for a social
service which goes beyond the supply in quantity of material commodities. For how can there be a society really

worth serving unless it is constituted of individuals of significant personal qualities?

The fact is that the opposition of high worth of personality to social efficiency is a product of a feudally organized
society with its rigid division of inferior and superior. The
latter are supposed to have time and opportunity to develop themselves as human beings; the former are confined
to providing external products. When social efficiency as
measured by product or output is urged as an ideal in a
would-be democratic society, it means that the depreciatory
estimate of the masses characteristic of an aristocratic community is accepted and carried over. But if democracy has
a moral and ideal meaning, it is that a social return be demanded from all and that opportunity for development of
distinctive capacities be afforded all. The separation of the
two aims in education is fatal to democracy; the adoption
of the narrower meaning of efficiency deprives it of its
essential justification.

The aim of efficiency (like any educational aim) must be
included within the process of experience. When it is
measured by tangible external products, and not by the
achieving of a distinctively valuable experience, it becomes
materialistic. Results in the way of commodities which
may be the outgrowth of an efficient personality are, in
the strictest sense, by-products of education: by-products
which are inevitable and important, but nevertheless by-
products. To set up an external aim strengthens by reaction
the false conception of culture which identifies it with
something purely "inner." And the idea of perfecting an
"inner" personality is a sure sign of social divisions. What
is called inner is simply that which does not connect with
others—which is not capable of free and full communication. What is termed spiritual culture has usually been
futile, with something rotten about it, just because it has
been conceived as a thing which a man might have inter-

nally—and therefore exclusively. What one is as a person is what one is as associated with others, in a free give and take of intercourse. This transcends both the efficiency which consists in supplying products to others and the culture which is an exclusive refinement and polish.

Any individual has missed his calling, farmer, physician, teacher, student, who does not find that the accomplishments of results of value to others in an accompaniment of a process of experience inherently worth while. Why then should it be thought that one must take his choice between sacrificing himself to doing useful things for others, or sacrificing them to pursuit of his own exclusive ends, whether the saving of his own soul or the building of an inner spiritual life and personality? What happens is that since neither of these things is persistently possible, we get a compromise and an alternation. One tries each course by turns. There is no greater tragedy than that so much of the professedly spiritual and religious thought of the world has emphasized the two ideals of self-sacrifice and spiritual self-perfecting instead of throwing its weight against this dualism of life. The dualism is too deeply established to be easily overthrown; for that reason, it is the particular task of education at the present time to struggle in behalf of an aim in which social efficiency and personal culture are synonyms instead of antagonists.

Summary.—General or comprehensive aims are points of view for surveying the specific problems of education. Consequently it is a test of the value of the manner in which any large end is stated to see if it will translate readily and consistently into the procedures which are suggested by another. We have applied this test to three general aims: Development according to nature, social efficiency, and culture or personal mental enrichment. In each case we have seen that the aims when partially stated come into conflict with each other. The partial statement of natural development takes the primitive powers in an alleged spontaneous development as the end-all. From this point of view training which renders them useful to others is an abnormal constraint; one which profoundly modifies them through deliberate nurture is corrupting. But when we recognize that natural activities mean native activities which develop only through the uses in which they are nurtured, the conflict disappears. Similarly a social efficiency which is defined in terms of rendering external service to others is of necessity opposed to the aim of enriching the meaning of experience, while a culture which is taken to consist in an internal refinement of a mind is opposed to a socialized disposition. But social efficiency as an educational purpose should mean cultivation of power to join freely and fully in shared or common activities. This is impossible without culture, while it brings a reward in culture, because one cannot share in intercourse with others without learning— without getting a broader point of view and perceiving things of which one would otherwise be ignorant. And there is perhaps no better definition of culture than that it is the capacity for constantly expanding the range and accuracy of one's perception of meanings.

VIII. Experience and Thinking

The Nature of Experience.—The nature of experience can be understood only by noting that it includes an active and a passive element peculiarly combined. On the active hand, experience is *trying*—a meaning which is made explicit in the connected term experiment. On the passive, it is *undergoing*. When we experience something we act upon it, we do something with it; then we suffer or undergo the consequences. We do something to the thing and then it does something to us in return: such is the peculiar combination. The connection of these two phases of experience measures the fruitfulness or value of the experience. Mere activity does not constitute experience. It is dispersive, centrifugal, dissipating. Experience as trying involves change, but change is meaningless transition unless it is consciously connected with the return wave of consequences which flow from it. When an activity is continued *into* the undergoing of consequences, when the change made by action is reflected back into a change made in us, the mere flux is loaded with significance. We learn something. It is not experience when a child merely sticks his finger into a flame; it is experience when the movement is connected with the pain which he undergoes in consequence. Henceforth the sticking of the finger into flame *means* a burn. Being burned is a mere physical change, like the burning of a stick of wood, if it is not perceived as a consequence of some other action.

Blind and capricious impulses hurry us on heedlessly from one thing to another. So far as this happens, everything is writ in water. There is none of that cumulative growth which makes an experience in any vital sense of that term. On the other hand, many things happen to us in the way of pleasure and pain which we do not connect with any prior activity of our own. They are mere accidents so far as we are concerned. There is no before or after to such experience; no retrospect nor outlook, and consequently no meaning. We get nothing which may be carried over to foresee what is likely to happen next, and no gain in ability to adjust ourselves to what is coming—no added control. Only by courtesy can such an experience be called experience. To "learn from experience" is to make a backward and forward connection between what we do to things and what we enjoy or suffer from things in consequence. Under such conditions, doing becomes a trying; an experiment with the world to find out what it is like; the undergoing becomes instruction—discovery of the connection of things.

Two conclusions important for education follow. (1) Experience is primarily an active-passive affair; it is not primarily cognitive. But (2) the *measure of the value* of an experience lies in the perception of relationships or continuities to which it leads up. It includes cognition in the degree in which it is cumulative or amounts to something, or has meaning. In schools, those under instruction are too customarily looked upon as acquiring knowledge as theoretical spectators, minds which appropriate knowledge by direct energy of intellect. The very word pupil has almost come to mean one who is engaged not in having fruitful experiences but in absorbing knowledge directly. Something which is called mind or consciousness is severed from the physical organs of activity. The former is then thought to be purely intellectual and cognitive; the latter to be an irrelevant and intruding physical factor. The intimate union of activity and undergoing its consequences which leads to recognition of meaning is broken; instead we have two fragments: mere bodily action on one side, and meaning directly grasped by "spiritual" activity on the other.

It would be impossible to state adequately the evil results which have flowed from this dualism of mind and body, much less to exaggerate them. Some of the more striking effects, may, however, be enumerated. (*a*) In part bodily activity becomes an intruder. Having nothing, so it is thought, to do with mental activity, it becomes a distraction, an evil to be contended with. For the pupil has a body, and brings it to school along with his mind. And the body is, of necessity, a wellspring of energy; it has to do something. But its activities, not being utilized in occupation with things which yield significant results, have to be frowned upon. They lead the pupil away from the lesson with which his "mind" ought to be occupied; they are sources of mischief. The chief source of the "problem of discipline" in schools is that the teacher has often to spend the larger part of the time in suppressing the bodily activities which take the mind away from its material. A premium is put on physical quietude; on silence, on rigid uniformity of posture and movement; upon a machine-like simulation of the attitudes of intelligent interest. The teachers' business is to hold the pupils up to these requirements and to punish the inevitable deviations which occur.

The nervous strain and fatigue which result with both teacher and pupil are a necessary consequence of the abnormality of the situation in which bodily activity is divorced from the perception of meaning. Callous indifference and explosions from strain alternate. The neglected body, having no organized fruitful channels of activity, breaks forth, without knowing why or how, into meaningless boisterousness, or settles into equally meaningless fooling—both very different from the normal play of children. Physically active children become restless and unruly; the more quiescent, so-called conscientious ones spend what energy they have in the negative task of keeping their instincts and active tendencies suppressed, instead of in a positive one of constructive planning and execution; they are thus educated not into responsibility for the significant and graceful use of bodily powers, but into an enforced duty not to give them free play. It may be seriously asserted that a chief cause for the remarkable achievements of Greek education was that it was never misled by false notions into an attempted separation of mind and body.

(b) Even, however, with respect to the lessons which have to be learned by the application of "mind," some bodily activities have to be used. The senses—especially the eye and ear—have to be employed to take in what the book, the map, the blackboard, and the teacher say. The lips and vocal organs, and the hands, have to be used to reproduce in speech and writing what has been stowed away. The senses are then regarded as a kind of mysterious conduit through which information is conducted from the external world into the mind; they are spoken of as gateways and avenues of knowledge. To keep the eyes on the book and the ears open to the teacher's words is a mysterious source of intellectual grace. Moreover, reading, writing, and figuring—important school arts—demand muscular or motor training. The muscles of eye, hand, and vocal organs accordingly have to be trained to act as pipes for carrying knowledge back out of the mind into external action. For it happens that using the muscles repeatedly in the same way fixes in them an automatic tendency to repeat.

The obvious result is a mechanical use of the bodily activities which (in spite of the generally obtrusive and interfering character of the body in mental action) have to be employed more or less. For the senses and muscles are used not as organic participants in having an instructive experience, but as external inlets and outlets of mind. Before the child goes to school, he learns with his hand, eye, and ear, because they are organs of the process of doing something from which meaning results. The boy flying a kite has to keep his eye on the kite, and has to note the various pressures of the string on his hand. His senses are avenues of knowledge not because external facts are somehow "conveyed" to the brain, but because they are *used* in doing something with a purpose. The qualities of seen and touched things have a bearing on what is done, and are alertly perceived; they have a meaning. But when pupils are expected to use their eyes to note the form of words, irrespective of their meaning, in order to reproduce them in spelling or reading, the resulting training is simply of isolated sense organs and muscles. It is such isolation of an act from a purpose which makes it mechanical. It is customary for teachers to urge children to read with expression, so as to bring out the meaning. But if they originally learned the sensory-motor technique of reading—the ability to identify forms and to reproduce the sounds they stand for —by methods which did not call for attention to meaning, a mechanical habit was established which makes it difficult to read subsequently with intelligence. The vocal organs have been trained to go their own way automatically in isolation; and meaning cannot be tied on at will. Drawing, singing, and writing may be taught in the same mechanical way; for, we repeat, any way *is* mechanical which narrows down the bodily activity so that a separation of body from mind—that is, from recognition of meaning—is set up. Mathematics, even in its higher branches, when undue emphasis is put upon the technique of calculation, and science, when laboratory exercises are given for their own sake, suffer from the same evil.

(c) On the intellectual side, the separation of "mind" from direct occupation with things throws emphasis on *things* at the expense of *relations* or connections. It is altogether too common to separate perceptions and even ideas from judgments. The latter are thought to come after the former in order to compare them. It is alleged that the mind perceives things apart from relations; that it forms ideas of them in isolation from their connections—with what goes before and comes after. Then judgment or thought is called upon to combine the separated items of "knowledge" so that their resemblance or casual connection shall be brought out. As matter of fact, every perception and every idea is a sense of the bearings, use, and cause, of a thing. We do not really know a chair or have an idea of it by inventorying and enumerating its various isolated qualities, but only by bringing these qualities into connection with something else—the purpose which makes it a chair and not a table; or its difference from the kind of chair we are accustomed to, or the "period" which it represents, and so on. A wagon is not perceived when all its parts are summed up; it is the characteristic connection of the parts which makes it a wagon. And these connections are not those of mere physical juxtaposition; they involve connection with the animals that draw it, the things that are carried on it, and so on. Judgment is employed in the perception; otherwise the perception is mere sensory excitation or else a recognition of the result of a prior judgment, as in the case of familiar objects.

Words, the counters for ideas, are, however, easily taken for ideas. And in just the degree in which mental activity is separated from active concern with the world, from doing something and connecting the doing with what is undergone, words, symbols, come to take the place of ideas. The substitution is the more subtle because *some* meaning is recognized. But we are very easily trained to be content with a minimum of meaning, and to fail to note how restricted is our perception of the relations which confer significance. We get so thoroughly used to a kind of pseudo-idea, a half perception, that we are not aware how half-dead our mental action is, and how much keener and more extensive our observations and ideas would be if we formed them under conditions of a vital experience which required us to use judgment: to hunt for the connections of the thing dealt with.

There is no difference of opinion as to the theory of the matter. All authorities agree that that discernment of relationships is the genuinely intellectual matter; hence, the educative matter. The failure arises in supposing that relationships can become perceptible without *experience*— without that conjoint trying and undergoing of which we have spoken. It is assumed that "mind" can grasp them if it will only give attention, and that this attention may be given at will irrespective of the situation. Hence the deluge of half-observations, of verbal ideas, and unassimilated "knowledge" which afflicts the world. An ounce of experience is better than a ton of theory simply because it is only in experience that any theory has vital and verifiable significance. An experience, a very humble experience, is capable of generating and carrying any amount of theory (or intellectual content), but a theory apart from an experience cannot be definitely grasped even as theory. It tends to become a mere verbal formula, a set of catchwords used to render thinking, or genuine theorizing, unnecessary and impossible. Because of our education we use words, thinking they are ideas, to dispose of questions, the disposal being in reality simply such an obscuring of perception as prevents us from seeing any longer the difficulty.

Reflection in Experience.—Thought or reflection, as we have already seen virtually if not explicitly, is the discernment of the relation between what we try to do and what happens in consequence. No experience having a meaning is possible without some element of thought. But we may contrast two types of experience according to the proportion of reflection found in them. All our experiences have a phase of "cut and try" in them—what psychologists call the method of trial and error. We simply do something, and when it fails, we do something else, and keep on trying till we hit upon something which works, and then we adopt that method as a rule of thumb measure in subsequent procedure. Some experiences have very little else in them than this hit and miss or succeed process. We see *that* a certain way of acting and a certain consequence are connected, but we do not see *how* they are. We do not see the details of the connection; the links are missing. Our discernment is very gross. In other cases we push our observation farther. We analyze to see just what lies between so as to bind together cause and effect, activity and consequence. This extension of our insight makes foresight more accurate and comprehensive. The action which rests simply upon the trial and error method is at the mercy of circumstances; they may change so that the act performed does not operate in the way it was expected to. But if we know in detail upon what the result depends, we can look to see whether the required conditions are there. The method extends our practical control. For if some of the conditions are missing, we may, if we know what the needed antecedents for an effect are, set to work to supply them; or, if they are such as to produce undesirable effects as well, we may eliminate some of the superfluous causes and economize effort.

In discovery of the detailed connections of our activities and what happens in consequence, the thought implied in cut and try experience is made explicit. Its quantity increases so that its proportionate value is very different. Hence the quality of the experience changes; the change is so significant that we may call this type of experience reflective—that is, reflective *par excellence*. The deliberate cultivation of this phase of thought constitutes thinking as a distinctive experience. Thinking, in other words, is the intentional endeavor to discover *specific* connections between something which we do and the consequences which result, so that the two become continuous. Their isolation, and consequently their purely arbitrary going together, is cancelled; a unified developing situation takes its place. The occurrence is now understood; it is explained; it is reasonable, as we say, that the thing should happen as it does.

Thinking is thus equivalent to an explicit rendering of the intelligent element in our experience. It makes it possible to act with an end in view. It is the condition of our having aims. As soon as an infant begins to *expect* he begins to use something which is now going on as a sign of something to follow; he is, in however simple a fashion, judging. For he takes one thing as *evidence* of something else, and so recognizes a relationship. Any future development, however elaborate it may be, is only an extending and a refining of this simple act of inference. All that the wisest man can do is to observe what is going on more widely and more minutely and then select more carefully from what is noted just those factors which point to something to happen. The opposites, once more, to thoughtful action are routine and capricious behavior. The former accepts what has been customary as a full measure of possibility and omits to take into account the connections of the particular things done. The latter makes the momentary act a measure of value, and ignores the connections of our personal action with the energies of the environment. It says, virtually, "things are to be just as I happen to like them at this instant," as routine says in effect "let things continue just as I have found them in the past." Both refuse to acknowledge responsibility for the future consequences which flow from present action. Reflection is the acceptance of such responsibility.

The starting point of any process of thinking is something going on, something which just as it stands is incomplete or unfulfilled. Its point, its meaning lies literally in what it is going to be, in how it is going to turn out. As this is written, the world is filled with the clang of contending armies. For an active participant in the war, it is clear that the momentous thing is the issue, the future consequences, of this and that happening. He is identified, for the time at least, with the issue; *his* fate hangs upon the course things are taking. But even for an onlooker in a neutral country, the significance of every move made, of every advance here and retreat there, lies in what it portends. To *think* upon the news as it comes to us is to attempt to see what is indicated as probable or possible regarding an outcome. To fill our heads, like a scrapbook, with this and that item as a finished and done-for thing, is not to think. It is to turn ourselves into a piece of registering apparatus. To consider the *bearing* of the occurrence upon what may be, but is not yet, is to think. Nor will the reflective experience be different in kind if we substitute distance in time for separation in space. Imagine the war done with, and a future historian giving an account of it. The episode is, by assumption, past. But he cannot give a thoughtful account of the war save as he preserves the time sequence; the meaning of each occurrence, as he deals with it, lies in what was future for *it*, though not for the historian. To take it by itself as a complete existence is to take it unreflectively.

Reflection also implies concern with the issue—a certain sympathetic identification of our own destiny, if only dramatic, with the outcome of the course of events. For the general in the war, or a common soldier, or a citizen of one of the contending nations, the stimulus to thinking is direct and urgent. For neutrals, it is indirect and dependent upon imagination. But the flagrant partisanship of human nature is evidence of the intensity of the tendency to identify ourselves with one possible course of events, and to reject the other as foreign. If we cannot take sides in overt action, and throw in our little weight to help determine the final balance, we take sides emotionally and imaginatively. We desire this or that outcome. One wholly indifferent to the outcome does not follow or think about what is happening at all. From this dependence of the act of thinking upon a sense of sharing in the consequences of what goes on, flows one of the chief paradoxes of thought. Born in partiality, in order to accomplish its tasks it must achieve a certain detached impartiality. The general who allows his hopes and desires to affect his observations and interpretations of the existing situation will surely make a mistake in calculation. While hopes and fears may be the chief motive for a thoughtful following of the war on the part of an onlooker in a neutral country, he too will think ineffectively in the degree in which his preferences modify the stuff of his observations and reasonings. There is, however, no incompatibility between the fact that the occasion of reflection lies in a personal sharing in what is going on and the fact that the value of the reflection lies upon keeping one's self out of the data. The almost insurmountable difficulty of achieving this detachment is evidence that thinking originates in situations where the course of thinking is an actual part of the course of events and is designed to influence the result.

Only gradually and with a widening of the area of vision through a growth of social sympathies does thinking develop to include what lies beyond our *direct* interests: a fact of great significance for education.

To say that thinking occurs with reference to situations which are still going on, and incomplete, is to say that thinking occurs when things are uncertain or doubtful or problematic. Only what is finished, completed, is wholly assured. Where there is reflection there is suspense. The object of thinking is to help *reach* a conclusion, to project a possible termination on the basis of what is already given. Certain other facts about thinking accompany this feature. Since the situation in which thinking occurs is a doubtful one, thinking is a process of inquiry, of looking into things, of investigating. Acquiring is always secondary, and instrumental to the act of *in*quiring. It is seeking, a quest, for something that is not at hand. We sometimes talk as if "original research" were a peculiar prerogative of scientists or at least of advanced students. But all thinking is research, and all research is native, original, with him who carries it on, even if everybody else in the world already is sure of what he is still looking for.

It also follows that all thinking involves a risk. Certainty cannot be guaranteed in advance. The invasion of the unknown is of the nature of an adventure; we cannot be sure in advance. The conclusions of thinking, till confirmed by the event, are, accordingly, more or less tentative or hypothetical. Their dogmatic assertion as final is unwarranted, short of the issue, in fact. The Greeks acutely raised the question: How can we learn? For either we know already what we are after, or else we do not know. In neither case is learning possible; on the first alternative because we know already; on the second, because we do not know what to look for, nor if, by chance, we find it can we tell that it is what we were after. The dilemma makes no provision for *coming* to know, for learning; it assumes either complete knowledge or complete ignorance. Nevertheless the twilight zone of inquiry, of thinking, exists. The possibility of *hypo-thetical* conclusions, of *tentative* results, is the fact which the Greek dilemma overlooked. The perplexities of the situation suggest certain ways out. We try these ways, and either push our way out, in which case we know we have found what we were looking for, or the situation gets darker and more confused—in which case, we know we are still ignorant. Tentative means trying out, feeling one's way along provisionally. Taken by itself, the Greek argument is a nice piece of formal logic. But it is also true that as long as men kept a sharp disjunction between knowledge and ignorance, science made only slow and accidental advance. Systematic advance in invention and discovery began when men recognized that they could utilize doubt for purposes of inquiry by forming conjectures to guide action in tentative explorations, whose development would confirm, refute, or modify the guiding conjecture. While the Greeks made knowledge more than learning, modern science makes conserved knowledge only a means to learning, to discovery.

To recur to our illustration. A commanding general cannot base his actions upon either absolute certainty or absolute ignorance. He has a certain amount of information at hand which is, we will assume, reasonably trustworthy. He then *infers* certain prospective movements, thus assigning meaning to the bare facts of the given situation. His inference is more or less dubious and hypothetical. But he acts upon it. He develops a plan of procedure, a method of dealing with the situation. The consequences which directly follow from his acting this way rather than that test and reveal the worth of his reflections. What he already knows functions and has value in what he learns. But will this account apply in the case of the one in a neutral country who is thoughtfully following as best he can the progress of events? In form, yes, though not of course in content. It is

self-evident that his guesses about the future indicated by
present facts, guesses by which he attempts to supply meaning to a multitude of disconnected data, cannot be the basis
of a method which shall take effect in the campaign. *That*
is not *his* problem. But in the degree in which he is actively
thinking, and not merely passively following the course of
events, his tentative inferences will take effect in *a* method
of procedure appropriate to *his* situation. He will anticipate
certain future moves, and will be on the alert to see whether
they happen or not. In the degree in which he is intellectually concerned, or thoughtful, he will be *actively* on the
lookout; he will take steps which although they do not affect
the campaign, modify in some degree *his* subsequent
actions. Otherwise his later "I told you so" has no intellectual quality at all; it does not mark any testing or verification of prior thinking, but only a coincidence that yields
emotional satisfaction—and includes a large factor of self-
deception.

The case is comparable to that of an astronomer who
from given data has been led to foresee (infer) a future
eclipse. No matter how great the mathematical probability,
the inference is hypothetical—a matter of probability.* The
hypothesis as to the date and position of the anticipated
eclipse becomes the material of forming a method of future
conduct. Apparatus is arranged; possibly an expedition is
made to some far part of the globe. In any case, some active
steps are taken which actually change *some* physical conditions. And apart from such steps and the consequent
modification of the situation, there is no completion of the
act of thinking. It remains suspended. Knowledge, already
attained knowledge, controls thinking and makes it fruitful.

So much for the general features of a reflective ex-

---

* It is most important for the practice of science that men in many cases
can calculate the degree of probability and the amount of probable error
involved, but that does not alter the features of the situation as described.
It refines them.

perience. They are (*i*) perplexity, confusion, doubt, due to the fact that one is implicated in an incomplete situation whose full character is not yet determined; (*ii*) a conjectural anticipation—a tentative interpretation of the given elements, attributing to them a tendency to effect certain consequences; (*iii*) a careful survey (examination, inspection, exploration, analysis) of all attainable consideration which will define and clarify the problem in hand; (*iv*) a consequent elaboration of the tentative hypothesis to make it more precise and more consistent, because squaring with a wider range of facts; (*v*) taking one stand upon the projected hypothesis as a plan of action which is applied to the existing state of affairs: doing something overtly to bring about the anticipated result, and thereby testing the hypothesis. It is the extent and accuracy of steps three and four which mark off a distinctive reflective experience from one on the trial and error plane. They make *thinking* itself into an experience. Nevertheless, we never get wholly beyond the trial and error situation. Our most elaborate and rationally consistent thought has to be tried in the world and thereby tried out. And since it can never take into account all the connections, it can never cover with perfect accuracy all the consequences. Yet a thoughtful survey of conditions is so careful, and the guessing at results so controlled, that we have a right to mark off the reflective experience from the grosser trial and error forms of action.

Summary.—In determining the place of thinking in experience we first noted that experience involves a connection of doing or trying with something which is undergone in consequence. A separation of the active doing phase from the passive undergoing phase destroys the vital meaning of an experience. Thinking is the accurate and deliberate instituting of connections between what is done and its consequences. It notes not only that they are connected, but the details of the connection. It makes con-

necting links explicit in the form of relationships. The
stimulus to thinking is found when we wish to determine
the significance of some act, performed or to be performed.
Then we anticipate consequences. This implies that the
situation as it stands is, either in fact or to us, incomplete
and hence indeterminate. The projection of consequences
means a proposed or tentative solution. To perfect this hypothesis, existing conditions have to be carefully scrutinized
and the implications of the hypothesis developed—an
operation called reasoning. Then the suggested solution—
the idea or theory—has to be tested by acting upon it. If it
brings about certain consequences, certain determinate
changes, in the world, it is accepted as valid. Otherwise it
is modified, and another trial made. Thinking includes all
of these steps,—the sense of a problem, the observation of
conditions, the formation and rational elaboration of a suggested conclusion, and the active experimental testing.
While all thinking results in knowledge, ultimately the
value of knowledge is subordinate to its use in thinking. For
we live not in a settled and finished world, but in one which
is going on, and where our main task is prospective, and
where retrospect—and all knowledge as distinct from
thought is retrospect—is of value in the solidity, security,
and fertility it affords our dealings with the future.

IX. Thinking in Education

Processes of instruction are unified in the degree in which they center in the production of good habits
of thinking. While we may speak, without error, of the
method of thought, the important thing is that thinking is
the method of an educative experience. The essentials of
method are therefore identical with the essentials of reflection. They are first that the pupil have a genuine situation
of experience—that there be a continuous activity in which
he is interested for its own sake; secondly, that a genuine

problem develop within this situation as a stimulus to thought; third, that he possess the information and make the observations needed to deal with it; fourth, that suggested solutions occur to him which he shall be responsible for developing in an orderly way; fifth, that he have opportunity and occasion to test his ideas by application, to make their meaning clear and to discover for himself their validity.

X. EDUCATIONAL VALUES

The Nature of Realization or Appreciation.— Much of our experience is indirect; it is dependent upon signs which intervene between the things and ourselves, signs which stand for or represent the former. It is one thing to have been engaged in war, to have shared its dangers and hardships; it is another thing to hear or read about it. All language, all symbols, are implements of an indirect experience; in technical language the experience which is procured by their means is "mediated." It stands in contrast with an immediate, direct experience, something in which we take part vitally and at first hand, instead of through the intervention of representative media. As we have seen, the scope of personal, vitally direct experience is very limited. If it were not for the intervention of agencies for representing absent and distant affairs, our experience would remain almost on the level of that of the brutes. Every step from savagery to civilization is dependent upon the invention of media which enlarge the range of purely immediate experience and give it deepened as well as wider meaning by connecting it with things which can only be signified or symbolized. It is doubtless this fact which is the cause of the disposition to identify an uncultivated person with an illiterate person—so dependent are we on letters for effective representative or indirect experience.

At the same time (as we have also had repeated occasion
to see) there is always a danger that symbols will not be
truly representative; danger that instead of really calling
up the absent and remote in a way to make it enter a
present experience, the linguistic media of representation
will become an end in themselves. Formal education is peculiarly exposed to this danger, with the result that when
literacy supervenes, mere bookishness, what is popularly
termed the academic, too often comes with it. In colloquial
speech, the phrase a "realizing sense" is used to express the
urgency, warmth, and intimacy of a direct experience in
contrast with the remote, pallid, and coldly detached quality of a representative experience. The terms "mental realization" and "appreciation" (or *genuine* appreciation) are
more elaborate names for the realizing sense of a thing. It
is not possible to define these ideas except by synonyms,
like "coming home to one," "really taking it in," etc., for the
only way to appreciate what is meant by a direct experience
of a thing is by having it. But it is the difference between
reading a technical description of a picture, and seeing it;
or between just seeing it and being moved by it; between
learning mathematical equations about light and being
carried away by some peculiarly glorious illumination of a
misty landscape.

We are thus met by the danger of the tendency of technique and other purely representative forms to encroach
upon the sphere of direct appreciations; in other words, the
tendency to assume that pupils have a foundation of direct
realization of situations sufficient for the superstructure of
representative experience erected by formulated school
studies. This is not simply a matter of quantity or bulk.
Sufficient direct experience is even more a matter of
quality; it must be of a sort to connect readily and fruit-
fully with the symbolic material of instruction. Before
teaching can safely enter upon conveying facts and ideas
through the media of signs, schooling must provide genuine

situations in which personal participation brings home the import of the material and the problems which it conveys. From the standpoint of the pupil, the resulting experiences are worth while on their own account; from the standpoint of the teacher, they are also means of supplying subject matter required for understanding instruction involving signs, and of evoking attitudes of open-mindedness and concern as to the material symbolically conveyed.

In the outline given of the theory of educative subject matter, the demand for this background of realization or appreciation is met by the provision made for play and active occupations embodying typical situations. Nothing need be added to what has already been said except to point out that while the discussion dealt explicitly with the subject matter of primary education, where the demand for the available background of direct experience is most obvious, the principle applies to the primary or elementary phase of every subject. The first and basic function of laboratory work, for example, in a high school or college in a new field, is to familiarize the student at first hand with a certain range of facts and problems—to give him a "feeling" for them. Getting command of technique and of methods of reaching and testing generalizations is at first secondary to getting appreciation. As regards the primary school activities, it is to be borne in mind that the fundamental intent is not to amuse nor to convey information with a minimum of vexation nor yet to acquire skill,—though these results may accrue as by-products,—but to enlarge and enrich the scope of experience, and to keep alert and effective the interest in intellectual progress.

The rubric of appreciation supplies an appropriate head for bringing out three further principles: the nature of effective or real (as distinct from nominal) standards of value; the place of the imagination in appreciative realizations; and the place of the fine arts in the course of study.

1. The nature of standards of valuation. Every adult has

acquired, in the course of his prior experience and education, certain measures of the worth of various sorts of experience. He has learned to look upon qualities like honesty, amiability, perseverance, loyalty, as moral goods; upon certain classics of literature, painting, music, as æsthetic values, and so on. Not only this, but he has learned certain rules for these values—the golden rule in morals; harmony, balance, etc., proportionate distribution in æsthetic goods; definition, clarity, system in intellectual accomplishments. These principles are so important as standards of judging the worth of new experiences that parents and instructors are always tending to teach them directly to the young. They overlook the danger that standards so taught will be *merely* symbolic; that is, largely conventional and verbal. In reality, working as distinct from professed standards depend upon what an individual has himself specifically appreciated to be deeply significant in concrete situations. An individual may have learned that certain characteristics are conventionally esteemed in music; he may be able to converse with some correctness about classic music; he may even honestly believe that these traits constitute his own musical standards. But if in his own past experience, what he has been most accustomed to and has most enjoyed is ragtime, his active or working measures of valuation are fixed on the ragtime level. The appeal actually made to him in his own personal realization fixes his attitude much more deeply than what he has been taught as the proper thing to say; his habitual disposition thus fixed forms his real "norm" of valuation in subsequent musical experiences.

Probably few would deny this statement as to musical taste. But it applies equally well in judgments of moral and intellectual worth. A youth who has had repeated experience of the full meaning of the value of kindliness toward others built into his disposition has a measure of the worth of generous treatment of others. Without this vital appreciation, the duty and virtue of unselfishness impressed upon him by others as a standard remains purely a matter of symbols which he cannot adequately translate into realities. His "knowledge" is second-handed; it is only a knowledge that others prize unselfishness as an excellence, and esteem him in the degree in which he exhibits it. Thus there grows up a split between a person's professed standards and his actual ones. A person may be aware of the *results* of this struggle between his inclinations and his theoretical opinions; he suffers from the conflict between doing what is really dear to him and what he has learned will win the approval of others. But of the split itself he is unaware; the result is a kind of unconscious hypocrisy, an instability of disposition. In similar fashion, a pupil who has worked through some confused intellectual situation and fought his way to clearing up obscurities in a definite outcome, appreciates the value of clarity and definition. He has a standard which can be depended upon. He may be trained externally to go through certain motions of analysis and division of subject matter and may acquire information about the value of these processes as standard logical functions, but unless it somehow comes home to him at some point as an appreciation of his own, the significance of the logical norms—so-called—remains as much an external piece of information as, say, the names of rivers in China. He may be able to recite, but the recital is a mechanical rehearsal.

It is, then, a serious mistake to regard appreciation as if it were confined to such things as literature and pictures and music. Its scope is as comprehensive as the work of education itself. The formation of habits is a purely mechanical thing unless habits are also *tastes*—habitual modes of preference and esteem, an effective sense of excellence. There are adequate grounds for asserting that the premium so often put in schools upon external "discipline," and upon marks and rewards, upon promotion and keeping back, are the obverse of the lack of attention given to life situations in which the meaning of facts, ideas, principles, and problems is vitally brought home.

2. Appreciative realizations are to be distinguished from symbolic or representative experiences. They are not to be distinguished from the work of the intellect or understanding. Only a personal response involving imagination can possibly procure realization even of pure "facts." The imagination is the medium of appreciation in every field. The engagement of the imagination is the only thing that makes any activity more than mechanical. Unfortunately, it is too customary to identify the imaginative with the imaginary, rather than with a warm and intimate taking in of the full scope of a situation. This leads to an exaggerated estimate of fairy tales, myths, fanciful symbols, verse, and something labeled "Fine Art," as agencies for developing imagination and appreciation; and, by neglecting imaginative vision in other matters, leads to methods which reduce much instruction to an unimaginative acquiring of specialized skill and amassing of load of information. Theory, and—to some extent—practice, have advanced far enough to recognize that play-activity is an imaginative enterprise. But it is still usual to regard this activity as a specially marked-off stage of childish growth, and to overlook the fact that the difference between play and what is regarded as serious employment should be not a difference between the presence and absence of imagination, but a difference in the materials with which imagination is occupied. The result is an unwholesome exaggeration of the phantastic and "unreal" phases of childish play and a deadly reduction of serious occupation to a routine efficiency prized simply for its external tangible results. Achievement comes to denote the sort of thing that a well-planned machine can do better than a human being can, and the main effect of education, the achieving of a life of rich significance, drops by the wayside. Meantime mind-wandering and wayward fancy are nothing but the

unsuppressible imagination cut loose from concern with what is done.

An adequate recognition of the play of imagination as the medium of realization of every kind of thing which lies beyond the scope of direct physical response is the sole way of escape from mechanical methods in teaching. The emphasis put in this book, in accord with many tendencies in contemporary education, upon activity, will be misleading if it is not recognized that the imagination is as much a normal and integral part of human activity as is muscular movement. The educative value of manual activities and of laboratory exercises, as well as of play, depends upon the extent in which they aid in bringing about a sensing of the *meaning* of what is going on. In effect, if not in name, they are dramatizations. Their utilitarian value in forming habits of skill to be used for tangible results is important, but not when isolated from the appreciative side. Were it not for the accompanying play of imagination, there would be no road from a direct activity to representative knowledge; for it is by imagination that symbols are translated over into a direct meaning and integrated with a narrower activity so as to expand and enrich it. When the representative creative imagination is made merely literary and mythological, symbols are rendered mere means of directing physical reactions of the organs of speech.

The Valuation of Studies.—The theory of educational values involves not only an account of the nature of appreciation as fixing the measure of subsequent valuations, but an account of the specific directions in which these valuations occur. To value means primarily to prize, to esteem; but secondarily it means to apprize, to estimate. It means, that is, the act of cherishing something, holding it dear, and also the act of passing judgment upon the nature and amount of its value as compared with something else. To value in the latter sense is to valuate or evaluate. The distinction coincides with that sometimes made between

intrinsic and instrumental values. Intrinsic values are not objects of judgment, they cannot (as intrinsic) be compared,
or regarded as greater and less, better or worse. They are
invaluable; and if a thing is invaluable, it is neither more
nor less so than any other invaluable. But occasions present
themselves when it is necessary to choose, when we must let
one thing go in order to take another. This establishes an
order of preference, a greater and less, better and worse.
Things judged or passed upon have to be estimated in relation to some third thing, some further end. With respect
to that, they are means, or instrumental values.

We may imagine a man who at one time thoroughly en-
joys converse with his friends, at another the hearing of a
symphony; at another the eating of his meals; at another
the reading of a book; at another the earning of money, and
so on. As an appreciative realization, each of these is an intrinsic value. It occupies a particular place in life; it serves
its own end, which cannot be supplied by a substitute.
There is no question of comparative value, and hence none
of valuation. Each is the specific good which it is, and that
is all that can be said. In its own place, none is a means to
anything beyond itself. But there may arise a situation in
which they compete or conflict, in which a choice has to be
made. Now comparison comes in. Since a choice has to
be made, we want to know the respective claims of each
competitor. What is to be said for it? What does it offer in
comparison with, as balanced over against, some other possibility? Raising these questions means that a particular
good is no longer an end in itself, an intrinsic good. For if
it were, its claims would be incomparable, imperative. The
question is now as to its status as a means of realizing something else, which is then the invaluable of *that* situation. If
a man has just eaten, or if he is well fed generally and the
opportunity to hear music is a rarity, he will probably
prefer the music to eating. In the given situation that will

render the greater contribution. If he is starving, or if he is satiated with music for the time being, he will naturally judge food to have the greater worth. In the abstract or at large, apart from the needs of a particular situation in which choice has to be made, there is no such thing as degrees or order of value.

Certain conclusions follow with respect to educational values. We cannot establish a hierarchy of values among studies. It is futile to attempt to arrange them in an order, beginning with one having least worth and going on to that of maximum value. In so far as any study has a unique or irreplaceable function in experience, in so far as it marks a characteristic enrichment of life, its worth is intrinsic or incomparable. Since education is not a means to living, but is identical with the operation of living a life which is fruitful and inherently significant, the only ultimate value which can be set up is just the process of living itself. And this is not an end to which studies and activities are subordinate means; it is the whole of which they are ingredients. And what has been said about appreciation means that every study in one of its aspects ought to have just such ultimate significance. It is as true of arithmetic as it is of poetry that in some place and at some time it ought to be a good to be appreciated on its own account—just as an enjoyable experience, in short. If it is not, then when the time and place come for it to be used as a means or instrumentality, it will be in just that much handicapped. Never having been realized or appreciated for itself, one will miss something of its capacity as a resource for other ends.

The point at issue in a theory of educational value is then the unity or integrity of experience. How shall it be full and varied without losing unity of spirit? How shall it be one and yet not narrow and monotonous in its unity? Ultimately, the question of values and a standard of values is the moral question of the organization of the interests of life. Educationally, the question concerns that organization of schools, materials, and methods which will operate to achieve breadth and richness of experience. . . . The term "value" has two quite different meanings. On the one hand, it denotes the attitude of prizing a thing, finding it worth while, for its own sake, or intrinsically. This is a name for a full or complete experience. To value in this sense is to appreciate. But to value also means a distinctively intellectual act—an operation of comparing and judging—to valuate. This occurs when direct full experience is lacking, and the question arises which of the various possibilities of a situation is to be preferred in order to reach a full realization, or vital experience.

We must not, however, divide the studies of the curriculum into the appreciative, those concerned with intrinsic value, and the instrumental, concerned with those which are of value or ends beyond themselves. The formation of proper standards in any subject depends upon a realization of the contribution which it makes to the immediate significance of experience, upon a direct appreciation. Literature and the fine arts are of peculiar value because they represent appreciation at its best—a heightened realization of meaning through selection and concentration. But every subject at some phase of its development should possess, what is for the individual concerned with it, an æsthetic quality.

Contribution to immediate intrinsic values in all their variety in experience is the only criterion for determining the worth of instrumental and derived values in studies. The tendency to assign separate values to each study and to regard the curriculum in its entirety as a kind of composite made by the aggregation of segregated values is a result of the isolation of social groups and classes. Hence it is the business of education in a democratic social group to struggle against this isolation in order that the various interests may reënforce and play into one another.

XI. LABOR AND LEISURE

. . . An education which should unify the disposition of the members of society would do much to unify
society itself.

Of the segregations of educational values . . . that between culture and utility is probably the most fundamental.
While the distinction is often thought to be intrinsic and
absolute, it is really historical and social. It originated, so
far as conscious formulation is concerned, in Greece, and
was based upon the fact that the truly human life was lived
only by a few who subsisted upon the results of the labor of
others. This fact affected the psychological doctrine of the
relation of intelligence and desire, theory and practice. It
was embodied in a political theory of a permanent division
of human beings into those capable of a life of reason and
hence having their own ends, and those capable only of desire and work, and needing to have their ends provided by
others. The two distinctions, psychological and political,
translated into educational terms, effected a division between a liberal education, having to do with the self-
sufficing life of leisure devoted to knowing for its own sake,
and a useful, practical training for mechanical occupations,
devoid of intellectual and æsthetic content. While the present situation is radically diverse in theory and much
changed in fact, the factors of the older historic situation
still persist sufficiently to maintain the educational distinction, along with compromises which often reduce the efficacy of the educational measures. The problem of education in a democratic society is to do away with the dualism
and to construct a course of studies which makes thought
a guide of free practice for all and which makes leisure a
reward of accepting responsibility for service, rather than
a state of exemption from it.

XII. Intellectual and Practical Studies

. . . Sensational empiricism represents neither the idea of experience justified by modern psychology nor the idea of knowledge suggested by modern scientific procedure. With respect to the former, it omits the primary position of active response which puts things to use and which learns about them through discovering the consequences that result from use. It would seem as if five minutes' unprejudiced observation of the way an infant gains knowledge would have sufficed to overthrow the notion that he is passively engaged in receiving impressions of isolated readymade qualities of sound, color, hardness, etc. For it would be seen that the infant reacts to stimuli by activities of handling, reaching, etc., in order to see what results follow upon motor response to a sensory stimulation; it would be seen that what is learned are not isolated qualities, but the behavior which may be expected from a thing, and the changes in things and persons which an activity may be expected to produce. In other words, what he learns are connections. Even such qualities as red color, sound of a high pitch, have to be discriminated and identified on the basis of the activities they call forth and the consequences these activities effect. We learn what things are hard and what are soft by finding out through active experimentation what they respectively will do and what can be done and what cannot be done with them. In like fashion, children learn about persons by finding out what responsive activities these persons exact and what these persons will do in reply to the children's activities. And the combination of what things *do* to us (not in impressing qualities on a passive mind) in modifying our actions, furthering some of them and resisting and checking others, and what we can do to *them* in producing new changes constitutes experience.

The methods of science by which the revolution in our knowledge of the world dating from the seventeenth century, was brought about, teach the same lesson. For these methods are nothing but experimentation carried out under conditions of deliberate control. To the Greek, it seemed absurd that such an activity as, say, the cobbler punching holes in leather, or using wax and needle and thread, could give an adequate knowledge of the world. It seemed almost axiomatic that for true knowledge we must have recourse to concepts coming from a reason above experience. But the introduction of the experimental method signified precisely that such operations, carried on under conditions of control, are just the ways in which fruitful ideas about nature are obtained and tested. In other words, it is only needed to conduct such an operation as the pouring of an acid on a metal for the purpose of getting knowledge instead of for the purpose of getting a trade result, in order to lay hold of the principle upon which the science of nature was henceforth to depend. Sense perceptions were indeed indispensable, but there was less reliance upon sense perceptions in their natural or customary form than in the older science. They were no longer regarded as containing within themselves some "form" or "species" of universal kind in a disguised mask of sense which could be stripped off by rational thought. On the contrary, the first thing was to alter and extend the data of sense perception: to act upon the *given* objects of sense by the lens of the telescope and microscope, and by all sorts of experimental devices. To accomplish this in a way which would arouse new ideas (hypotheses, theories) required even more general ideas (like those of mathematics) than were at the command of ancient science. But these general conceptions were no longer taken to give knowledge in themselves. They were implements for instituting, conducting, interpreting experimental inquiries and formulating their results.

The logical outcome is a new philosophy of experience

and knowledge, a philosophy which no longer puts experience in opposition to rational knowledge and explanation. Experience is no longer a mere summarizing of what has been done in a more or less chance way in the past; it is a deliberate control of what is done with reference to making what happens to us and what we do to things as fertile as possible of suggestions (of suggested meanings) and a means for trying out the validity of the suggestions. When trying, or experimenting, ceases to be blinded by impulse or custom, when it is guided by an aim and conducted by measure and method, it becomes reasonable—rational. When what we suffer from things, what we undergo at their hands, ceases to be a matter of chance circumstance, when it is transformed into a consequence of our own prior purposive endeavors, it becomes rationally significant—enlightening and instructive. The antithesis of empiricism and rationalism loses the support of the human situation which once gave it meaning and relative justification.

The bearing of this change upon the opposition of purely practical and purely intellectual studies is self-evident. The distinction is not intrinsic but is dependent upon conditions, and upon conditions which can be regulated. Practical activities *may* be intellectually narrow and trivial; they *will* be so in so far as they are routine, carried on under the dictates of authority, and having in view *merely* some external result. But childhood and youth, the period of schooling, is just the time when it is possible to carry them on in a different spirit. It is inexpedient to repeat the discussions of our previous chapters on thinking and on the evolution of educative subject matter from childlike work and play to logically organized subject matter. The discussions of this chapter and the prior one should, however, give an added meaning to those results.

(*i*) Experience itself primarily consists of the *active* relations subsisting between a human being and his natural and social surroundings. In some cases, the initiative in activity is on the side of the environment; the human being undergoes or suffers certain checkings and deflections of endeavors. In other cases, the behavior of surrounding things and persons carries to a successful issue the active tendencies of the individual, so that in the end what the individual undergoes are consequences which he has himself tried to produce. In just the degree in which connections are established between what happens to a person and what he does in response, and between what he does to his environment and what it does in response to him, his acts and the things about him acquire meaning. He learns to understand both himself and the world of men and things. Purposive education or schooling should present such an environment that this interaction will effect acquisition of those meanings which are so important that they become, in turn, instruments of further learnings. As has been repeatedly pointed out, activity out of school is carried on under conditions which have not been deliberately adapted to promoting the function of understanding and formation of effective intellectual dispositions. The results are vital and genuine as far as they go, but they are limited by all kinds of circumstances. Some powers are left quite undeveloped and undirected; others get only occasional and whimsical stimulations; others are formed into habits of a routine skill at the expense of aims and resourceful initiative and inventiveness. It is not the business of the school to transport youth from an environment of activity into one of cramped study of the records of other men's learning; but to transport them from an environment of relatively chance activities (accidental in the relation they bear to insight and thought) into one of activities selected with reference to guidance of learning. A slight inspection of the improved methods which have already shown themselves effective in education will reveal that they have laid hold, more or less consciously, upon the fact that "intellectual" studies instead of being opposed to active pursuits represent an intellectualizing of practical pursuits. It remains to grasp the principle with greater firmness.

(*ii*) The changes which are taking place in the content of social life tremendously facilitate selection of the sort of activities which will intellectualize the play and work of the school. When one bears in mind the social environment of the Greeks and the people of the Middle Ages, where such practical activities as could be successfully carried on were mostly of a routine and external sort and even servile in nature, one is not surprised that educators turned their back upon them as unfitted to cultivate intelligence. But now that even the occupations of the household, agriculture, and manufacturing as well as transportation and intercourse are instinct with applied science, the case stands otherwise. It is true that many of those who now engage in them are not aware of the intellectual content upon which their personal actions depend. But this fact only gives an added reason why schooling should use these pursuits so as to enable the coming generation to acquire a comprehension now too generally lacking, and thus enable persons to carry on their pursuits intelligently instead of blindly.

(*iii*) The most direct blow at the traditional separation of doing and knowing and at the traditional prestige of purely "intellectual" studies, however, has been given by the progress of experimental science. If this progress has demonstrated anything, it is that there is no such thing as genuine knowledge and fruitful understanding except as the offspring of *doing*. The analysis and rearrangement of facts which is indispensable to the growth of knowledge and power of explanation and right classification cannot be attained purely mentally—just inside the head. Men have to *do* something to the things when they wish to find out something; they have to alter conditions. This is the lesson of the laboratory method, and the lesson which all education has to learn. The laboratory is a discovery of the conditions under which *labor* may become intellectually fruitful and not merely externally productive. If, in too many cases at present, it results only in the acquisition of an additional mode of technical skill, that is because it still remains too largely but an isolated resource, not resorted to until pupils are mostly too old to get the full advantage of it, and even then is surrounded by other studies where traditional methods isolate intellect from activity.

Summary.—The Greeks were induced to philosophize by the increasing failure of their traditional customs and beliefs to regulate life. Thus they were led to criticize custom adversely and to look for some other source of authority in life and belief. Since they desired a rational standard for the latter, and had identified with experience the customs which had proved unsatisfactory supports, they were led to a flat opposition of reason and experience. The more the former was exalted, the more the latter was depreciated. Since experience was identified with what men do and suffer in particular and changing situations of life, doing shared in the philosophic depreciation. This influence fell in with many others to magnify, in higher education, all the methods and topics which involved the least use of sense-observation and bodily activity. The modern age began with a revolt against this point of view, with an appeal to experience, and an attack upon so-called purely rational concepts on the ground that they either needed to be ballasted by the results of concrete experiences, or else were mere expressions of prejudice and institutionalized class interest, calling themselves rational for protection. But various circumstances led to considering experience as pure cognition, leaving out of account its intrinsic active and emotional phases, and to identifying it with a passive reception of isolated "sensations." Hence the educational reform effected by the new theory was confined mainly to doing away with some of the bookishness of prior methods; it did not accomplish a consistent reorganization.

Meantime, the advance of psychology, of industrial

methods, and of the experimental method in science makes another conception of experience explicitly desirable and possible. This theory reinstates the idea of the ancients that experience is primarily practical, not cognitive—a matter of doing and undergoing the consequences of doing. But the ancient theory is transformed by realizing that doing may be directed so as to take up into its own content all which thought suggests, and so as to result in securely tested knowledge. "Experience" then ceases to be empirical and becomes experimental. Reason ceases to be a remote and ideal faculty, and signifies all the resources by which activity is made fruitful in meaning.

XIII. Philosophy as the Generalized Theory of Education

. . . We have already virtually described, though not defined, philosophy in terms of the problems with which it deals; and we have pointed out that these problems originate in the conflicts and difficulties of social life. The problems are such things as the relations of mind and matter; body and soul; humanity and physical nature; the individual and the social; theory—or knowing, and practice—or doing. The philosophical systems which formulate these problems record the main lineaments and difficulties of contemporary social practice. They bring to explicit consciousness what men have come to think, in virtue of the quality of their current experience, about nature, themselves, and the reality they conceive to include or to govern both.

As we might expect, then, philosophy has generally been defined in ways which imply a certain totality, generality, and ultimateness of both subject matter and method. With respect to subject matter, philosophy is an attempt to *comprehend*—that is, to gather together the varied details of the world and of life into a single inclusive whole, which shall either be a unity, or, as in the dualistic systems, shall reduce the plural details to a small number of ultimate principles. On the side of the attitude of the philosopher and of those who accept his conclusions, there is the endeavor to attain as unified, consistent, and complete an outlook upon experience as is possible. This aspect is expressed in the word "philosophy"—love of wisdom. Whenever philosophy has been taken seriously, it has always been assumed that it signified achieving a wisdom which would influence the conduct of life. Witness the fact that almost all ancient schools of philosophy were also organized ways of living, those who accepted their tenets being committed to certain distinctive modes of conduct; witness the intimate connection of philosophy with the theology of the Roman church in the middle ages, its frequent association with religious interests, and, at national crises, its association with political struggles.

This direct and intimate connection of philosophy with an outlook upon life obviously differentiates philosophy from science. Particular facts and laws of science evidently influence conduct. They suggest things to do and not do, and provide means of execution. When science denotes not simply a report of the particular facts discovered about the world but a *general attitude* toward it—as distinct from special things to do—it merges into philosophy. For an underlying disposition represents an attitude not to this and that thing nor even to the aggregate of known things, but to the considerations which govern conduct.

Hence philosophy cannot be defined simply from the side of subject matter. For this reason, the definition of such conceptions as generality, totality, and ultimateness is most readily reached from the side of the disposition toward the world which they connote. In any literal and quantitative sense, these terms do not apply to the subject matter of knowledge, for completeness and finality are out of the question. The very nature of experience as an ongoing, changing process forbids. In a less rigid sense, they apply to *science* rather than to philosophy. For obviously it is to mathematics, physics, chemistry, biology, anthropology, history, etc. that we must go, not to philosophy, to find out the facts of the world. It is for the sciences to say what generalizations are tenable about the world and what they specifically are. But when we ask what *sort* of permanent disposition of action toward the world the scientific disclosures exact of us we are raising a philosophic question.

From this point of view, "totality" does not mean the hopeless task of a quantitative summation. It means rather *consistency* of mode of response in reference to the plurality of events which occur. Consistency does not mean literal identity; for since the same thing does not happen twice, an exact repetition of a reaction involves some maladjustment. Totality means continuity—the carrying on of a former habit of action with the readaptation necessary to keep it alive and growing. Instead of signifying a ready-made complete scheme of action, it means keeping the balance in a multitude of diverse actions, so that each borrows and gives significance to every other. Any person who is open-minded and sensitive to new perceptions, and who has concentration and responsibility in connecting them has, in so far, a philosophic disposition. One of the popular senses of philosophy is calm and endurance in the face of difficulty and loss; it is even supposed to be a power to bear pain without complaint. This meaning is a tribute to the influence of the Stoic philosophy rather than an attribute of philosophy in general. But in so far as it suggests that the wholeness characteristic of philosophy is a power to learn, or to extract meaning, from even the unplesant vicissitudes of experience and to embody what is learned in an ability to go on learning, it is justified in any scheme. An analogous interpretation applies to the generality and ultimateness of philosophy. Taken literally, they are absurd pretensions; they indicate insanity. Finality does not mean, however, that experience is ended and exhausted, but means the disposition to penetrate to deeper levels of meaning—to go below the surface and find out the connections of any event or object, and to keep at it. In like manner the philosophic attitude is general in the sense that it is averse to taking anything as isolated; it tries to place an act in its context—which constitutes its significance.

It is of assistance to connect philosophy with thinking in its distinction from knowledge. Knowledge, grounded knowledge, is science; it represents objects which have been settled, ordered, disposed of rationally. Thinking, on the other hand, is prospective in reference. It is occasioned by an *un*settlement and it aims at overcoming a disturbance. Philosophy is thinking what the known demands of us— what responsive attitude it exacts. It is an idea of what is possible, not a record of accomplished fact. Hence it is hypothetical, like all thinking. It presents an assignment of something to be done—something to be tried. Its value lies not in furnishing solutions (which can be achieved only in action) but in defining difficulties and suggesting methods for dealing with them. Philosophy might almost be described as thinking which has become conscious of itself— which has generalized its place, function, and value in experience.

More specifically, the demand for a "total" attitude arises because there is the need of integration in action of the conflicting various interests in life. Where interests are so superficial that they glide readily into one another, or where they are not sufficiently organized to come into conflict with one another, the need for philosophy is not perceptible. But when the scientific interest conflicts with, say, the religious, or the economic with the scientific or æsthetic, or when the conservative concern for order is at odds with the progressive interest in freedom, or when institutionalism clashes with individuality, there is a stimulus to discover some more comprehensive point of view from which the divergencies may be brought together, and consistency or continuity of experience recovered. Often these clashes may be settled by an individual for himself; the area of the struggle of aims is limited and a person works out his own rough accommodations. Such homespun philosophies are genuine and often adequate. But they do not result in systems of philosophy. These arise when the discrepant claims of different ideals of conduct affect the community as a whole, and the need for readjustment is general.

These traits explain some things which are often brought as objections against philosophies, such as the part played in them by individual speculation, and their controversial diversity, as well as the fact that philosophy seems to be repeatedly occupied with much the same questions differently stated. Without doubt, all these things characterize historic philosophies more or less. But they are not objections to philosophy so much as they are to human nature, and even to the world in which human nature is set. If there are genuine uncertainties in life, philosophies must reflect that uncertainty. If there are different diagnoses of the cause of a difficulty, and different proposals for dealing with it; if, that is, the conflict of interests is more or less embodied in different sets of persons, there must be divergent competing philosophies. With respect to what has happened, sufficient evidence is all that is needed to bring agreement and certainty. The thing itself is sure. But with reference to what it is wise to do in a complicated situation, discussion is inevitable precisely because the thing itself is still indeterminate. One would not expect a ruling class living at ease to have the same philosophy of life as those who were having a hard struggle for existence. If the possessing and the dispossessed had the same fundamental disposition toward the world, it would argue either insincerity or lack of seriousness. A community devoted to industrial pursuits, active in business and commerce, is not likely to

see the needs and possibilities of life in the same way as a
country with high æsthetic culture and little enterprise in
turning the energies of nature to mechanical account. A
social group with a fairly continuous history will respond
mentally to a crisis in a very different way from one which
has felt the shock of abrupt breaks. Even if the same data
were present, they would be evaluated differently. But the
different sorts of experience attending different types of
life prevent just the same data from presenting themselves,
as well as lead to a different scheme of values. As for the
similarity of problems, this is often more a matter of appearance than of fact, due to old discussions being translated into the terms of contemporary perplexities. But in
certain fundamental respects the same predicaments of life
recur from time to time with only such changes as are due
to change of social context, including the growth of the
sciences.

The fact that philosophic problems arise because of widespread and widely felt difficulties in social practice is
disguised because philosophers become a specialized class
which uses a technical language, unlike the vocabulary in
which the direct difficulties are stated. But where a system
becomes influential, its connection with a conflict of interests calling for some program of social adjustment may
always be discovered. At this point, the intimate connection
between philosophy and education appears. In fact, education offers a vantage ground from which to penetrate to
the human, as distinct from the technical, significance of
philosophic discussions. The student of philosophy "in itself" is always in danger of taking it as so much nimble or
severe intellectual exercise—as something said by philosophers and concerning them alone. But when philosophic
issues are approached from the side of the kind of mental
disposition to which they correspond, or the differences in
educational practice they make when acted upon, the life-
situations which they formulate can never be far from view.

If a theory makes no difference in educational endeavor, it must be artificial. The educational point of view enables one to envisage the philosophic problems where they arise and thrive, where they are at home, and where acceptance or rejection makes a difference in practice.

If we are willing to conceive education as the process of forming fundamental dispositions, intellectual and emotional, toward nature and fellow men, philosophy may even be defined *as the general theory of education*. Unless a philosophy is to remain symbolic—or verbal—or a sentimental indulgence for a few, or else mere arbitrary dogma, its auditing of past experience and its program of values must take effect in conduct. Public agitation, propaganda, legislative and administrative action are effective in producing the change of disposition which a philosophy indicates as desirable, but only in the degree in which they are educative—that is to say, in the degree in which they modify mental and moral attitudes. And at the best, such methods are compromised by the fact they are used with those whose habits are already largely set, while education of youth has a fairer and freer field of operation. On the other side, the business of schooling tends to become a routine empirical affair unless its aims and methods are animated by such a broad and sympathetic survey of its place in contemporary life as it is the business of philosophy to provide.

Positive science always implies *practically* the ends which the community is concerned to achieve. Isolated from such ends, it is matter of indifference whether its disclosures are used to cure disease or to spread it; to increase the means of sustenance of life or to manufacture war material to wipe life out. If society is interested in one of these things rather than another, science shows the way of attainment. Philosophy thus has a double task: that of criticizing existing aims with respect to the existing state of science, pointing out values which have become obsolete with the command of new resources, showing what values are merely sentimental because there are no means for their realization; and also that of interpreting the results of specialized science in their bearing on future social endeavor. It is impossible that it should have any success in these tasks without educational equivalents as to what to do and what not to do. For philosophic theory has no Aladdin's lamp to summon into immediate existence the values which it intellectually constructs. In the mechanical arts, the sciences become methods of managing things so as to utilize their energies for recognized aims. By the educative arts philosophy may generate methods of utilizing the energies of human beings in accord with serious and thoughtful conceptions of life. Education is the laboratory in which philosophic distinctions become concrete and are tested.

It is suggestive that European philosophy originated (among the Athenians) under the direct pressure of educational questions. The earlier history of philosophy, developed by the Greeks in Asia Minor and Italy, so far as its range of topics is concerned, is mainly a chapter in the history of science rather than of philosophy as that word is understood to-day. It had nature for its subject, and speculated as to how things are made and changed. Later the traveling teachers, known as the Sophists, began to apply the results and the methods of the natural philosophers to human conduct.

When the Sophists, the first body of professional educators in Europe, instructed the youth in virtue, the political arts, and the management of city and household, philosophy began to deal with the relation of the individual to the universal, to some comprehensive class, or to some group; the relation of man and nature, of tradition and reflection, of knowledge and action. Can virtue, approved excellence in any line, be learned, they asked? What is learning? It has to do with knowledge. What, then, is knowledge? How is it achieved? Through the senses, or by apprenticeship in

some form of doing, or by reason that has undergone a
preliminary logical discipline? Since learning is *coming* to
know, it involves a passage from ignorance to wisdom, from
privation to fullness, from defect to perfection, from non-
being to being, in the Greek way of putting it. How is such
a transition possible? Is change, becoming, development
really possible and if so, how? And supposing such questions answered, what is the relation of instruction, of
knowledge, to virtue?   .

This last question led to opening the problem of the relation of reason to action, of theory to practice, since virtue
clearly dwelt in action. Was not knowing, the activity of
reason, the noblest attribute of man? And consequently was
not purely intellectual activity itself the highest of all excel-
lences, compared with which the virtues of neighborliness
and the citizen's life were secondary? Or, on the other
hand, was the vaunted intellectual knowledge more than
empty and vain pretense, demoralizing to character and
destructive of the social ties that bound men together
in their community life? Was not the only true, because
the only moral, life gained through obedient habituation
to the customary practices of the community? And was not
the new education an enemy to good citizenship, because
it set up a rival standard to the established traditions of the
community?

In the course of two or three generations such questions
were cut loose from their original practical bearing upon
education and were discussed on their own account; that is,
as matters of philosophy as an independent branch of inquiry. But the fact that the stream of European philosophical thought arose as a theory of educational procedure
remains an eloquent witness to the intimate connection of
philosophy and education. "Philosophy of education" is not
an external application of ready-made ideas to a system of
practice having a radically different origin and purpose: it

is only an explicit formulation of the problems of the formation of right mental and moral habitudes in respect to the difficulties of contemporary social life. The most penetrating definition of philosophy which can be given is, then, that it is the theory of education in its most general phases.

The reconstruction of philosophy, of education, and of social ideals and methods thus go hand in hand. If there is especial need of educational reconstruction at the present time, if this need makes urgent a reconsideration of the basic ideas of traditional philosophic systems, it is because of the thoroughgoing change in social life accompanying the advance of science, the industrial revolution, and the development of democracy. Such practical changes cannot take place without demanding an educational re-formation to meet them, and without leading men to ask what ideas and ideals are implicit in these social changes, and what revisions they require of the ideas and ideals which are inherited from older and unlike cultures.

. . . Philosophy was defined as the generalized theory of education. Philosophy was stated to be a form of thinking, which, like all thinking, finds its origin in what is uncertain in the subject matter of experience, which aims to locate the nature of the perplexity and to frame hypotheses for its clearing up to be tested in action. Philosophic thinking has for its differentia the fact that the uncertainties with which it deals are found in widespread social conditions and aims, consisting in a conflict of organized interests and institutional claims. Since the only way of bringing about a harmonious readjustment of the opposed tendencies is through a modification of emotional and intellectual disposition, philosophy is at once an explicit formulation of the various interests of life and a propounding of points of view and methods through which a better balance of interests may be effected. Since education is the process through

which the needed transformation may be accomplished
and not remain a mere hypothesis as to what is desirable,
we reach a justification of the statement that philosophy is
the theory of education as a deliberately conducted practice.

XIV. Theories of Morals: the Social
and the Moral

. . . Morals are as broad as acts which concern our relationships with others. And potentially this
includes all our acts, even though their social bearing
may not be thought of at the time of performance. For
every act, by the principle of habit, modifies disposition
—it sets up a certain kind of inclination and desire. And
it is impossible to tell when the habit thus strengthened
may have a direct and perceptible influence on our association with others. Certain traits of character have such
an obvious connection with our social relationships that
we call them "moral" in an emphatic sense—truthfulness,
honesty, chastity, amiability, etc. But this only means that
they are, as compared with some other attitudes, central:—that they carry other attitudes with them. They
are moral in an emphatic sense not because they are isolated and exclusive, but because they are so intimately
connected with thousands of other attitudes which we do
not explicitly recognize—which perhaps we have not even
names for. To call them virtues in their isolation is like
taking the skeleton for the living body. The bones are
certainly important, but their importance lies in the fact
that they support other organs of the body in such a way
as to make them capable of integrated effective activity.
And the same is true of the qualities of character which
we specifically designate virtues. Morals concern nothing
less than the whole character, and the whole character
is identical with the man in all his concrete make-up and

manifestations. To possess virtue does not signify to have cultivated a few nameable and exclusive traits; it means to be fully and adequately what one is capable of becoming through association with others in all the offices of life.

The moral and the social quality of conduct are, in the last analysis, identical with each other. It is then but to restate explicitly the import of our earlier chapters regarding the social function of education to say that the measure of the worth of the administration, curriculum, and methods of instruction of the school is the extent to which they are animated by a social spirit. And the great danger which threatens school work is the absence of conditions which make possible a permeating social spirit; this is the great enemy of effective moral training. For this spirit can be actively present only when certain conditions are met.

(*i*) In the first place, the school must itself be a community life in all which that implies. Social perceptions and interests can be developed only in a genuinely social medium—one where there is give and take in the building up of a common experience. Informational statements about things can be acquired in relative isolation by any one who previously has had enough intercourse with others to have learned language. But realization of the *meaning* of the linguistic signs is quite another matter. That involves a context of work and play in association with others. The plea which has been made for education through continued constructive activities in this book rests upon the fact they afford an opportunity for a social atmosphere. In place of a school set apart from life as a place for learning lessons, we have a miniature social group in which study and growth are incidents of present shared experience. Playgrounds, shops, workrooms, laboratories not only direct the natural active tendencies of youth, but they involve intercourse, communication, and coöperation,—all extending the perception of connections.

(*ii*) The learning in school should be continuous with

that out of school. There should be a free interplay between
the two. This is possible only when there are numerous
points of contact between the social interests of the one
and of the other. A school is conceivable in which there
should be a spirit of companionship and shared activity,
but where its social life would no more represent or typify
that of the world beyond the school walls than that of
a monastery. Social concern and understanding would be
developed, but they would not be available outside; they
would not carry over. The proverbial separation of town
and gown, the cultivation of academic seclusion, operate in
this direction. So does such adherence to the culture of the
past as generates a reminiscent social spirit, for this makes
an individual feel more at home in the life of other days
than in his own. A professedly cultural education is peculiarly exposed to this danger. An idealized past becomes
the refuge and solace of the spirit; present-day concerns
are found sordid, and unworthy of attention. But as a rule,
the absence of a social environment in connection with
which learning is a need and a reward is the chief reason
for the isolation of the school; and this isolation renders
school knowledge inapplicable to life and so infertile in
character.

A narrow and moralistic view of morals is responsible for
the failure to recognize that all the aims and values which
are desirable in education are themselves moral. Discipline,
natural development, culture, social efficiency, are moral
traits—marks of a person who is a worthy member of that
society which it is the business of education to further.
There is an old saying to the effect that it is not enough for
a man to be good; he must be good for something. The something for which a man must be good is capacity to live as a
social member so that what he gets from living with others
balances with what he contributes. What he gets and gives

as a human being, a being with desires, emotions, and ideas, is not external possessions, but a widening and deepening of conscious life—a more intense, disciplined, and expanding realization of meanings. What he *materially* receives and gives is at most opportunities and means for the evolution of conscious life. Otherwise, it is neither giving nor taking, but a shifting about of the position of things in space, like the stirring of water and sand with a stick. Discipline, culture, social efficiency, personal refinement, improvement of character are but phases of the growth of capacity nobly to share in such a balanced experience. And education is not a mere means to such a life. Education is such a life. To maintain capacity for such education is the essence of morals. For conscious life is a continual beginning afresh.

Summary.—The most important problem of moral education in the school concerns the relationship of knowledge and conduct. For unless the learning which accrues in the regular course of study affects character, it is futile to conceive the moral end as the unifying and culminating end of education. When there is no intimate organic connection between the methods and materials of knowledge and moral growth, particular lessons and modes of discipline have to be resorted to: knowledge is not integrated into the usual springs of action and the outlook on life, while morals become moralistic—a scheme of separate virtues.

The two theories chiefly associated with the separation of learning from activity, and hence from morals, are those which cut off inner disposition and motive—the conscious personal factor—and deeds as purely physical and outer; and which set action from interest in opposition to that from principle. Both of these separations are overcome in an educational scheme where learning is the accompaniment of continuous activities or occupations which have a social aim and utilize the materials of typical social situations. For un-

der such conditions, the school becomes itself a form of social life, a miniature community and one in close interaction
with other modes of associated experience beyond school
walls. All education which develops power to share effectively in social life is moral. It forms a character which not
only does the particular deed socially necessary but one
which is interested in that continuous readjustment which
is essential to growth. Interest in learning from all the contacts of life is the essential moral interest.

IV ♦ Human Nature and Conduct

I. The Place of Habit in Conduct*

HABITS may be profitably compared to physiological functions, like breathing, digesting. The latter are, to be sure, involuntary, while habits are acquired. But important as is this difference for many purposes it should not conceal the fact that habits are like functions in many respects, and especially in requiring the coöperation of organism and environment. Breathing is an affair of the air as truly as of the lungs; digesting an affair of food as truly as of tissues of stomach. Seeing involves light just as certainly as it does the eye and optic nerve. Walking implicates the ground as well as the legs; speech demands physical air and human companionship and audience as well as vocal organs. We may shift from the biological to the mathematical use of the word function, and say that natural operations like breathing and digesting, acquired ones like speech and honesty, are functions of the surroundings as truly as of a person. They are things done *by* the environment by means of organic structures or acquired dispositions. The same air that under certain conditions ruffles the pool or wrecks buildings, under other conditions purifies the blood and conveys thought. The outcome depends upon what air acts upon. The social environment acts through

* From *Human Nature and Conduct* by John Dewey. By permission of Henry Holt and Company. Copyright 1922. Copyright 1950 by John Dewey. New York: Modern Library, 1930.

native impulses and speech and moral habitudes manifest
themselves. There are specific good reasons for the usual
attribution of acts to the person from whom they immediately proceed. But to convert this special reference into a
belief of exclusive ownership is as misleading as to suppose
that breathing and digesting are complete within the human body. To get a rational basis for moral discussion we
must begin with recognizing that functions and habits are
ways of using and incorporating the environment in which
the latter has its say as surely as the former.

We may borrow words from a context less technical than
that of biology, and convey the same idea by saying that
habits are arts. They involve skill of sensory and motor
organs, cunning or craft, and objective materials. They assimilate objective energies, and eventuate in command of
environment. They require order, discipline, and manifest
technique. They have a beginning, middle and end. Each
stage marks progress in dealing with materials and tools,
advance in converting material to active use. We should
laugh at any one who said that he was master of stone working, but that the art was cooped up within himself and in
no wise dependent upon support from objects and assistance from tools.

II. The Place of Impulse in Conduct

I

Habits as organized activities are secondary
and acquired, not native and original. They are outgrowths
of unlearned activities which are part of man's endowment
at birth. The order of topics followed in our discussion may
accordingly be questioned. Why should what is derived
and therefore in some sense artificial in conduct be discussed before what is primitive, natural and inevitable?
Why did we not set out with an examination of those instinc-

tive activities upon which the acquisition of habits is conditioned?

The query is a natural one, yet it tempts to flinging forth a paradox. In conduct the acquired is the primitive. Impulses although first in time are never primary in fact; they are secondary and dependent. The seeming paradox in statement covers a familiar fact. In the life of the individual, instinctive activity comes first. But an individual begins life as a baby, and babies are dependent beings. Their activities could continue at most for only a few hours were it not for the presence and aid of adults with their formed habits. And babies owe to adults more than procreation, more than the continued food and protection which preserve life. They owe to adults the opportunity to express their native activities in ways which have meaning. Even if by some miracle original activity could continue without assistance from the organized skill and art of adults, it would not amount to anything. It would be mere sound and fury.

In short, the *meaning* of native activities is not native; it is acquired. It depends upon interaction with a matured social medium. In the case of a tiger or eagle, anger may be identified with a serviceable life-activity, with attack and defense. With a human being it is as meaningless as a gust of wind on a mudpuddle apart from a direction given it by the presence of other persons, apart from the responses they make to it. It is a physical spasm, a blind dispersive burst of wasteful energy. It gets quality, significance, when it becomes a smouldering sullenness, an annoying interruption, a peevish irritation, a murderous revenge, a blazing indignation. And although these phenomena which have a meaning spring from original native reactions to stimuli, yet they depend also upon the responsive behavior of others. They and all similar human displays of anger are not pure impulses; they are habits formed under the influence of association with others who have habits already and who show their habits in the treatment which converts a blind physical discharge into a significant anger.

After ignoring impulses for a long time in behalf of sensations, modern psychology now tends to start out with an inventory and description of instinctive activities. This is an undoubted improvement. But when it tries to explain complicated events in personal and social life by direct reference to these native powers, the explanation becomes hazy and forced. It is like saying the flea and the elephant, the lichen and the redwood, the timid hare and the ravening wolf, the plant with the most inconspicuous blossom and the plant with the most glaring color are alike products of natural selection. There may be a sense in which the statement is true; but till we know the specific environing conditions under which selection took place we really know nothing. And so we need to know about the social conditions which have educated original activities into definite and significant dispositions before we can discuss the psychological element in society. This is the true meaning of social psychology.

At some place on the globe, at some time, every kind of practice seems to have been tolerated or even praised. How is the tremendous diversity of institutions (including moral codes) to be accounted for? The native stock of instincts is practically the same everywhere. Exaggerate as much as we like the native differences of Patagonians and Greeks, Sioux Indians and Hindoos, Bushmen and Chinese, their original differences will bear no comparison to the amount of difference found in custom and culture. Since such a diversity cannot be attributed to an original identity, the development of native impulse must be stated in terms of acquired habits, not the growth of customs in terms of instincts. The wholesale human sacrifices of Peru and the tenderness of St. Francis, the cruelties of pirates and the philanthropies of Howard, the practice of Suttee and the cult of the Virgin, the war and peace dances of the Comanches and the parliamentary institutions of the British, the communism of the southsea islander and the proprietary thrift of the Yankee, the magic of the medicine man and the experiments of the chemist in his laboratory, the non-resistance of Chinese and the aggressive militarism of an imperial Prussia, monarchy by divine right and government by the people; the countless diversity of habits suggested by such a random list springs from practically the same capital-stock of native instincts.

It would be pleasant if we could pick and choose those institutions which we like and impute them to human nature, and the rest to some devil; or those we like to our kind of human nature, and those we dislike to the nature of despised foreigners on the ground they are not really "native" at all. It would appear to be simpler if we could point to certain customs, saying that they are the unalloyed products of certain instincts, while those other social arrangements are to be attributed wholly to other impulses. But such methods are not feasible. The same original fears, angers, loves and hates are hopelessly entangled in the most opposite institutions. The thing we need to know is how a native stock has been modified by interaction with different environments.

Yet it goes without saying that original, unlearned activity has its distinctive place and that an important one in conduct. Impulses are the pivots upon which the re-organization of activities turn, they are agencies of deviation, for giving new directions to old habits and changing their quality. Consequently whenever we are concerned with understanding social transition and flux or with projects for reform, personal and collective, our study must go to analysis of native tendencies. Interest in progress and reform is, indeed, the reason for the present great development of scientific interest in primitive human nature. If we inquire why men were so long blind to the existence of powerful and varied instincts in human beings, the answer seems to be found in the lack of a conception of orderly progress. It is fast becoming incredible that psychologists disputed as to whether they should choose between innate ideas and an empty, passive, wax-like mind. For it seems as if a glance at a child would have revealed that the truth lay in neither doctrine, so obvious is the surging of specific native activities. But this obtuseness to facts was evidence of lack of interest in what could be done with impulses, due, in turn, to lack of interest in modifying existing institutions. It is no accident that men became interested in the psychology of savages and babies when they became interested in doing away with old institutions.

A combination of traditional individualism with the recent interest in progress explains why the discovery of the scope and force of instincts has led many psychologists to think of them as the fountain head of all conduct, as occupying a place before instead of after that of habits. The orthodox tradition in psychology is built upon isolation of individuals from their surroundings. The soul or mind or consciousness was thought of as self-contained and self-enclosed. Now in the career of an individual if it is regarded as complete in itself instincts clearly come before habits. Generalize this individualistic view, and we have an assumption that all customs, all significant episodes in the life of individuals can be carried directly back to the operation of instincts.

But, as we have already noted, if an individual be isolated in this fashion, along with the fact of primacy of instinct we find also the fact of death. The inchoate and scattered impulses of an infant do not coordinate into serviceable powers except through social dependencies and companionships. His impulses are merely starting points for assimilation of the knowledge and skill of the more matured beings upon whom he depends. They are tentacles sent out to gather that nutrition from customs which will in time render the infant capable of independent action. They are agencies for transfer of existing social power into personal ability; they are means of reconstructive growth. Abandon an impossible individualistic psychology, and we arrive at the fact that native activities are organs of re-organization and re-adjustment. The hen precedes the egg. But nevertheless this particular egg may be so treated as to modify the future type of hen.

II

In the case of the young it is patent that impulses are highly flexible starting points for activities which are diversified according to the ways in which they are used. Any impulse may become organized into almost any disposition according to the way it interacts with surroundings. Fear may become abject cowardice, prudent caution, reverence for superiors or respect for equals; an agency for credulous swallowing of absurd superstitions or for wary scepticism. A man may be chiefly afraid of the spirits of his ancestors, of officials, of arousing the disapproval of his associates, of being deceived, of fresh air, or of Bolshevism. The actual outcome depends upon how the impulse of fear is interwoven with other impulses. This depends in turn upon the outlets and inhibitions supplied by the social environment.

In a definite sense, then, a human society is always starting afresh. It is always in process of renewing, and it endures only because of renewal. We speak of the peoples of southern Europe as Latin peoples. Their existing languages depart widely from one another and from the Latin mother tongue. Yet there never was a day when this alteration of speech was intentional or explicit. Persons always meant to reproduce the speech they heard from their elders and supposed they were succeeding. This fact may stand as a kind of symbol of the reconstruction wrought in habits because of the fact that they can be transmitted and be made to endure only through the medium of the crude activities of the young or through contact with persons having different habits.

For the most part, this continuous alteration has been unconscious and unintended. Immature, undeveloped activity has succeeded in modifying adult organized activity accidentally and surreptitiously. But with the dawn of the idea of progressive betterment and an interest in new uses of impulses, there has grown up some consciousness of the extent to which a future new society of changed purposes and desires may be created by a deliberate humane treatment of the impulses of youth. This is the meaning of education; for a truly humane education consists in an intelligent direction of native activities in the light of the possibilities and necessities of the social situation. But for the most part, adults have given training rather than education. An impatient, premature mechanization of impulsive activity after the fixed pattern of adult habits of thought and affection has been desired. The combined effect of love of power, timidity in the face of the novel and a self-admiring complacency has been too strong to permit immature impulse to exercise its reorganizing potentialities. The younger generation has hardly even knocked frankly at the door of adult customs, much less been invited in to rectify through better education the brutalities and inequities established in adult habits. Each new generation has crept blindly and furtively through such chance gaps as have happened to be left open. Otherwise it has been modeled after the old.

We have already noted how original plasticity is warped and docility is taken mean advantage of. It has been used to signify not capacity to learn liberally and generously, but willingness to learn the customs of adult associates, ability to learn just those special things which those having power and authority wish to teach. Original modifiability has not been given a fair chance to act as a trustee for a better human life. It has been loaded with convention, biased by adult convenience. It has been practically rendered into an

equivalent of non-assertion of originality, a pliant accommodation to the embodied opinions of others.

Consequently docility has been identified with imitative-
ness, instead of with power to re-make old habits, to
re-create. Plasticity and originality have been opposed to
each other. That the most precious part of plasticity consists
in ability to form habits of independent judgment and of
inventive initiation has been ignored. For it demands a more
complete and intense docility to form flexible easily re-ad-
justed habits than it does to acquire those which rigidly
copy the ways of others. In short, among the native activities of the young are some that work towards accommodation, assimilation, reproduction, and others that work toward exploration, discovery and creation. But the weight of
adult custom has been thrown upon retaining and strength-
ening tendencies toward conformity, and against those
which make for variation and independence. The habits of
the growing person are jealously kept within the limit of
adult customs. The delightful originality of the child is
tamed. Worship of institutions and personages themselves
lacking in imaginative foresight, versatile observation and
liberal thought, is enforced.

We return to the original proposition. The position of impulse in conduct is intermediary. Morality is an endeavor
to find for the manifestation of impulse in special situations
an office of refreshment and renewal. The endeavor is not
easy of accomplishment. It is easier to surrender the main
and public channels of action and belief to the sluggishness
of custom, and idealize tradition by emotional attachment
to its ease, comforts and privileges instead of idealizing it in
practice by making it more equably balanced with present
needs. Again, impulses not used for the work of rejuvenation
and vital recovery are sidetracked to find their own lawless
barbarities or their own sentimental refinements. Or they
are perverted to pathological careers—some of which have
been mentioned.

In the course of time custom becomes intolerable because of what it suppresses and some accident of war or inner catastrophe releases impulses for unrestrained expression. At such times we have philosophies which identify progress with motion, blind spontaneity with freedom, and which under the name of the sacredness of individuality or a return to the norms of nature make impulse a law unto itself. The oscillation between impulse arrested and frozen in rigid custom and impulse isolated and undirected is seen most conspicuously when epochs of conservatism and revolutionary ardor alternate. But the same phenomenon is repeated on a smaller scale in individuals. And in society the two tendencies and philosophies exist simultaneously; they waste in controversial strife the energy that is needed for specific criticism and specific reconstruction.

The release of some portion of the stock of impulses is an opportunity, not an end. In its origin it is the product of chance; but it affords imagination and invention *their* chance. The moral correlate of liberated impulse is not immediate activity, but reflection upon the way in which to use impulse to renew disposition and reorganize habit. Escape from the clutch of custom gives an opportunity to do old things in new ways, and thus to construct new ends and means. Breach in the crust of the cake of custom releases impulses; but it is the work of intelligence to find the ways of using them. There is an alternative between anchoring a boat in the harbor till it becomes a rotting hulk and letting it loose to be the sport of every contrary gust. To discover and define this alternative is the business of mind, of observant, remembering, contriving disposition.

Habit as a vital art depends upon the animation of habit by impulse; only this inspiriting stands between habit and stagnation. But art, little as well as great, anonymous as well as that distinguished by titles of dignity, cannot be improvised. It is impossible without spontaneity, but it is not spontaneity. Impulse is needed to arouse thought, incite reflection and enliven belief. But only thought notes obstructions, invents tools, conceives aims, directs technique, and thus converts impulse into an art which lives in objects. Thought is born as the twin of impulse in every moment of impeded habit. But unless it is nurtured, it speedily dies, and habit and instinct continue their civil warfare. There is instinctive wisdom in the tendency of the young to ignore the limitations of the environment. Only thus can they discover their own power and learn the differences in different kinds of environing limitations. But this discovery when once made marks the birth of intelligence; and with its birth comes the responsibility of the mature to observe, to recall, to forecast. Every moral life has its radicalism; but this radical factor does not find its full expression in direct action but in the courage of intelligence to go deeper than either tradition or immediate impulse goes. To the study of intelligence in action we now turn our attention.

We are going far afield from any direct moral issue. But the problem of the place of knowledge and judgment in conduct depends upon getting the fundamental psychology of thought straightened out. So the excursion must be continued. We compare life to a traveler faring forth. We may consider him first at a moment where his activity is confident, straightforward, organized. He marches on giving no direct attention to his path, nor thinking of his destination. Abruptly he is pulled up, arrested. Something is going wrong in his activity. From the standpoint of an onlooker, he has met an obstacle which must be overcome before his behavior can be unified into a successful ongoing. From his own standpoint, there is shock, confusion, perturbation, uncertainty. For the moment he doesn't know what hit him, as we say, nor where he is going. But a new impulse is stirred which becomes the starting point of an investigation, a looking into things, a trying to see them, to find out what is going on. Habits which were interfered with begin to get a new direction as they cluster about the impulse to

look and see. The blocked habits of locomotion give him a
sense of where he *was* going, of what he had set out to do,
and of the ground already traversed. As he looks, he sees
definite things which are not just things at large but which
are related to his course of action. The momentum of the
activity entered upon persists as a sense of direction, of
aim; it is an anticipatory project. In short, he recollects,
observes and plans.

The trinity of these forecasts, perceptions and remem-
brances form a subject-matter of discriminated and identified objects. These objects represent habits turned inside
out. They exhibit both the onward tendency of habit and
the objective conditions which have been incorporated
within it. Sensations in immediate consciousness are
elements of action dislocated through the shock of interruption. They never, however, completely monopolize the
scene; for there is a body of residual undisturbed habits
which is reflected in remembered and perceived objects
having a meaning. Thus out of shock and puzzlement there
gradually emerges a figured framework of objects, past,
present, future. These shade off variously into a vast
penumbra of vague, unfigured things, a setting which is
taken for granted and not at all explicitly presented. The
complexity of the figured scene in its scope and refinement
of contents depends wholly upon prior habits and their organization. The reason a baby can know little and an experienced adult know much when confronting the same things
is not because the latter has a "mind" which the former has
not, but because one has already formed habits which the
other has still to acquire. The scientific man and the philosopher like the carpenter, the physician and politician know
with their habits not with their "consciousness." The latter
is eventual, not a source. Its occurrence marks a peculiarly
delicate connection between highly organized habits and
unorganized impulses. Its contents or objects, observed,

recollected, projected and generalized into principles, represent the incorporated material of habits coming to the surface, because habits are disintegrating at the touch of conflicting impulses. But they also gather themselves together to comprehend impulse and make it effective.

V ♦ Intelligence and Inquiry

I. The Biological Basis of Inquiry*

WHATEVER else organic life is or is not, it is a process of activity that involves an environment. It is a transaction extending beyond the spatial limits of the organism. An organism does not live *in* an environment; it lives by means of an environment. Breathing, the ingestion of food, the ejection of waste products, are cases of *direct* integration; the circulation of the blood and the energizing of the nervous system are relatively *indirect*. But every organic function is an interaction of intra-organic and extra-organic energies, either directly or indirectly. For life involves expenditure of energy and the energy expended can be replenished only as the activities performed succeed in making return drafts upon the environment—the only source of restoration of energy. Not even a hibernating animal can live indefinitely upon itself. The energy that is drawn is not forced in from without; it is a consequence of energy expended. If there is a surplus balance, growth occurs. If there is a deficit balance, degeneration commences. There are things in the world that are indifferent to the life-activities of an organism. But they are not parts of *its* environment, save potentially. The processes of living are enacted by the environment as truly as by the organism; for they *are* an integration.

It follows that with every differentiation of structure the

* From *Logic* by John Dewey. By permission of Henry Holt and Company. Copyright 1938.

environment expands. For a new organ provides a new way of interacting in which things in the world that were previously indifferent enter into life-functions. The environment of an animal that is locomotor differs from that of a sessile plant; that of a jelly fish differs from that of a trout, and the environment of any fish differs from that of a bird. So, to repeat what was just said, the difference is not just that a fish lives *in* the water and a bird *in* the air, but that the characteristic functions of these animals are what they are because of the special way in which water and air enter into their respective activities.

With differentiation of interactions comes the need of maintaining a balance among them; or, in objective terms, a unified environment. The balance has to be maintained by a mechanism that responds both to variations that occur within the organism and in surroundings. For example, such an apparently self-contained function as that of respiration is kept constant by means of active exchanges between the alkaline and carbon dioxide contents of changing pressures exerted by the blood and the carbon dioxide in the lungs. The lungs in turn are dependent upon interactions effected by kidneys and liver, which effect the interactions of the circulating blood with materials of the digestive tract. This whole system of accurately timed interchanges is regulated by changes in the nervous system.

The effect of this delicate and complex system of internal changes is the maintenance of a fairly uniform integration with the environment, or—what amounts to the same thing —a fairly unified environment. The interactions of inanimate things with their surroundings are not such as to maintain a stable relation between the things involved. The blow of a hammer, for example, breaks a stone into bits. But as long as life normally continues, the interactions in which organic and environmental energies enter are such as to maintain the conditions in both of them needed for later interactions. The processes, in other words, are self-maintaining, in a sense in which they are not in the case of the interactions of non-living things.

Capacity for maintenance of a constant form of interaction between organism and environment is not confined to the individual organism. It is manifested also, in the reproduction of similar organisms. The stone is presumably indifferent as to how it reacts mechanically and chemically (within the limits of its potentialities) to other things. The stone may lose its individuality but basic mechanical and chemical processes go on uninterruptedly. As long as life continues, its processes are such as continuously to maintain and restore the enduring relationship which is characteristic of the life-activities of a given organism.

Each particular activity prepares the way for the activity that follows. These form not a mere succession but a series. This seriated quality of life activities is effected through the delicate balance of the complex factors in each particular activity. When the balance within a given activity is disturbed—when there is a proportionate excess or deficit in some factor—then there is exhibited need, search and fulfilment (or satisfaction) in the objective meaning of those terms. The greater the differentiation of structures and their corresponding activities becomes, the more difficult it is to keep the balance. Indeed, living may be regarded as a continual rhythm of disequilibrations and recoveries of equilibrium. The "higher" the organism, the more serious become the disturbances and the more energetic (and often more prolonged) are the efforts necessary for its reestablishment. The state of disturbed equilibration constitutes *need*. The movement towards its restoration is search and exploration. The recovery is fulfilment or satisfaction.

Modification of both organic and environmental energies is involved in life-activity. This organic fact foreshadows learning and discovery, with the consequent outgrowth of new needs and new problematic situations. Inquiry, in settling the disturbed relation of organism-environment (which defines doubt) does not merely remove doubt by recurrence to a prior adaptive integration. It institutes new environing conditions that occasion new problems. What the organism learns during this process produces new powers that make new demands upon the environment. In short, as special problems are resolved, new ones tend to emerge. There is no such thing as a final settlement, because every settlement introduces the conditions of some degree of a new unsettling. In the stage of development marked by the emergence of science, deliberate institution of problems becomes an objective of inquiry. Philosophy, in case it has not lost touch with science, may play an important role in determining formulation of these problems and in suggesting hypothetical solutions. But the moment philosophy supposes it can find a final and comprehensive solution, it ceases to be inquiry and becomes either apologetics or propaganda.

II. The Pattern of Inquiry

The existence of inquiries is not a matter of doubt. They enter into every area of life and into every aspect of every area. In everyday living, men examine; they turn things over intellectually; they infer and judge as "naturally" as they reap and sow, produce and exchange commodities. As a mode of conduct, inquiry is as accessible to objective study as are these other modes of behavior. Because of the intimate and decisive way in which inquiry and its conclusions enter into the management of all affairs of life, no study of the latter is adequate save as it is noted how they are affected by the methods and instruments of inquiry that currently obtain. Quite apart, then, from the particular hypothesis about logical forms that is put forth, study of the objective facts of inquiry is a matter of tremendous import, practically and intellectually. . . .

Everybody knows that today there are in vogue methods of farming generally followed in the past which compare very unfavorably in their results with those obtained by practices that have already been introduced and tested. When an expert tells a farmer he *should* do thus and so, he is not setting up for a bad farmer an ideal drawn from the blue. He is instructing him in methods that have been tried and that have proved successful in procuring results. In a similar way we are able to contrast various kinds of inquiry that are in use or that have been used in respect to their economy and efficiency in reaching warranted conclusions. We know that some methods of inquiry are better than others in just the same way in which we know that some methods of surgery, farming, road-making, navigating or whatnot are better than others. It does not follow in any of these cases that the "better" methods are ideally perfect, or that they are regulative or "normative" because of conformity to some absolute form. They are the methods which experience up to the present time shows to be the best methods available for achieving certain results, while abstraction of these methods does supply a (relative) norm or standard for further undertakings.

The search for the pattern of inquiry is, accordingly, not one instituted in the dark or at large. It is checked and controlled by knowledge of the kinds of inquiry that have and that have not worked; methods which, as was pointed out earlier, can be so compared as to yield reasoned or rational conclusions. For, through comparison-contrast, we ascertain *how and why* certain means and agencies have provided warrantably assertible conclusions, while others have not and *cannot* do so in the sense in which "cannot" expresses an intrinsic incompatibility between means used and consequences attained.

We may now ask: What is the *definition* of Inquiry? That is, what is the most highly generalized conception of inquiry which can be justifiably formulated? The definition that will be expanded, directly in the present chapter and indirectly in the following chapters, is as follows: *Inquiry is the controlled or directed transformation of an indeterminate situation into one that is so determinate in its constituent distinctions and relations as to convert the elements of the original situation into a unified whole.*

The original indeterminate situation is not only "open" to inquiry, but it is open in the sense that its constituents do not hang together. The determinate situation on the other hand, *qua* outcome of inquiry, is a closed and, as it were, finished situation or "universe of experience." "Controlled or directed" in the above formula refers to the fact that inquiry is competent in any given case in the degree in which the operations involved in it actually do terminate in the establishment of an objectively unified existential situation. In the intermediate course of transition and transformation of the indeterminate situation, *discourse* through use of symbols is employed as means. In received logical terminology, propositions, or terms and the relations between them, are intrinsically involved.

The Antecedent Conditions of Inquiry: The Indeterminate Situation.—Inquiry and questioning, up to a certain point, are synonymous terms. We inquire when we question; and we inquire when we seek for whatever will provide an answer to a question asked. Thus it is of the very nature of the indeterminate situation which evokes inquiry to be *questionable;* or, in terms of actuality instead of potentiality, to be uncertain, unsettled, disturbed. The peculiar quality of what pervades the given materials, constituting them a situation, is not just uncertainty at large; it is a unique doubtfulness which makes that situation to be just and only the situation it is. It is this unique quality that not only evokes the particular inquiry engaged in but that exercises control over its special procedures. Otherwise, one procedure in inquiry would be as likely to occur and to be effective as any other. Unless a situation is uniquely quali-

fied in its very indeterminateness, there is a condition of
complete panic; response to it takes the form of blind and
wild overt activities. Stating the matter from the personal
side, we have "lost our heads." A variety of names serves to
characterize indeterminate situations. They are disturbed,
troubled, ambiguous, confused, full of conflicting tendencies, obscure, etc.

It is the *situation* that has these traits. *We* are doubtful
because the situation is inherently doubtful. Personal states
of doubt that are not evoked by and are not relative to some
existential situation are pathological; when they are extreme they constitute the mania of doubting. Consequently,
situations that are disturbed and troubled, confused or obscure, cannot be straightened out, cleared up and put in
order, by manipulation of our personal states of mind. The
attempt to settle them by such manipulations involves what
psychiatrists call "withdrawal from reality." Such an attempt is pathological as far as it goes, and when it goes far
it is the source of some form of actual insanity. The habit of
disposing of the doubtful as if it belonged only to *us* rather
than to the existential situation in which we are caught and
implicated is an inheritance from subjectivistic psychology.
The biological antecedent conditions of an unsettled situation are involved in that state of imbalance in organic-envi-
ronmental interactions which has already been described.
Restoration of integration can be effected, in one case as in
the other, only by operations which actually modify existing
conditions, not by merely "mental" processes.

It is, accordingly, a mistake to suppose that a situation is
doubtful only in a "subjective" sense. The notion that in
actual existence everything is completely determinate has
been rendered questionable by the progress of physical
science itself. Even if it had not been, complete determination would not hold of existences as an *environment*. For
Nature is an environment only as it is involved in interac-

tion with an organism, or self, or whatever name be used.*

Every such interaction is a temporal process, not a momentary cross-sectional occurrence. The situation in which it occurs is indeterminate, therefore, with respect to its *issue*. If we call it *confused*, then it is meant that its outcome cannot be anticipated. It is called *obscure* when its course of movement permits of final consequences that cannot be clearly made out. It is called *conflicting* when it tends to evoke discordant responses. Even were existential conditions unqualifiedly determinate in and of themselves, they are indeterminate in *significance*: that is, in what they import and portend in their interaction with the organism. The organic responses that enter into the production of the state of affairs that is temporally later and sequential are just as existential as are environing conditions.

The immediate *locus* of the problem concerns, then, what kind of responses the organism shall make. It concerns the interaction of organic responses and environing conditions in their movement toward an existential issue. It is a commonplace that in any troubled state of affairs *things* will come out differently according to what is done. The farmer won't get grain unless he plants and tills; the general will win or lose the battle according to the way he conducts it, and so on. Neither the grain nor the tilling, neither the outcome of the battle nor the conduct of it, are "mental" events. Organic interaction becomes inquiry when existential consequences are anticipated; when environing conditions are examined with reference to their potentialities; and when responsive activities are selected and ordered with reference to actualization of some of the potentialities, rather than others, in a final existential situation. Resolution of the

---

* Except of course a purely mentalistic name, like *consciousness*. The alleged problem of "interactionism" versus automatism, parallelism, etc., is a problem (and an insoluble one) because of the assumption involved in its statement—the assumption, namely, that the interaction in question is with something mental instead of with biological-cultural human beings.

indeterminate situation is active and operational. If the inquiry is adequately directed, the final issue is the unified situation that has been mentioned.

Institution of a Problem.—The unsettled or indeterminate situation might have been called a *problematic* situation. This name would have been, however, proleptic and anticipatory. The indeterminate situation becomes problematic in the very process of being subjected to inquiry. The indeterminate situation comes into existence from existential causes, just as does, say, the organic imbalance of hunger. There is nothing intellectual or cognitive in the existence of such situations, although they are the necessary condition of cognitive operations or inquiry. In themselves they are precognitive. The first result of evocation of inquiry is that the situation is taken, adjudged, to be problematic. To see that a situation requires inquiry is the initial step in inquiry.*

Qualification of a situation as problematic does not, however, carry inquiry far. It is but an initial step in institution of a problem. A problem is not a task to be performed which a person puts upon himself or that is placed upon him by others—like a so-called arithmetical "problem" in school work. A problem represents the partial transformation by inquiry of a problematic situation into a determinate situation. It is a familiar and significant saying that a problem well put is half-solved. To find out *what* the problem and problems are which a problematic situation presents to be inquired into, is to be well along in inquiry. To mistake the problem involved is to cause subsequent inquiry to be irrelevant or to go astray. Without a problem, there is blind groping in the dark. The way in which the problem is conceived decides what specific suggestions are entertained and which are dismissed; what data are selected and which

---

* If by "two-valued logic" is meant a logic that regards "true and false" as the sole logical values, then such a logic is necessarily so truncated that clearness and consistency in logical doctrine are impossible. Being the matter of a problem is a primary logical property.

rejected; it is the criterion for relevancy and irrelevancy of hypotheses and conceptual structures. On the other hand, to set up a problem that does not grow out of an actual situation is to start on a course of dead work, nonetheless dead because the work is "busy work." Problems that are self-set are mere excuses for seeming to do something intellectual, something that has the semblance but not the substance of scientific activity.

The Determination of a Problem-Solution.—Statement of a problematic situation in terms of a problem has no meaning save as the problem instituted has, in the very terms of its statement, reference to a possible solution. Just because a problem well stated is on its way to solution, the determining of a genuine problem is a *progressive* inquiry; the cases in which a problem and its probable solution flash upon an inquirer are cases where much prior ingestion and digestion have occurred. If we assume, prematurely, that the problem involved is definite and clear, subsequent inquiry proceeds on the wrong track. Hence the question arises: How is the formation of a genuine problem so controlled that further inquiries will move toward a solution?

The first step in answering this question is to recognize that no situation which is *completely* indeterminate can possibly be converted into a problem having definite constituents. The first step then is to search out the *constituents* of a given situation which, as constituents, are settled. When an alarm of fire is sounded in a crowded assembly hall, there is much that is indeterminate as regards the activities that may produce a favorable issue. One may get out safely or one may be trampled and burned. The fire is characterized, however, by some settled traits. It is, for example, located *somewhere*. Then the aisles and exits are at fixed places. Since they are settled or determinate in *existence*, the first step in institution of a problem is to settle them in *observation*. There are other factors which, while they are not as temporally and spatially fixed, are yet ob-

servable constituents; for example, the behavior and movements of other members of the audience. All of these
observed conditions taken together constitute "the facts of
the case." They constitute the terms of the problem, because they are conditions that must be reckoned with or
taken account of in any relevant solution that is proposed.

A *possible* relevant solution is then suggested by the
determination of factual conditions which are secured by
observation. The possible solution presents itself, therefore,
as an *idea*, just as the terms of the problem (which are
facts) are instituted by observation. Ideas are anticipated
consequences (forecasts) of what will happen when certain
operations are executed under and with respect to observed
conditions.* Observation of facts and suggested meanings
or ideas arise and develop in correspondence with each
other. The more the facts of the case come to light in consequence of being subjected to observation, the clearer and
more pertinent become the conceptions of the way the
problem constituted by these facts is to be dealt with. On
the other side, the clearer the idea, the more definite, as a
truism, become the operations of observation and of execution that must be performed in order to resolve the situation.

An idea is first of all an anticipation of something that
may happen; it marks a *possibility*. When it is said, as it
sometimes is, that science is *prediction*, the anticipation that
constitutes every idea an idea is grounded in a set of controlled observations and of regulated conceptual ways of
interpreting them. Because inquiry is a progressive determination of a problem and its possible solution, ideas differ

* The theory of *ideas* that has been held in psychology and epistemology
since the time of Locke's successors is completely irrelevant and obstructive
in logical theory. For in treating them as copies of perceptions or "impressions," it ignores the prospective and anticipatory character that defines
being an idea. Failure to define ideas functionally, in the reference they
have to a solution of a problem, is one reason they have been treated as
merely "mental." The notion, on the other hand, that ideas are fantasies is
a derivative. Fantasies arise when the function an idea performs is ruled out
when it is entertained and developed.

in grade according to the stage of inquiry reached. At first, save in highly familiar matters, they are vague. They occur at first simply as suggestions; suggestions just spring up, flash upon us, occur to us. They may then become stimuli to direct an overt activity but they have as yet no logical status. Every idea originates as a suggestion, but not every suggestion is an idea. The suggestion becomes an idea when it is examined with reference to its functional fitness; its capacity as a means of resolving the given situation.

This examination takes the form of reasoning, as a result of which we are able to appraise better than we were at the outset, the pertinency and weight of the meaning now entertained with respect to its functional capacity. But the final test of its possession of these properties is determined when it actually functions—that is, when it is put into operation so as to institute by means of observations facts not previously observed, and is then used to organize them with other facts into a coherent whole.

Because suggestions and ideas are of that which is not present in given existence, the meanings which they involve must be embodied in some symbol. Without some kind of symbol no idea; a meaning that is completely disembodied can not be entertained or used. Since an existence (which *is* an existence) is the support and vehicle of a meaning and is a symbol instead of a merely physical existence only in this respect, embodied meanings or ideas are capable of objective survey and development. To "look at an idea" is not a mere literary figure of speech.

"Suggestions" have received scant courtesy in logical theory. It is true that when they just "pop into our heads," because of the workings of the psycho-physical organism, they are not logical. But they are both the conditions and the primary stuff of logical ideas. The traditional empiristic theory reduced them, as has already been pointed out, to mental copies of physical things and assumed that they were *per se* identical with ideas. Consequently it ignored the function of ideas in directing observation and in ascertaining relevant facts. The rationalistic school, on the other hand, saw clearly that "facts" apart from ideas are trivial, that they acquire import and significance only in relation to ideas. But at the same time it failed to attend to the operative and functional nature of the latter. Hence it treated ideas as equivalent to the ultimate structure of "Reality." The Kantian formula that apart from each other "perceptions are blind and conceptions empty" marks a profound logical insight. The insight, however, was radically distorted because perceptual and conceptual contents were supposed to originate from different sources and thus required a third activity, that of synthetic understanding, to bring them together. In logical fact, perceptual and conceptual materials are instituted in functional correlativity with each other, in such a manner that the former locates and describes the problem while the latter represents a possible method of solution. Both are determinations in and by inquiry of the original problematic situation whose pervasive quality controls their institution and their contents. Both are finally checked by their capacity to work together to introduce a resolved unified situation. As distinctions they represent logical divisions of labor.

Reasoning.—The necessity of developing the meaning-contents of ideas in their relations to one another has been incidentally noted. This process, operating with symbols (constituting propositions) is reasoning in the sense of ratiocination or rational discourse.* When a suggested meaning is immediately accepted, inquiry is cut short. Hence the conclusion reached is not grounded, even if it happens to be correct. The check upon immediate acceptance is the examination of the meaning as a meaning. This examination consists in noting what the meaning in question implies in

---

* "Reasoning" is sometimes used to designate *inference* as well as ratiocination. When so used in logic the tendency is to identify inference and implication and thereby seriously to confuse logical theory.

relation to other meanings in the system of which it is a member, the formulated relation constituting a proposition. If such and such a relation of meanings is accepted, then we are committed to such and such other relations of meanings because of their membership in the same system. Through a series of intermediate meanings, a meaning is finally reached which is more clearly *relevant* to the problem in hand than the originally suggested idea. It indicates operations which can be performed to test its applicability, whereas the original idea is usually too vague to determine crucial operations. In other words, the idea or meaning when developed in discourse directs the activities which, when executed, provide needed evidential material.

The point made can be most readily appreciated in connection with scientific reasoning. An hypothesis, once suggested and entertained, is developed in relation to other conceptual structures until it receives a form in which it can instigate and direct an experiment that will disclose precisely those conditions which have the maximum possible force in determining whether the hypothesis should be accepted or rejected. Or it may be that the experiment will indicate what modifications are required in the hypothesis so that it may be applicable, i.e., suited to interpret and organize the facts of the case. In many familiar situations, the meaning that is most relevant has been settled because of the eventuations of experiments in prior cases so that it is applicable almost immediately upon its occurrence. But, indirectly, if not directly, an idea or suggestion that is not developed in terms of the constellation of meanings to which it belongs can lead only to overt response. Since the latter terminates inquiry, there is then no adequate inquiry into the meaning that is used to settle the given situation, and the conclusion is in so far logically ungrounded.

VI ♦ The Human Uses of Freedom

I. THE PROBLEM OF FREEDOM*

WHAT is freedom and why is it prized? Is desire for freedom inherent in human nature or is it a product of special circumstances? Is it wanted as an end or as a means of getting other things? Does its possession entail responsibilities, and are these responsibilities so onerous that the mass of men will readily surrender liberty for the sake of greater ease? Is the struggle for liberty so arduous that most men are easily distracted from the endeavor to achieve and maintain it? Does freedom in itself and in the things it brings with it seem as important as security of livelihood; as food, shelter, clothing, or even as having a good time? Did man ever care as much for it as we in this country have been taught to believe? Is there any truth in the old notion that the driving force in political history has been the effort of the common man to achieve freedom? Was our own struggle for political independence in any genuine sense animated by desire for freedom, or were there a number of discomforts that our ancestors wanted to get rid of, things having nothing in common save that they were felt to be troublesome?

Is love of liberty ever anything more than a desire to be liberated from some special restriction? And when it is got rid of does the desire for liberty die down until something

* From *Freedom and Culture* by John Dewey. New York: G. P. Putnam's Sons, 1939. By permission of G. P. Putnam's Sons.

else feels intolerable? Again, how does the desire for freedom compare in intensity with the desire to feel equal with others, especially with those who have previously been called superiors? How do the fruits of liberty compare with the enjoyments that spring from a feeling of union, of solidarity, with others? Will men surrender their liberties if they believe that by so doing they will obtain the satisfaction that comes from a sense of fusion with others and that respect by others which is the product of the strength furnished by solidarity?

The present state of the world is putting questions like these to citizens of all democratic countries. It is putting them with special force to us in a country where democratic institutions have been bound up with a certain tradition, the "ideology" of which the Declaration of Independence is the classic expression. This tradition has taught us that attainment of freedom is the goal of political history; that self-government is the inherent right of free men and is that which, when it is achieved, men prize above all else. Yet as we look at the world we see supposedly free institutions in many countries not so much overthrown as abandoned willingly, apparently with enthusiasm. We may infer that what has happened is proof they never existed in reality but only in name. Or we may console ourselves with a belief that unusual conditions, such as national frustration and humiliation, have led men to welcome any kind of government that promised to restore national self-respect. But conditions in our country as well as the eclipse of democracy in other countries compel us to ask questions about the career and fate of free societies, even our own.

There perhaps was a time when the questions asked would have seemed to be mainly or exclusively political. Now we know better. For we know that a large part of the causes which have produced the conditions that are expressed in the questions is the dependence of politics upon other forces, notably the economic. The problem of the constitution of human nature is involved, since it is part of our tradition that love of freedom is inherent in its make-up. Is the popular psychology of democracy a myth? The old doctrine about human nature was also tied up with the ethical belief that political democracy is a moral right and that the laws upon which it is based are fundamental moral laws which every form of social organization should obey. If belief in natural rights and natural laws as the foundation of free government is surrendered, does the latter have any other moral basis? For while it would be foolish to believe that the American colonies fought the battles that secured their independence and that they built their government consciously and deliberately upon a foundation of psychological and moral theories, yet the democratic tradition, call it dream or call it penetrating vision, was so closely allied with beliefs about human nature and about the moral ends which political institutions should serve, that a rude shock occurs when these affiliations break down. Is there anything to take their place, anything that will give the kind of support they once gave?

The problems behind the questions asked, the forces which give the questions their urgency, go beyond the particular beliefs which formed the early psychological and moral foundation of democracy. After retiring from public office, Thomas Jefferson in his old age carried on a friendly philosophical correspondence with John Adams. In one of his letters he made a statement about existing American conditions and expressed a hope about their future estate: "The advance of liberalism encourages a hope that the human mind will some day get back to the freedom it enjoyed two thousand years ago. This country, which has given to the world the example of physical liberty, owes to it that of moral emancipation also, for as yet it is but nominal with us. The inquisition of public opinion overwhelms in practice the freedom asserted by the laws in theory." The situation that has developed since his time may well lead us to reverse the ideas he expressed, and inquire whether political freedom can be maintained without that freedom of culture which he expected to be the final result of political freedom. It is no longer easy to entertain the hope that given political freedom as the one thing necessary all other things will in time be added to it—and so to us. For we now know that the relations which exist between persons, outside of political institutions, relations of industry, of communication, of science, art and religion, affect daily associations, and thereby deeply affect the attitudes and habits expressed in government and rules of law. If it is true that the political and legal react to shape the other things, it is even more true that political institutions are an effect, not a cause.

It is this knowledge that sets the theme to be discussed. For this complex of conditions which taxes the terms upon which human beings associate and live together is summed up in the word *Culture*. The problem is to know what kind of culture is so free in itself that it conceives and begets political freedom as its accompaniment and consequence. What about the state of science and knowledge; of the arts, fine and technological; of friendships and family life; of business and finance; of the attitudes and dispositions created in the give and take of ordinary day by day associations? No matter what is the native make-up of human nature, its working activities, those which respond to institutions and rules and which finally shape the pattern of the latter, are created by the whole body of occupations, interests, skills, beliefs that constitute a given culture. As the latter changes, especially as it grows complex and intricate in the way in which American life has changed since our political organization took shape, new problems take the place of those governing the earlier formation and distribution of political powers. The view that love of freedom is so inherent in man that, if it only has a chance given it by abolition of oppressions exercised by church and state, it will produce and maintain free institutions is no longer adequate. The idea naturally arose when settlers in a new country felt that the distance they had put between themselves and the forces that oppressed them effectively symbolized everything that stood between them and permanent achievement of freedom. We are now forced to see that positive conditions, forming the prevailing state of culture, are required. Release from oppressions and repressions which previously existed marked a necessary transition, but transitions are but bridges to something different.

Early republicans were obliged even in their own time to note that general conditions, such as are summed up under the name of culture, had a good deal to do with political institutions. For they held that oppressions of state and church had exercised a corrupting influence upon human nature, so that the original impulse to liberty had either been lost or warped out of shape. This was a virtual admission that surrounding conditions may be stronger than native tendencies. It proved a degree of plasticity in human nature that required exercise of continual solicitude—expressed in the saying that eternal vigilance is the price of liberty. The Founding Fathers were aware that love of power is a trait of human nature, so strong a one that definite barriers had to be erected to keep persons who get into positions of official authority from encroachments that undermine free institutions. Admission that men may be brought by long habit to hug their chains implies a belief that second or acquired nature is stronger than original nature.

Jefferson at least went further than this. For his fear of the growth of manufacturing and trade and his preference for agrarian pursuits amounted to acceptance of the idea that interests bred by certain pursuits may fundamentally alter original human nature and the institutions that are congenial to it. That the development Jefferson dreaded has come about and to a much greater degree than he could have anticipated is an obvious fact. We face today the consequences of the fact that an agricultural and rural people has become an urban industrial population.

Proof is decisive that economic factors are an intrinsic part of the culture that determines the actual turn taken by political measures and rules, no matter what verbal beliefs are held. Although it later became the fashion to blur the connection which exists between economics and politics, and even to reprove those who called attention to it, Madison as well as Jefferson was quite aware of the connection and of its bearing upon democracy. Knowledge that the connection demanded a general distribution of property and the prevention of rise of the extremely poor and the extremely rich, was however different from explicit recognition of a relation between culture and nature so intimate that the former may shape the patterns of thought and action.

Economic relations and habits cannot be set apart in isolation any more than political institutions can be. The state of knowledge of nature, that is, of physical science, is a phase of culture upon which industry and commerce, the production and distribution of goods and the regulation of services directly depend. Unless we take into account the rise of the new science of nature in the seventeenth century and its growth to its present state, our economic agencies of production and distribution and ultimately of consumption cannot be understood. The connection of the events of the industrial revolution with those of the advancing scientific revolution is an incontrovertible witness.

It has not been customary to include the arts, the fine arts, as an important part of the social conditions that bear upon democratic institutions and personal freedom. Even after the influence of the state of industry and of natural science has been admitted, we still tend to draw the line at the idea that literature, music, painting, the drama, architecture, have any intimate connection with the cultural

bases of democracy. Even those who call themselves good
democrats are often content to look upon the fruits of these
arts as adornments of culture rather than as things in whose
enjoyment all should partake, if democracy is to be a reality. The state of things in totalitarian countries may induce
us to revise this opinion. For it proves that no matter what
may be the case with the impulses and powers that lead the
creative artist to do his work, works of art once brought into
existence are the most compelling of the means of communication by which emotions are stirred and opinions formed.
The theater, the movie and music hall, even the picture
gallery, eloquence, popular parades, common sports and re-
creative agencies, have all been brought under regulation
as part of the propaganda agencies by which dictatorship
is kept in power without being regarded by the masses as
oppressive. We are beginning to realize that emotions and
imagination are more potent in shaping public sentiment
and opinion than information and reason.

Indeed, long before the present crisis came into being
there was a saying that if one could control the songs of a
nation, one need not care who made its laws. And historical study shows that primitive religions owe their power in
determining belief and action to their ability to reach emotions and imagination by rites and ceremonies, by legend
and folklore, all clothed with the traits that mark works of
art. The Church that has had by far the greatest influence
in the modern world took over their agencies of esthetic
appeal and incorporated them into its own structure, after
adapting them to its own purpose, in winning and holding
the allegiance of the masses.

A totalitarian regime is committed to control of the
whole life of all its subjects by its hold over feelings, desires, emotions, as well as opinions. This indeed is a mere
truism, since a totalitarian state has to be total. But save as
we take it into account we shall not appreciate the intensity
of the revival of the warfare between state and church that

exists in Germany and Russia. The conflict is not the expression of the whim of a leader. It is inherent in any regime that demands the *total* allegiance of all its subjects. It must first of all, and most enduringly of all, if it is to be permanent, command the imagination, with all the impulses and motives we have been accustomed to call *inner*. Religious organizations are those which rule by use of these means, and for that reason are an inherent competitor with any political state that sets out on the totalitarian road. Thus it is that the very things that seem to us in democratic countries the most obnoxious features of the totalitarian state are the very things for which its advocates recommend it. They are the things for whose absence they denounce democratic countries. For they say that failure to enlist the whole make-up of citizens, emotional as well as ideological, condemns democratic states to employ merely external and mechanical devices to hold the loyal support of its citizens. We may regard all this as a symptom of a collective hallucination, such as at times seems to have captured whole populations. But even so, we must recognize the influence of this factor if we are ourselves to escape collective delusion—that totalitarianism rests upon external coercion alone.

Finally, the moral factor is an intrinsic part of the complex of social forces called culture. For no matter whether or not one shares the view, now held on different grounds by different groups, that there is no scientific ground or warrant for moral conviction and judgments—it is certain that human beings hold some things dearer than they do others, and that they struggle for the things they prize, spending time and energy in their behalf: doing so indeed to such an extent that the best measure we have of what is valued is the effort spent in its behalf. Not only so, but for a number of persons to form anything that can be called a community in its pregnant sense there must be values prized in common. Without them, any so-called social group, class, people, nation, tends to fall apart into molecules having but mechanically enforced connections with one another. For the present at least we do not have to ask whether values are moral, having a kind of life and potency of their own, or are but by-products of the working of other conditions, biological, economic or whatever.

The qualification will indeed seem quite superfluous to most, so habituated have most persons become to believing, at least nominally, that moral forces are the ultimate determinants of the rise and fall of all human societies—while religion has taught many to believe that cosmic as well as social forces are regulated in behalf of moral ends. The qualification is introduced, nevertheless, because of the existence of a school of philosophy holding that opinions about the values which move conduct are lacking in any scientific standing, since (according to them) the only things that can be *known* are physical events. The denial that values have any influence in the long run course of events is also characteristic of the Marxist belief that forces of production ultimately control every human relationship. The idea of the impossibility of intellectual regulation of ideas and judgments about values is shared by a number of intellectuals who have been dazzled by the success of mathematical and physical science. These last remarks suggest that there is at least one other factor in culture which needs some attention:—namely, the existence of schools of social philosophy, of competing ideologies.

The intent of the previous discussion should be obvious. The problem of freedom and of democratic institutions is tied up with the question of what kind of culture exists; with the necessity of free culture for free political institutions. The import of this conclusion extends far beyond its contrast with the simpler faith of those who formulated the democratic tradition. The question of human psychology, of the make-up of human nature in its original state, is involved. It is involved not just in a general way but with respect to its special constituents and their significance in their relations to one another. For every social and political philosophy currently professed will be found upon examination to involve a certain view about the constitution of human nature: in itself and in its relation to physical nature. What is true of this factor is true of every factor in culture, so that they need not here be listed again, although it is necessary to bear them all in mind if we are to appreciate the variety of factors involved in the problem of human freedom.

Running through the problem of the relation of this and that constituent of culture to social institutions in general and political democracy in particular is a question rarely asked. Yet it so underlies any critical consideration of the principles of each of them that some conclusion on the matter ultimately decides the position taken on each special issue. The question is whether any one of the factors is so predominant that it is *the* causal force, so that other factors are secondary and derived effects. Some kind of answer in what philosophers call a *monistic* direction has been usually given. The most obvious present example is the belief that economic conditions are ultimately the controlling forces in human relationships. It is perhaps significant that this view is comparatively recent. At the height of the eighteenth century, Enlightenment, the prevailing view, gave final supremacy to reason, to the advance of science and to education. Even during the last century, a view was held which is expressed in the motto of a certain school of historians: "History is past politics and politics is present history."

Because of the present fashion of economic explanation, this political view may now seem to have been the crotchet of a particular set of historical scholars. But, after all, it only formulated an idea consistently acted upon during the period of the formation of national states. It is possible to

regard the present emphasis upon economic factors as a
sort of intellectual revenge taken upon its earlier all but
total neglect. The very word "political economy" suggests
how completely economic considerations were once subordinated to political. The book that was influential in putting an end to this subjection, Adam Smith's *Wealth of
Nations,* continued in its title, though not its contents, the
older tradition. In the Greek period, we find that Aristotle
makes the political factor so controlling that all normal
economic activities are relegated to the household, so that
all morally justifiable economic practice is literally domestic economy. And in spite of the recent vogue of the Marxist theory, Oppenheim has produced a considerable body
of evidence in support of the thesis that political states are
the result of military conquests in which defeated people
have become subjects of their conquerors, who, by assuming rule over the conquered, begot the first political states.

The rise of totalitarian states cannot, because of the bare
fact of their totalitarianism, be regarded as mere reversions
to the earlier theory of supremacy of the political institutional factor. Yet as compared with theories that had subordinated the political to the economic, whether in the
Marxist form or in that of the British classical school, it
marks reversion to ideas and still more to practices which
it was supposed had disappeared forever from the conduct
of any modern state. And the practices have been revived
and extended with the benefit of scientific technique of
control of industry, finance and commerce in ways which
show the earlier governmental officials who adopted "mer-
cantile" economics in the interest of government were the
veriest bunglers at their professed job.

The idea that morals ought to be, even if it is not, the
supreme regulator of social affairs is not so widely entertained as it once was, and there are circumstances which
support the conclusion that when moral forces were as
influential as they were supposed to be it was because

morals were identical with customs which happened in fact
to regulate the relations of human beings with one another.
However, the idea is still advanced by sermons from the
pulpit and editorials from the press that adoption of say
the Golden Rule would speedily do away with all social
discord and trouble; and as I write the newspapers report
the progress of a campaign for something called "moral re-
armament." Upon a deeper level, the point made about
the alleged identity of ethics with established customs
raises the question whether the effect of the disintegration
of customs that for a long time held men together in social
groups can be overcome save by development of new generally accepted traditions and customs. This development,
upon this view, would be equivalent to the creation of a
new ethics.

However, such questions are here brought up for the
sake of the emphasis they place upon the question already
raised: Is there any one factor or phase of culture which
is dominant, or which tends to produce and regulate others,
or are economics, morals, art, science, and so on only so
many aspects of the interaction of a number of factors,
each of which acts upon and is acted upon by the others?
In the professional language of philosophy: shall our point
of view be monistic or pluralistic? The same question re-
curs moreover about each one of the factors listed:—about
economics, about politics, about science, about art. I shall
here illustrate the point by reference not to any of these
things but to theories that have at various times been influential about the make-up of human nature. For these psychological theories have been marked by serious attempts
to make some one constituent of human nature *the* source
of motivation of action; or at least to reduce all conduct to
the action of a small number of alleged native "forces."
A comparatively recent example was the adoption by the
classic school of economic theory of self-interest as the main
motivating force of human behavior; an idea linked up on

its technical side with the notion that pleasure and pain are the causes and the ends-in-view of all conscious human conduct, in desire to obtain one and avoid the other. Then there was a view that self-interest and sympathy are the two components of human nature, as opposed and balanced centrifugal and centripetal tendencies are the moving forces of celestial nature.

Just now the favorite ideological psychological candidate for control of human activity is love of power. Reasons for its selection are not far to seek. Success of search for economic profit turned out to be largely conditioned in fact upon possession of superior power while success reacted to increase power. Then the rise of national states has been attended by such vast and flagrant organization of military and naval force that politics have become more and more markedly power-politics, leading to the conclusion that there is not any other kind, although in the past the power-element has been more decently and decorously covered up. One interpretation of the Darwinian struggle for existence and survival of the fittest was used as ideological support; and some writers, notably Nietzsche (though not in the crude form often alleged), proposed an ethics of power in opposition to the supposed Christian ethics of sacrifice.

Because human nature is the factor which in one way or another is always interacting with environing conditions in production of culture, the theme receives special attention later. But the shift that has occurred from time to time in theories that have gained currency about the "ruling motive" in human nature suggests a question which is seldom asked. It is the question whether these psychologies have not in fact taken the cart to be the horse. Have they not gathered their notion as to the ruling element in human nature from observation of tendencies that are marked in contemporary collective life, and then bunched these tendencies together in some alleged psychological "force" as their cause? It is significant that human nature was taken to be strongly moved by an inherent love of freedom at the time when there was a struggle for representative government; that the motive of self-interest appeared when conditions in England enlarged the role of money, because of new methods of industrial production; that the growth of organized philanthropic activities brought sympathy into the psychological picture, and that events today are readily converted into love of power as the mainspring of human action.

In any case, the idea of culture that has been made familiar by the work of anthropological students points to the conclusion that whatever are the native constituents of human nature, the culture of a period and group is the determining influence in their arrangement; it is that which determines the patterns of behavior that mark out the activities of any group, family, clan, people, sect, faction, class. It is at least as true that the state of culture determines the order and arrangement of native tendencies as that human nature produces any particular set or system of social phenomena so as to obtain satisfaction for itself. The problem is to find out the way in which the elements of a culture interact with each other and the way in which the elements of human nature are caused to interact with one another under conditions set by their interaction with the existing environment. For example, if our American culture is largely a pecuniary culture, it is not because the original or innate structure of human nature tends of itself to obtaining pecuniary profit. It is rather that a certain complex culture stimulates, promotes and consolidates native tendencies so as to produce a certain pattern of desires and purposes. If we take all the communities, peoples, classes, tribes and nations that ever existed, we may be sure that since human nature in its native constitution is the relative constant, it cannot be appealed to, in isolation, to account for the multitude of diversities presented by different forms of association.

Primitive peoples for reasons that are now pretty evident attribute magical qualities to blood. Popular beliefs about race and inherent race differences have virtually perpetuated the older superstitions. Anthropologists are practically all agreed that the differences we find in different "races" are not due to anything in inherent physiological structure but to the effects exercised upon members of various groups by the cultural conditions under which they are reared; conditions that act upon raw or original human nature unremittingly from the very moment of birth. It has always been known that infants, born without ability in any language, come to speak the language, whatever it may be, of the community in which they were born. Like most uniform phenomena the fact aroused no curiosity and led to no generalization about the influence of cultural conditions. It was taken for granted; as a matter of course it was so "natural" as to appear inevitable. Only since the rise of systematic inquiries carried on by anthropological students has it been noted that the conditions of culture which bring about the common language of a given group produce other traits they have in common;—traits which like the mother tongue differentiate one group or society from others.

Culture as a complex body of customs tends to maintain itself. It can reproduce itself only through effecting certain differential changes in the original or native constitutions of its members. Each culture has its own pattern, its own characteristic arrangement of its constituent energies. By the mere force of its existence as well as by deliberately adopted methods systematically pursued, it perpetuates itself through transformation of the raw or original human nature of those born immature.

These statements do not signify that biological heredity and native individual differences are of no importance. They signify that as they operate within a given social form, they are shaped and take effect *within* that particular form. They are not indigenous traits that mark off one people, one group, one class, from another, but mark differences in every group. Whatever the "white man's burden," it was not imposed by heredity.

We have traveled a seemingly long way from the questions with which we set out, so that it may appear that they had been forgotten on the journey. But the journey was undertaken for the sake of finding out something about the nature of the problem that is expressed in the questions asked. The maintenance of democratic institutions is not such a simple matter as was supposed by some of the Founding Fathers—although the wiser among them realized how immensely the new political experiment was favored by external circumstances—like the ocean that separated settlers from the governments that had an interest in using the colonists for their own purposes; the fact that feudal institutions had been left behind; that so many of the settlers had come here to escape restrictions upon religious beliefs and form of worship; and especially the existence of a vast territory with free land and immense unappropriated natural resources.

The function of culture in determining what elements of human nature are dominant and their pattern or arrangement in connection with one another goes beyond any special point to which attention is called. It affects the very idea of individuality. The idea that human nature is inherently and exclusively individual is itself a product of a cultural individualistic movement. The idea that mind and consciousness are intrinsically individual did not even occur to any one for much the greater part of human history. It would have been rejected as the inevitable source of disorder and chaos if it had occurred to anyone to suggest it:—not that their ideas of human nature on that account were any better than later ones but that they also were functions of culture. All that we can safely say is that hu-

man nature, like other forms of life, tends to differentiation,
and this moves in the direction of the distinctively individual, and that it also tends toward combination, association.
In the lower animals, physical-biological factors determine
which tendency is dominant in a given animal or plant
species and the ratio existing between the two factors—
whether, for example, insects are what students call "solitary" or "social." With human beings, cultural conditions
replace strictly physical ones. In the earlier periods of human history they acted almost like physiological conditions
as far as deliberate intention was concerned. They were
taken to be "natural" and change in them to be unnatural.
At a later period the cultural conditions were seen to be
subject in some degree to deliberate formation. For a time
radicals then identified their policies with the belief that if
only artificial social conditions could be got rid of human
nature would produce almost automatically a certain kind
of social arrangements, those which would give it free scope
in its supposed exclusively individual character.

Tendencies toward sociality, such as sympathy, were
admitted. But they were taken to be traits of an individual isolated by nature, quite as much as, say, a tendency
to combine with others in order to get protection against
something threatening one's own private self. Whether
complete identification of human nature with individuality
would be desirable or undesirable if it existed is an idle
academic question. For it does not exist. Some cultural
conditions develop the psychological constituents that lead
toward differentiation; others stimulate those which lead in
the direction of the solidarity of the beehive or anthill. The
human problem is that of securing the development of each
constituent so that it serves to release and mature the other.
Cooperation—called fraternity in the classic French formula—is as much a part of the democratic ideal as is personal initiative. That cultural conditions were allowed to
develop (markedly so in the economic phase) which subor-

dinated cooperativeness to liberty and equality serves to explain the decline in the two latter. Indirectly, this decline is responsible for the present tendency to give a bad name to the very word *individualism* and to make *sociality* a term of moral honor beyond criticism. But that association of nullities on even the largest scale would constitute a realization of human nature is as absurd as to suppose that the latter can take place in beings whose only relations to one another are those entered into in behalf of exclusive private advantage.

The problem of freedom of cooperative individualities is then a problem to be viewed in the context of culture. The state of culture is a state of interaction of many factors, the chief of which are law and politics, industry and commerce, science and technology, the arts of expression and communication, and of morals, or the values men prize and the ways in which they evaluate them; and finally, though indirectly, the system of general ideas used by men to justify and to criticize the fundamental conditions under which they live, their social philosophy. We are concerned with the problem of freedom rather than with solutions: in the conviction that solutions are idle until the problem has been placed in the context of the elements that constitute culture as they interact with elements of native human nature. The fundamental postulate of the discussion is that isolation of any one factor, no matter how strong its workings at a given time, is fatal to understanding and to intelligent action. Isolations have abounded, both on the side of taking some one thing in human nature to be a supreme "motive" and in taking some one form of social activity to be supreme. Since the problem is here thought of as that of the ways in which a great number of factors within and without human nature interact, our next task is to ask concerning the reciprocal connections raw human nature and culture bear to one another.

II. Culture and Human Nature

In the American as in the English liberal tradition, the idea of freedom has been connected with the idea of individuality, of *the* individual. The connection has been so close and so often reiterated that it has come to seem inherent. Many persons will be surprised if they hear that freedom has ever been supposed to have another source and foundation than the very nature of individuality. Yet in the continental European tradition the affiliation of the idea of freedom is with the idea of rationality. Those are free who govern themselves by the dictates of reason; those who follow the promptings of appetite and sense are so ruled by them as to be unfree. Thus it was that Hegel at the very time he was glorifying the State wrote a philosophy of history according to which the movement of historical events was from the despotic state of the Oriental World in which only one was free to the era dawning in Germany in the Western World in which *all* are free. The same difference in contexts that give freedom its meaning is found when representatives of totalitarian Germany at the present time claim their regime is giving the subjects of their state a "higher" freedom than can be found in democratic states, individuals in the latter being unfree because their lives are chaotic and undisciplined. The aroma of the continental tradition hangs about the sayings of those who settle so many social problems to their own satisfaction by invoking a distinction between liberty and license, identifying the former with "liberty under law"—for in the classic tradition law and reason are related as child and parent. So far as the saying assigns to law an origin and authority having nothing to do with freedom, so far, that is, as it affirms the impossibility of free conditions determining their own law, it points directly, even if unintentionally, to the totalitarian state.

We do not, however, have to go as far abroad as the European continent to note that freedom has had its practical significance fixed in different ways in different cultural contexts. For in the early nineteenth century there was a great practical difference between the English and the American theories, although both associated freedom with qualities that cause human beings to be *individuals* in the distinctive sense of that word. The contrast is so flat that it would be amusing if it were not so instructive. Jefferson, who was the original and systematic promulgator of the doctrine of free, self-governing institutions, found that the properties of individuals with which these institutions were most closely associated were traits found in the farming class. In his more pessimistic moments he even went so far as to anticipate that the development of manufacturing and commerce would produce a state of affairs in which persons in this country "would eat one another" as they did in Europe. In England, on the other hand, landed proprietors were the great enemy of the new freedom, which was connected in its social and political manifestations with the activities and aims of the manufacturing class.

It is not, of course, the bare fact of contrast which is instructive but the causes for its existence. They are not far to seek. Landed proprietors formed the aristocracy in Great Britain. The hold landed interests had over law-making bodies due to feudalism was hostile to the development of manufacturing and commerce. In the United States traces of feudalism were so faint that laws against primogeniture were about all that was needed to erase them. It was easy in this country to idealize the farmers as the sturdy yeomanry who embodied all the virtues associated with the original Anglo-Saxon love of liberty, the Magna Charta, and the struggle against the despotism of the Stuarts. Farmers were the independent self-supporting class that had no favors to ask from anybody, since they were not dependent for their livelihood nor their ideas

upon others, owning and managing their own farms. It is a
history that again would be amusing, were it not instructive, to find that as this country changed from an agrarian
one to an urban industrial one, the qualities of initiative, invention, vigor and intrinsic contribution to progress which
British *laissez-faire* liberalism had associated with manufacturing pursuits were transferred by American Courts
and by the political representatives of business and finance
from Jeffersonian individuals and given to the entrepre-
neurs who were individuals in the British sense.

In such considerations as these—which would be reinforced by an extensive survey of the history of the meaning
given to freedom under different conditions—we have one
instance and an important one of the relation of culture to
the whole problem of freedom. The facts fall directly in line
with the conclusion of the previous chapter:—a conclusion
summed up in saying that the idea of Culture, which has
become a central idea of anthropology, has such a wide
sociological application that it puts a new face upon the
old, old problem of the relation of the individual and the
social. The idea of culture even outlaws the very terms in
which the problem has been conceived, independently of
its effect upon solutions proposed. For most statements of
the problem have been posed as if there were some inherent
difference amounting to opposition between what is called
the individual and the social. As a consequence there was
a tendency for those who were interested in theory to line
up in two parties, which at the poles were so far apart that
one denied whatever the other asserted. One party held
that social conventions, traditions, institutions, rules are
maintained only by some form of coercion, overt or covert,
which encroaches upon the natural freedom of individuals;
while the other school held that individuals are such by
nature that the one standing social problem is the agencies
by which recalcitrant individuals are brought under social
control or "socialized." The term of honor of one school has

been that of reproach of the other. The two extremes serve
to define the terms in which the problem was put. Most
persons occupy an intermediate and compromise position,
one whose classic expression is that the basic problem of
law and politics is to find the line which separates legitimate liberty from the proper exercise of law and political
authority, so that each can maintain its own province under
its own jurisdiction; law operating only when liberty over-
steps its proper bounds, an operation supposed, during the
heights of *laissez-faire* liberalism, to be legitimate only
when police action was required to keep the peace.

Few persons today hold the extreme view of Hobbes,
according to which human nature is so inherently anti-
social that only experiences of the evil consequences of
the war of all against all, reigning when human nature has
free play, leads men, in connection with the motive of fear,
to submit to authority—human nature even then remaining
so intractable that the only assurance of safety against
its marauding instincts is subjection to sovereignty. But in
reading books on sociology it is still not uncommon to find
the basic problem stated as if it were to list and analyze
agencies by which individuals are tamed or "socialized."
The chief difference of these writers from Hobbes consists
in the fact that much less emphasis is laid upon merely political pressure, while it is recognized that there are tendencies in original human nature which render it amenable
to social rules and regulations. As a result of the successful
struggle of the new industrial class in England against the
restrictions which existed even after the disappearance of
feudalism in its grosser obvious forms, the favorite formula
weighted the scales on the side of liberty, holding that each
person was free as long as his actions did not restrict the
freedom of others. The latter question, moreover, was never
decided by going into the concrete consequences produced
by the action of one person upon other persons. It was settled by a formal legal principle such as the equal right of

every sane individual of a certain age to enter into contractual relations with others—no matter whether actual conditions gave equally free scope of action on both sides or made "free" contract a jug-handled affair.

However, the purpose is not to thrash over the old straw of these issues or similar issues on the moral side such as the respective parts of altruistic and egoistic tendencies in human nature. The point concerns the situation in which the problems were envisaged; the context of ideas in which as problems they were placed irrespective of the solution reached. With the intellectual resources now available, we can see that such opinions about the inherent make-up of human nature neglected the fundamental question of how its constituents are stimulated and inhibited, intensified and weakened; how their pattern is determined by interaction with cultural conditions. In consequence of this failure the views held regarding human nature were those appropriate to the purposes and policies a given group wanted to carry through. Those who wished to justify the exercise of authority over others took a pessimistic view of the constitution of human nature; those who wanted relief from something oppressive discovered qualities of great promise in its native makeup. There is here a field which has hardly been entered by intellectual explorers:—the story of the way in which ideas put forth about the makeup of human nature, ideas supposed to be the results of psychological inquiry, have been in fact only reflections of practical measures that different groups, classes, factions wished to see continued in existence or newly adopted, so that what passed as psychology was a branch of political doctrine.

We are thus brought back to the earlier statement of principle. The primary trouble has been that issues have been formulated as if they were matters of the structure of human beings on one side and of the very nature of social rules and authority on the other side, when in reality the underlying issue is that of the relation of the "natural" and the "cultural." Rousseau's attack upon the arts and sciences (as well as upon existing law and government) shocked his eighteenth century contemporaries, since the things he claimed to be operating to corrupt human nature, by creating inequality, were the very things they relied upon to generate unending human progress. Nevertheless, he stated, in a way, the problem of culture versus nature; putting, himself, all emphasis upon and giving all advantage to human nature; since to him, in spite of its raw unrefined condition, it retained its natural goodness as long as loss of original equality had not produced conditions that corrupted it. Kant and his German successors took up the challenge presented in the unpopular paradoxes of Rousseau. They tried to reverse his position; they interpreted all history as the continuing process of culture by which the original animal nature of man becomes refined and is transformed from the animal into the distinctively human.

But Rousseau and his opponents carried over into their discussion of the problem in its new form many of the elements derived from the traditional way of putting it. In German philosophy, the issue was further complicated by the rise of Nationalism which followed the encroachments of Napoleon. Though the Germans were defeated in war, in culture they were to be superior—an idea that still persists in the use of *Kultur* in German nationalistic propaganda, since superiority in culture gives the kind of rightful authority over peoples of less culture that the human has over the animal. The French Revolution, as well as the writings of Rousseau, had the effect, in addition, of identifying in the minds of German thinkers the cause of culture with that of law and authority. The individual freedom, which was the "natural right" of mankind according to the philosophers of the Revolution, was to the German philosophers of the reaction but the freedom of primitive sensuous animality. A period of subjection to universal law, express-

ing the higher non-natural essence of humanity, was required to bring about a condition of "higher" and true
freedom. Events in Germany, including the rise of totalitarianism, since the time this view was formulated, have
borne the stamp of this idea. Anticipation of the existence
of some ultimate and a final social state, different from
original "natural" freedom and from present subordination,
has played a role in all social philosophies—like the Marxist
—framed under German intellectual influences. It has had
the function once exercised by the idea of the Second
Coming.

In no case, however, could the problem have taken its
new form without the material made available by anthropological research. For what has been disclosed about the
immense variety of cultures shows that the problem of the
relation of individuals and their freedom to social convention, custom, tradition and rules has been stated in a
wholesale form, and hence not capable of intelligent and
scientific attack. Judged by the methods of the natural
sciences, the procedure in the social field has been pre-
scientific and anti-scientific. For science has developed by
analytic observation, and by interpretations of observed
facts on the basis of their relations to one another. Social
theory has operated on the basis of general "forces,"
whether those of inherent natural "motives" or those
alleged to be social.

Were it not for the inertia of habit (which applies to
opinion as well as to overt acts) it would be astonishing to
find today writers who are well acquainted with the procedure of physical science and yet appeal to "forces" in
explanation of human and social phenomena. For in the
former case, they are aware that electricity, heat, light, etc.,
are names for ways in which definite observable concrete
phenomena behave in relation to one another, and that all
description and explanation have to be made in terms of
verifiable relations of observed singular events. They know

that reference to electricity or heat, etc., is but a shorthand reference to relations between events which have been established by investigation of actual occurrences. But in the field of social phenomena they do not hesitate to explain concrete phenomena by reference to motives as forces (such as love of power), although these so-called forces are but reduplication, in the medium of abstract words, of the very phenomena to be explained.

Statement in terms of the relations of culture and nature to one another takes us away from vague abstractions and glittering generalities. Approach in its terms compels attention to go to the variety of cultures that exist and to the variety of constituents of human nature, including native differences between one human being and another—differences which are not just differences in quantity. The business of inquiry is with the ways in which specified constituents of human nature, native or already modified, *interact* with specified definite constituents of a given culture; conflicts and agreements between human nature on one side and social customs and rules on the other being *products* of specifiable modes of interaction. In a given community some individuals are in practical agreement with its existing institutions and others are in revolt—varying from a condition of moderate irritation and discontent to one of violent rebellion. The resulting differences when they are sufficiently marked to be labelled are the sources of the names conservative and radical, forward-looking or progressive and reactionary, etc. They cut across economic classes. For even revolutionaries have to admit that part of their problem is to create in an oppressed class consciousness of their servitude so as to arouse active protest.

This fact, so patent to even superficial observation, is sufficient disproof of the notion that the problem can be stated as one of the relation of *the* individual and *the* social, as if these names stood for any actual existences. It indicates that *ways of interaction* between human nature and

cultural conditions are the first and the fundamental thing
to be examined, and that the problem is to ascertain the
effects of interactions between different components of different human beings and different customs, rules, traditions, institutions—the things called "social." A fallacy has
controlled the traditional statement of the problem. It took
results, good or bad—or both—of specific interactions as if
they were original causes, on one side or the other, of what
existed or else of what should exist.

It is just as certain, for example, that slaves have at times
been contented with their estate of servitude as that a slave
class has existed. It is certain that persons who have personally experienced no discomfort—except that commonly
called moral—from existing conditions of oppression and
injustice have been leaders in campaigns for equality and
freedom. It is just as certain that inherent so-called social
"instincts" have led men to form criminal gangs marked by
certain mutual loyalties as that they have led men to cooperative activities. Now analytic observation of actual
interactions to determine the elements operative on each
side and their consequences is not easy in any case to execute. But recognition of its necessity is the condition of
adequate judgment of actual events. Estimate of the value
of any proposed policy is held back by taking the problem
as if it were one of individual "forces" on one side and of
social forces on the other, the nature of the forces being
known in advance. We must start from another set of premises if we are to put the problem of freedom in the context
where it belongs.

The questions which are asked at the beginning of the
last chapter are genuine questions. But they are not questions in the abstract and cannot be discussed in a wholesale
way. They are questions that demand discussion of cultural conditions, conditions of science, art, morals, religion,
education and industry, so as to discover which of them in
actuality promote and which retard the development of the

native constituents of human nature. If we want individuals to be free we must see to it that suitable conditions exist:—a truism which at least indicates the direction in which to look and move.

It tells us among other things to get rid of the ideas that lead us to believe that democratic conditions automatically maintain themselves, or that they can be identified with fulfillment of prescriptions laid down in a constitution. Beliefs of this sort merely divert attention from what is going on, just as the patter of the prestidigitator enables him to do things that are not noticed by those whom he is engaged in fooling. For what is actually going on may be the formation of conditions that are hostile to any kind of democratic liberties. This would be too trite to repeat were it not that so many persons in the high places of business talk as if they believed or could get others to believe that the observance of formulae that have become ritualistic are effective safeguards of our democratic heritage. The same principle warns us to beware of supposing that totalitarian states are brought about by factors so foreign to us that "It can't happen here";—to beware especially of the belief that these states rest only upon unmitigated coercion and intimidation. For in spite of the wide use of purges, executions, concentration camps, deprivation of property and of means of livelihood, no regime can endure long in a country where a scientific spirit has once existed unless it has the support of so-called idealistic elements in the human constitution. There is a tendency in some quarters to treat remarks of this sort as if they were a sort of apology or justification of dictatorships and totalitarian states. This way of reacting to an attempt to find out what it is that commends, at least for a time, totalitarian conditions to persons otherwise intelligent and honorable, is dangerous. It puts hate in place of attempt at understanding; hate once aroused can be directed by skillful manipulation against other objects than those which first aroused it. It also leads us to think that we

are immune from the disease to which others have given
way so long as the evil things we see in totalitarianism are
not known to be developing among us. The belief that only
such things operate to harm democracy keeps us from being
on our guard against the causes that may be at work undermining the values we nominally prize. It even leads us to
ignore beams in our own eyes such as our own racial preju-
dices.

It is extremely difficult at a distance to judge just what
are the appeals made to better elements in human nature
by, say, such policies as form the Nazi faith. We may believe that aside from appeal to fear; from desire to escape
responsibilities imposed by free citizenship; from impulses
to submission strengthened by habits of obedience bred in
the past; from desire for compensation for past humili-
ations, and from the action of nationalistic sentiments growing in intensity for over a century (and not in Germany
alone), there is also love for novelty which in this particular case has taken the form of idealistic faith, among the
youth in particular, of being engaged in creating a pattern
for new institutions which the whole world will in time
adopt. For one of the elements of human nature that is often discounted in both idea and practice is the satisfaction
derived from a sense of sharing in creative activities; the
satisfaction increasing in direct ratio to the scope of the
constructive work engaged in.

Other causes may be mentioned, though with the admission that it is quite possible in good faith to doubt or deny
their operation. There is the satisfaction that comes from
a sense of union with others, a feeling capable of being
intensified till it becomes a mystical sense of fusion with
others and being mistaken for love on a high level of manifestation. The satisfaction obtained by the sentiment of
communion with others, of the breaking down of barriers,
will be intense in the degree in which it has previously been
denied opportunity to manifest itself. The comparative ease

with which provincial loyalties, which in Germany had
been at least as intense and as influential as state-rights sentiments ever were in this country, were broken down; the
similar ease, though less in degree, with which habitual
religious beliefs and practices were subordinated to a feeling of racial and social union, would seem to testify that
underneath there was yearning for emotional fusion. Something of this kind showed itself in most countries when they
were engaged in the World War. For the time being it
seemed as if barriers that separated individuals from one
another had been swept away. Submission to abolition of
political parties and to abolition of labor unions which had
had great power, would hardly have come about so readily
had there not been some kind of a void which the new regime promised to fill. Just how far the fact of uniformity is
accompanied by a sense of equality in a nation where class
distinctions had been rigid, one can only guess at. But there
is considerable ground for believing that it has been a
strong factor in reconciling "humbler" folk to enforced deprivation of material benefits, so that, at least for a time, a
sense of honorable equality more than compensates for less
to eat, harder and longer hours of work—since it is psycho-
logically true that man does not live by bread alone.

It might seem as if belief in operation of "idealistic" factors was contradicted by the cruel persecutions that have
taken place, things indicative of a reign of sadism rather
than of desire for union with others irrespective of birth
and locale. But history shows that more than once social
unity has been promoted by the presence, real or alleged,
of some hostile group. It has long been a part of the technique of politicians who wish to maintain themselves in
power to foster the idea that the alternative is the danger of
being conquered by an enemy. Nor does what has been
suggested slur over in any way the effect of powerful and
unremitting propaganda. For the intention has been to indicate some of the conditions whose interaction produces the

social spectacle. Other powerful factors in the interaction
are those technologies produced by modern science which
have multiplied the means of modifying the dispositions of
the mass of the population; and which, in conjunction with
economic centralization, have enabled mass opinion to become like physical goods a matter of mass production. Here
also is both a warning and a suggestion to those concerned
with cultural conditions which will maintain democratic
freedom. The warning is obvious as to the role of propaganda, which now operates with us in channels less direct
and less official. The suggestion is that the printing press
and radio have made the problem of the intelligent and
honest use of means of communication in behalf of openly
declared public ends a matter of fundamental concern.

What has been said is stated by way of illustration, and
it may, if any one desires, be treated as hypothetical. For
even so, the suggestions serve to enforce the point that a
social regime can come into enduring existence only as it
satisfies some elements of human nature not previously afforded expression. On the other hand getting relief from
saturation of elements that have become stale makes almost
anything welcome if only it is different. The general principle holds even if the elements that are provided a new
outlet are the baser things in human nature: fear, suspicion,
jealousy, inferiority complexes; factors that were excited by
earlier conditions but that are now given channels of fuller
expression. Common observation, especially of the young,
shows that nothing is more exasperating and more resented
than stirring up certain impulses and tendencies and then
checking their manifestation. We should also note that a
period of uncertainty and insecurity, accompanied as it is
by more or less unsettlement and disturbance, creates a feeling that anything would be better than what exists, together
with desire for order and stability upon almost any terms—
the latter being a reason why revolutions are so regularly
followed by reaction, and explain the fact that Lenin ex-

pressed by saying revolutions are authoritative, though not for the reason he gave.

Just which of these factors are involved in our own maintenance of democratic conditions or whether any of them are so involved is, at this juncture, not so pertinent as is the principle they illustrate. Negatively speaking, we have to get away from the influence of belief in bald single forces, whether they are thought of as intrinsically psychological or sociological. This includes getting away from mere hatred of abominable things, and it also means refusing to fall back on such a generalized statement as that Fascist institutions are expressions of the sort of thing to be expected in a stage of contracting capitalism, since they are a kind of final spasm of protest against approaching dissolution. We cannot reject out of hand any cause assigned; it may have some truth. But the primary need is to escape from wholesale reasons, as totalitarian as are the states ruled by dictators. We have to analyze conditions by observations, which are as discriminating as they are extensive, until we discover specific interactions that are taking place, and learn to think in terms of interactions instead of force. We are led to search even for the conditions which have given the interacting factors the power they possess.

The lesson is far from being entirely new. The founders of American political democracy were not so naively devoted to pure theory that they were unaware of the necessity of cultural conditions for the successful working of democratic forms. I could easily fill pages from Thomas Jefferson in which he insists upon the necessity of a free press, general schooling and local neighborhood groups carrying on, through intimate meetings and discussions, the management of their own affairs, if political democracy was to be made secure. These sayings could be backed up by almost equally numerous expressions of his fears for the success of republican institutions in South American countries that had thrown off the Spanish yoke.

He expressly set forth his fear that their traditions were such that domestic military despotisms would be substituted for foreign subjugations. A background of "ignorance, bigotry and superstition" was not a good omen. On one occasion he even went so far as to suggest that the best thing that could happen would be for the South American states to remain under the nominal supremacy of Spain, under the collective guarantee of France, Russia, Holland and the United States, until experience in self-government prepared them for complete independence.

The real source of the weakness that has developed later in the position of our democratic progenitors is not that they isolated the problem of freedom from the positive conditions that would nourish it, but that they did not—and in their time could not—carry their analysis far enough. The outstanding examples of this inability are their faith in the public press and in schooling. They certainly were not wrong in emphasizing the need of a free press and of common public schools to provide conditions favorable to democracy. But to them the enemy of freedom of the press was official governmental censorship and control; they did not foresee the non-political causes that might restrict its freedom, nor the economic factors that would put a heavy premium on centralization. And they failed to see how education in literacy could become a weapon in the hands of an oppressive government, nor that the chief cause for promotion of elementary education in Europe would be increase of military power.

The inefficacy of education in general, that is, apart from constant attention to all the elements of its constitution, is illustrated in Germany itself. Its schools were so efficient that the country had the lowest rate of illiteracy in the world, the scholarship and scientific researches of its universities were known throughout the civilized globe. In fact it was not so many years ago that a distinguished American educator held them up as models to be followed in this country if the weaknesses of our higher institutions were to be remedied. Nevertheless German lower schools furnished the intellectual fodder for totalitarian propaganda, and the higher schools were the centers of reaction against the German Republic.

The illustrations are simple, and perhaps too familiar to carry much force. Nevertheless they proclaim that while free institutions over a wide territory are not possible without a mechanism, like the press, for quick and extensive communication of ideas and information, and without general literacy to take advantage of the mechanism, yet these very factors create a problem for a democracy instead of providing a final solution. Aside from the fact that the press may distract with trivialities or be an agent of a faction, or be an instrument of inculcating ideas in support of the hidden interest of a group or class (all in the name of public interest), the wide-world present scene is such that individuals are overwhelmed and emotionally confused by publicized reverberation of isolated events. And after a century of belief that the Common School system was bound by the very nature of its work to be what its earlier apostles called a "pillar of the republic," we are learning that everything about the public schools, its official agencies of control, organization and administration, the status of teachers, the subjects taught and methods of teaching them, the prevailing modes of discipline, set *problems;* and that the problems have been largely ignored as far as the relation of schools to democratic institutions is concerned. In fact the attention these things have received from various technical standpoints has been one reason why the central question has been obscured.

After many centuries of struggle and following of false gods, the natural sciences now possess methods by which particular facts and general ideas are brought into effective cooperation with one another. But with respect to means for understanding social events, we are still living in the pre-scientific epoch, although the events to be understood are the consequences of application of scientific knowledge to a degree unprecedented in history. With respect to information and understanding of social events, our state is that on one side of an immense number of undigested and unrelated facts, reported in isolation (and hence easily colored by some twist of interest) and large untested generalizations on the other side.

The generalizations are so general in the sense of remoteness from the events to which they are supposed to apply that they are matters of opinion, and frequently the rallying cries and slogans of factions and classes. They are often expressions of partisan desire clothed in the language of intellect. As matters of opinion, they are batted hither and yon in controversy and are subject to changes of popular fashion. They differ at practically every point from scientific generalizations, since the latter express the relations of facts to one another and, as they are employed to bring together more facts, are tested by the material to which they are applied.

If a glance at an editorial page of a newspaper shows what is meant by untested opinions put forth in the garb of the general principles of sound judgment, the items of the news columns illustrate what is meant by a multitude of diverse unrelated facts. The popular idea of "sensational," as it is derived from the daily press, is more instructive as to meaning of *sensations* than is the treatment accorded that subject in books on psychology. Events are sensational in the degree in which they make a strong impact in isolation from the relations to other events that give them their significance. They appeal to those who like things raw. Ordinary reports of murders, love nests, etc., are of this sort, with an artificial intensity supplied by unusual size or color of type. To say that a response is intellectual, not sensational, in the degree in which its significance is supplied by relations to other things is to state a truism.

They are two sets of words used to describe the same thing.

One effect of literacy under existing conditions has been to create in a large number of persons an appetite for the momentary "thrills" caused by impacts that stimulate nerve endings but whose connections with cerebral functions are broken. Then stimulation and excitation are not so ordered that intelligence is produced. At the same time the habit of using judgment is weakened by the habit of depending on external stimuli. Upon the whole it is probably a tribute to the powers of endurance of human nature that the consequences are not more serious than they are.

The new mechanisms resulting from application of scientific discoveries have, of course, immensely extended the range and variety of particular events, or "news items" which are brought to bear upon the senses and the emotions connected with them. The telegraph, telephone, and radio report events going on over the whole face of the globe. They are for the most part events about which the individuals who are told of them can do nothing, except to react with a passing emotional excitation. For, because of lack of relation and organization in reference to one another, no imaginative reproduction of the situation is possible, such as might make up for the absence of personal response. Before we engage in too much pity for the inhabitants of our rural regions before the days of invention of modern devices for circulation of information, we should recall that they knew more about the things that affected their own lives than the city dweller of today is likely to know about the causes of his affairs. They did not possess nearly as many separate items of information, but they were compelled to know, in the sense of *understanding*, the conditions that bore upon the conduct of their own affairs. Today the influences that affect the actions performed by individuals are so remote as to be unknown. We are at the mercy of events acting upon us in unexpected, abrupt, and violent ways.

The bearing of these considerations upon the cultural conditions involved in maintenance of freedom is not far to seek. It is very directly connected with what now seems to us the over-simplification of the democratic idea indulged in by the authors of our republican government. They had in mind persons whose daily occupations stimulated initiative and vigor, and who possessed information which even if narrow in scope, bore pretty directly upon what they had to do, while its sources were pretty much within their control. Their judgment was exercised upon things within the range of their activities and their contacts. The press, the telegraph, the telephone and radio have broadened indefinitely the range of information at the disposal of the average person. It would be foolish to deny that a certain quickening of sluggish minds has resulted. But quite aside from having opened avenues through which organized propaganda may operate continuously to stir emotion and to leave behind a deposit of opinion, there is much information about which judgment is not called upon to respond, and where even if it wanted to, it cannot act effectively so dispersive is the material about which it is called upon to exert itself. The average person is surrounded today by readymade intellectual goods as he is by readymade foods, articles, and all kinds of gadgets. He has not the personal share in making either intellectual or material goods that his pioneer ancestors had. Consequently they knew better what they themselves were about, though they knew infinitely less concerning what the world at large was doing.

Self-government of the town-meeting type is adequate for management of local affairs, such as school buildings, district revenues, school local roads and local taxation. Participation in these forms of self-government was a good preparation for self-government on a larger scale. But such matters as roads and schools under existing conditions have more than local import even in country districts; and while participation in town meetings is good as far as it arouses public spirit, it cannot provide the information that enables a citizen to be an intelligent judge of national affairs—now also affected by world conditions. Schooling in literacy is no substitute for the dispositions which were formerly provided by direct experiences of an educative quality. The void created by lack of relevant personal experiences combines with the confusion produced by impact of multitudes of unrelated incidents to create attitudes which are responsive to organized propaganda, hammering in day after day the same few and relatively simple beliefs asseverated to be "truths" essential to national welfare. In short, we have to take into account the attitudes of human nature that have been created by the immense development in mechanical instrumentalities if we are to understand the present power of organized propaganda.

The effect of the increase in number and diversity of unrelated facts that now play pretty continuously upon the average person is more easily grasped than is the influence of popular generalities, not checked by observed facts, over the interpretation put upon practical events, one that provokes acquiescence rather than critical inquiry. One chief reason for underestimation of the influence of generalities or "principles" is that they are so embodied in habits that those actuated by them are hardly aware of their existence. Or, if they are aware of them, they take them to be self-evident truths of common sense. When habits are so ingrained as to be second nature, they seem to have all of the inevitability that belongs to the movement of the fixed stars. The "principles" and standards which are stated in words and which circulate widely at a given time are usually only formulations of things which men do not so much believe in the intellectual sense of belief as live by unconsciously. Then when men who have lived under different conditions and have formed different life habits put forth different "principles," the latter are rejected as sources of some contagion introduced by foreigners hostile to our institutions.

Opinions are at once the most superficial and the most steel-plated of all human affairs. This difference between them is due to connection or lack of connection with habits that operate all but unconsciously. Verbal habits also exist and have power. Men continue to give assent to formulae after they have ceased to be more than linguistic rituals. Even lip-service has practical effect, that of creating intellectual and emotional divisions. The latter may not be deliberate hypocrisy. But they constitute that kind of insincerity, that incompatibility of actions with professions, which startles us in those cases in which it is clear that a person "believes" what he says in the sense that he is not even aware of its inconsistency with what he does. These gaps, these insincerities, become deeper and wider in times like the present when great change in events and practical affairs is attended with marked cultural lags in verbal formulations. And the persons who have first deceived themselves are most effective in misleading others. One of the most perplexing of human phenomena is the case of persons who do "in good faith" the sort of things which logical demonstration can easily prove to be incompatible with good faith.

Insincerities of this sort are much more frequent than deliberate hypocrisies and more injurious. They exist on a wide scale when there has been a period of rapid change in environment accompanied by change in what men do in response and by a change in overt habits, but without corresponding readjustment of the basic emotional and moral attitudes formed in the period prior to change of environment. This "cultural lag" is everywhere in evidence at the present time. The rate of change in conditions has been so much greater than anything the world has known before that it is estimated that the last century has seen more changes in the conditions under which people live and associate than occurred in thousands of previous years. The pace has been so swift that it was practically impossible for underlying traditions and beliefs to keep step. Not merely individuals here and there but large numbers of people habitually respond to conditions about them by means of actions having no connection with their familiar verbal responses. And yet the latter express dispositions saturated with emotions that find an outlet in words but not in acts.

No estimate of the effects of culture upon the elements that now make up freedom begins to be adequate that does not take into account the moral and religious splits that are found in our very make-up as persons. The problem of creation of genuine democracy cannot be successfully dealt with in theory or in practice save as we create intellectual and moral integration out of present disordered conditions. Splits, divisions, between attitudes emotionally and congenially attuned to the past and habits that are forced into existence because of the necessity of dealing with present conditions are a chief cause of continued profession of devotion to democracy by those who do not think nor act day by day in accord with the moral demands of the profession. The consequence is a further weakening of the environing conditions upon which genuine democracy occurs, whether the division is found in business men, in clergymen, in educators or in politicians. The serious threat to our democracy is not the existence of foreign totalitarian states. It is the existence within our own personal attitudes and within our own institutions of conditions similar to those which have given a victory to external authority, discipline, uniformity and dependence upon The Leader in foreign countries. The battlefield is also accordingly here—within ourselves and our institutions.

III. Democracy and America

I make no apology for linking what is said in this chapter with the name of Thomas Jefferson. For he was

the first modern to state in human terms the principles of
democracy. Were I to make an apology, it would be that in
the past I have concerned myself unduly, if a comparison
has to be made, with the English writers who have attempted to state the ideals of self-governing communities
and the methods appropriate to their realization. If I now
prefer to refer to Jefferson it is not, I hope, because of American provincialism, even though I believe that only one who
was attached to American soil and who took a consciously
alert part in the struggles of the country to attain its independence, could possibly have stated as thoroughly and
intimately as did Jefferson the aims embodied in the American tradition: "the definitions and axioms of a free government," as Lincoln called them. Nor is the chief reason for
going to him, rather than to Locke or Bentham or Mill, his
greater sobriety of judgment due to that constant tempering
of theory with practical experience which also kept his
democratic doctrine within human bounds.

The chief reason is that Jefferson's formulation is moral
through and through: in its foundations, its methods, its
ends. The heart of his faith is expressed in his words "Nothing is unchangeable but inherent and inalienable rights of
man." The words in which he stated the moral basis of free
institutions have gone out of vogue. We repeat the opening
words of the Declaration of Independence, but unless we
translate them they are couched in a language that, even
when it comes readily to our tongue, does not penetrate today to the brain. He wrote: "These truths are self-evident:
that all men are created equal; that they are endowed by
their Creator with inherent and unalienable rights; that
among these are life, liberty and the pursuit of happiness."
Today we are wary of anything purporting to be self-
evident truths; we are not given to associating politics with
the plans of the Creator; the doctrine of natural rights
which governed his style of expression has been weakened
by historic and by philosophic criticism.

To put ourselves in touch with Jefferson's position we have therefore to translate the word "natural" into *moral*. Jefferson was under the influence of the Deism of his time. Nature and the plans of a benevolent and wise Creator were never far apart in his reflections. But his fundamental beliefs remain unchanged in substance if we forget all special associations with the word *Nature* and speak instead of ideal aims and values to be realized—aims which, although ideal, are not located in the clouds but are backed by something deep and indestructible in the needs and demands of humankind.

Were I to try to connect in any detail what I have to say with the details of Jefferson's speeches and letters—he wrote no theoretical treatises—I should probably seem to be engaged in a partisan undertaking; I should at times be compelled to indulge in verbal exegesis so as to attribute to him ideas not present in his mind. Nevertheless, there are three points contained in what has to be said about American democracy that I shall here explicitly connect with his name. In the first place, in the quotation made, it was the *ends* of democracy, the rights of *man*—not of men in the plural—which are unchangeable. It was not the forms and mechanisms through which inherent moral claims are realized that are to persist without change. Professed Jeffersonians have often not even followed the words of the one whose disciples they say they are, much less his spirit. For he said: "I know that laws and institutions must go hand in hand with the progress of the human mind. . . . As new discoveries are made, new truths disclosed, and manners and opinions change with the change of circumstances, institutions must change also and keep pace with the times. We might as well require a man to wear the coat which fitted him when a boy, as civilized society to remain ever under the regime of their barbarous ancestors."

Because of the last sentence his idea might be interpreted to be a justification of the particular change in government he was championing against earlier institutions. But he goes on to say: "Each generation has a right to choose for itself the form of government it believes the most promotive of its own happiness." Hence he also said: "The idea that institutions established for the use of a nation cannot be touched or modified, even to make them answer their end . . . may perhaps be a salutary provision against the abuses of a monarch, but is most absurd against the nation itself." "A generation holds all the rights and powers their predecessors once held and may change their laws and institutions to suit themselves." He engaged in certain calculations based on Buffon, more ingenious than convincing, to settle upon a period of eighteen years and eight months that fixed the natural span of the life of a generation; thereby indicating the frequency with which it is desirable to overhaul "laws and institutions" to bring them into accord with "new discoveries, new truths, change of manners and opinions." The word *culture* is not used; Jefferson's statement would have been weakened by its use. But it is not only professed followers of Jefferson who have failed to act upon his teaching. It is true of all of us so far as we have set undue store by established mechanisms. The most flagrantly obvious violation of Jefferson's democratic point of view is found in the idolatry of the Constitution as it stands that has been sedulously cultivated. But it goes beyond this instance. As believers in democracy we have not only the right but the duty to question existing mechanisms of, say, suffrage and to inquire whether some functional organization would not serve to formulate and manifest public opinion better than the existing methods. It is not irrelevant to the point that a score of passages could be cited in which Jefferson refers to the American Government as an *experiment*.

The second point of which I would speak is closely bound up with an issue which has become controversial and partisan, namely, states rights versus federal power. There is no question of where Jefferson stood on that issue, nor as to

his fear in general of governmental encroachment on liberty
—inevitable in his case, since it was the cause of the Rebellion against British domination and was also the ground of
his struggle against Hamiltonianism. But any one who stops
with this particular aspect of Jefferson's doctrine misses an
underlying principle of utmost importance. For while he
stood for state action as a barrier against excessive power
at Washington, and while on the *practical side* his concern
with it was most direct, in his theoretical writings chief importance is attached to local self-governing units on something like the New England town-meeting plan. His project
for general political organization on the basis of small units,
small enough so that all its members could have direct communication with one another and take care of all community affairs was never acted upon. It never received much
attention in the press of immediate practical problems.

But without forcing the significance of this plan, we may
find in it an indication of one of the most serious of present
problems regarding democracy. I spoke earlier of the way
in which individuals at present find themselves in the grip
of immense forces whose workings and consequences they
have no power of affecting. The situation calls emphatic
attention to the need for face-to-face associations, whose
interactions with one another may offset if not control the
dread impersonality of the sweep of present forces. There
is a difference between a society, in the sense of an association, and a community. Electrons, atoms and molecules are
in association with one another. Nothing exists in isolation
anywhere throughout nature. Natural associations are conditions for the existence of a community, but a community
adds the function of communication in which emotions
and ideas are shared as well as joint undertakings engaged
in. Economic forces have immensely widened the scope of
associational activities. But it has done so largely at the
expense of the intimacy and directness of communal group
interests and activities. The American habit of "joining"

is a tribute to the reality of the problem but has not gone far in solving it. The power of the rabblerouser, especially in the totalitarian direction, is mainly due to his power to create a factitious sense of direct union and communal solidarity—if only by arousing the emotion of common intolerance and hate.

I venture to quote words written some years ago: "Evils which are uncritically and indiscriminately laid at the door of industrialism and democracy might, with greater intelligence, be referred to the dislocation and unsettlement of local communities. Vital and thorough attachments are bred only in the intimacy of an intercourse which is of necessity restricted in range. . . . Is it possible to restore the reality of the less communal organizations and to penetrate and saturate their members with a sense of local community life? . . . Democracy must begin at home, and its home is the neighborly community." * On account of the vast extension of the field of association, produced by elimination of distance and lengthening of temporal spans, it is obvious that social agencies, political and non-political, cannot be confined to localities. But the problem of harmonious adjustment between extensive activities, precluding direct contacts, and the intensive activities of community intercourse is a pressing one for democracy. It involves even more than apprenticeship in the practical processes of self-government, important as that is, which Jefferson had in mind. It involves development of local agencies of communication and cooperation, creating stable loyal attachments, to militate against the centrifugal forces of present culture, while at the same time they are of a kind to respond flexibly to the demands of the larger unseen and indefinite public. To a very considerable extent, groups having a functional basis will probably have to replace those based on physical contiguity. In the family both factors combine.

* *The Public and Its Problems*, pp. 212-213.

The third point of which I would make express mention as to Jefferson and democracy has to do with his ideas about property. It would be absurd to hold that his personal views were "radical" beyond fear of concentrated wealth and a positive desire for general distribution of wealth without great extremes in either direction. However, it is sometimes suggested that his phrase "pursuit of happiness" stood for economic activity, so that life, liberty, and property were the rights he thought organized society should maintain. But just here is where he broke most completely with Locke. In connection with property, especially property in land, he makes his most positive statements about the inability of any generation to bind its successors. Jefferson held that property rights are created by the "social pact" instead of representing inherent individual moral claims which government is morally bound to maintain.

The right to pursue happiness stood with Jefferson for nothing less than the claim of every human being to choose his own career and to act upon his own choice and judgment free from restraints and constraints imposed by the arbitrary will of other human beings—whether these others are officials of government, of whom Jefferson was especially afraid, or are persons whose command of capital and control of the opportunities for engaging in useful work limits the ability of others to "pursue happiness." The Jeffersonian principle of equality of rights without special favor to any one justifies giving supremacy to personal rights when they come into conflict with property rights. While his views are properly enough cited against ill-considered attacks upon the economic relations that exist at a given time, it is sheer perversion to hold that there is anything in Jeffersonian democracy that forbids political action to bring about equalization of economic conditions in order that the equal right of all to free choice and free action be maintained.

I have referred with some particularity to Jefferson's ideas upon special points because of the proof they afford that the source of the American democratic tradition is moral—not technical, abstract, narrowly political nor materially utilitarian. It is moral because based on faith in the ability of human nature to achieve freedom for individuals accompanied with respect and regard for other persons and with social stability built on cohesion instead of coercion. Since the tradition is a moral one, attacks upon it, however they are made, wherever they come from, from within or from without, involve moral issues and can be settled only upon moral grounds. In as far as the democratic ideal has undergone eclipse among us, the obscuration is moral in source and effect. The dimming is both a product and a manifestation of the confusion that accompanies transition from an old order to a new one for the arrival of the latter was heralded only as conditions plunged it into an economic regime so novel that there was no adequate preparation for it and which dislocated the established relations of persons with one another.

Nothing is gained by attempts to minimize the novelty of the democratic order, nor the scope of the change it requires in old and long cherished traditions. We have not even as yet a common and accepted vocabulary in which to set forth the order of moral values involved in realization of democracy. The language of Natural Law was once all but universal in educated Christendom. The conditions which gave it force disappeared. Then there was an appeal to natural rights, supposed by some to center in isolated individuals—although not in the original American formulation. At present, appeal to the individual is dulled by our inability to locate the individual with any assurance. While we are compelled to note that his freedom can be maintained only through the working together toward a single end of a large number of different and complex factors, we do not know how to coordinate them on the basis of voluntary purpose.

The intimate association that was held to exist between

individualism and business activity for private profit gave, on one side, a distorted meaning to individualism. Then the weakening, even among persons who nominally retain older theological beliefs, of the imaginative ideas and emotions connected with the sanctity of the individual, disturbed democratic individualism on the positive moral side. The moving energy once associated with things called spiritual has lessened; we use the word *ideal* reluctantly, and have difficulty in giving the word *moral* much force beyond, say, a limited field of mutually kindly relations among individuals. That such a syllogism as the following once had a vital meaning to a man of affairs like Jefferson today seems almost incredible: "Man was created for social intercourse, but social intercourse cannot be maintained without a sense of justice; then man must have been created with a sense of justice."

Even if we have an abiding faith in democracy, we are not likely to express it as Jefferson expressed his faith: "I have no fear but that the result of our experiment will be that men may be trusted to govern themselves without a master. Could the contrary of this be proved, I should conclude either there is no God or that he is a malevolent being." The belief of Jefferson that the sole legitimate object of government among men "is to secure the greatest degree of happiness possible to the general mass of those associated under it" was connected with his belief that Nature—or God—benevolent in intent, had created men for happiness on condition they attained knowledge of natural order and observed the demands of that knowledge in their actions. The obsolescence of the language for many persons makes it the more imperative for all who would maintain and advance the ideals of democracy to face the issue of the moral ground of political institutions and the moral principles by which men acting together may attain freedom of individuals which will amount to fraternal associations with one another. The weaker our faith in Nature, in its laws and rights and its benevolent intentions for human welfare, the more urgent is the need for a faith based on ideas that are now intellectually credible and that are consonant with present economic conditions, which will inspire and direct action with something of the ardor once attached to things religious.

Human power over the physical energies of nature has immensely increased. In moral ideal, power of man over physical nature should be employed to reduce, to eliminate progressively, the power of man over man. By what means shall we prevent its use to effect new, more subtle, more powerful agencies of subjection of men to other men? Both the issue of war or peace between nations, and the future of economic relations for years and generations to come in contribution either to human freedom or human subjection are involved. An increase of power undreamed of a century ago, one to whose further increase no limits can be put as long as scientific inquiry goes on, is an established fact. The thing still uncertain is what we are going to do with it. That it is power signifies of itself it is electrical, thermic, chemical. What will be done with it is a moral issue.

Physical interdependence has increased beyond anything that could have been foreseen. Division of labor in industry was anticipated and was looked forward to with satisfaction. But it is relatively the least weighty phase of the present situation. The career of individuals, their lives and security as well as prosperity is now affected by events on the other side of the world. The forces back of these events he cannot touch or influence—save perhaps by joining in a war of nations against nations. For we seem to live in a world in which nations try to deal with the problems created by the new situation by drawing more and more into themselves, by more and more extreme assertions of independent nationalist sovereignty, while everything they do in the direction of autarchy leads to ever closer mixture with other nations—but in war.

War under existing conditions compels nations, even those professedly the most democratic, to turn authoritarian and totalitarian as the World War of 1914-18 resulted in Fascist totalitarianism in non-democratic Italy and Germany and in Bolshevist totalitarianism in non-democratic Russia, and promoted political, economic and intellectual reaction in this country. The necessity of transforming physical interdependence into moral—into human—interdependence is part of the democratic problem: and yet war is said even now to be the path of salvation for democratic countries!

Individuals can find the security and protection that are prerequisites for freedom only in association with others— and then the organization these associations take on, as a measure of securing their efficiency, limits the freedom of those who have entered into them. The importance of organization has increased so much in the last hundred years that the word is now quite commonly used as a synonym for association and society. Since at the very best organization is but the mechanism through which association operates, the identification is evidence of the extent in which a servant has become a master; in which means have usurped the place of the end for which they are called into existence. The predicament is that individuality demands association to develop and sustain it and association requires arrangement and coordination of its elements, or organization—since otherwise it is formless and void of power. But we have now a kind of molluscan organization, soft individuals within and a hard constrictive shell without. Individuals voluntarily enter associations which have become practically nothing but organizations; and then conditions under which they act take control of what they do whether they want it or not.

Persons acutely aware of the dangers of regimentation when it is imposed by government remain oblivious of the millions of persons whose behavior is regimented by an economic system through whose intervention alone they obtain a livelihood. The contradiction is the more striking because the new organizations were for the most part created in the name of freedom, and, at least at the outset, by exercise of voluntary choice. But the kind of working-together which has resulted is too much like that of the parts of a machine to represent a cooperation which expresses freedom and also contributes to it. No small part of the democratic problem is to achieve associations whose ordering of parts provides the strength that comes from stability, while they promote flexibility of response to change.

Lastly, in this brief survey, there is the problem of the relation of human nature and physical nature. The ancient world solved the problem, in abstract philosophical theory, by endowing all nature, in its cosmic scope, with the moral qualities of the highest and most ideal worth in humanity. The theology and rites of the Church gave this abstract theory direct significance in the lives of the peoples of the western world. For it provided practical agencies by means of which the operation of the power creating and maintaining the universe were supposed to come to the support of individuals in this world and the next. The rise of physical science rendered an ever increasing number of men skeptical of the intellectual foundation provided by the old theory. The unsettlement, going by the name of the conflict of science and religion, proves the existence of the division in the foundations upon which our culture rests, between ideas in the form of knowledge and ideas that are emotional and imaginative and that directly actuate conduct.

This disturbance on the moral side has been enormously aggravated by those who are remote from the unsettlement due to intellectual causes. It comes home to everyone by the effects of the practical application of the new physical

science. For all the physical features of the present regime
of production and distribution of goods and services are
products of the new physical science, while the distinctively
human consequences of science are still determined by
habits and beliefs established before its origin. That democracy should not as yet have succeeded in healing the breach
is no cause for discouragement: provided there is effected
a union of human possibilities and ideals with the spirit and
methods of science on one side and with the workings of the
economic system on the other side. For a considerable period *laissez-faire* individualism prevented the problem from
being even seen. It treated the new economic movement as
if it were simply an expresson of forces that were fundamental in the human constitution but were only recently
released for free operation. It failed to see that the great expansion which was occurring was in fact due to release of
physical energies; that as far as human action and human
freedom is concerned, a problem, not a solution, was
thereby instituted: the problem, namely, of management
and direction of the new physical energies so they would
contribute to realizaticn of human possibilities.

The reaction that was created by the inevitable collapse
of a movement that failed so disastrously in grasp of the
problem has had diverse results, the diversity of which is
part of the present confused state of our lives. Production
of the material means of a secure and free life has been
indefinitely increased and at an accelerated rate. It is not
surprising that there is a large group which attributes the
gains which have accrued, actually and potentially, to the
economic regime under which they have occurred—instead
of to the scientific knowledge which is the source of physical control of natural energies. The group is large. It is composed not only of the immediate beneficiaries of the system
but also of the much larger number who hope that they, or
at least their children, are to have full share in its benefits.
Because of the opportunities furnished by free land, large

unused natural resources and the absence of fixed class differences (which survive in European countries in spite of
legal abolition of feudalism), this group is particularly large
in this country. It is represented by those who point to the
higher standard of living in this country and by those who
have responded to the greater opportunities for advancement this country has afforded to them. In short, this group,
in both categories of its constituents, is impressed by actual
gains that have come about. They have a kind of blind and
touching faith that improvement is going to continue in
some more or less automatic way until it includes them and
their offspring.

Then there is a much smaller group who are as sensitive,
perhaps more so, to the immense possibilities represented
by the physical means now potentially at our command,
but who are acutely aware of our failure to realize them;
who see instead the miseries, cruelties, oppressions and frus-
trations which exist. The weakness of this group has been
that it has also failed to realize the involvement of the new
scientific method in producing the existing state of affairs,
and the need for its further extensive and unremitting application to determine analytically—in detail—the causes
of present ills, and to project means for their elimination.
In social affairs, the wholesale mental attitude that has
been referred to persists with little change. It leads to formation of ambitious and sweeping beliefs and policies. The
human *ideal* is indeed comprehensive. As a standpoint from
which to view existing conditions and judge the direction
change should take, it cannot be too inclusive. But the problem of production of change is one of infinite attention to
means; and means can be determined only by definite analysis of the conditions of each problem as it presents itself.
Health is a comprehensive, a "sweeping" ideal. But progress
toward it has been made in the degree in which recourse to
panaceas has been abandoned and inquiry has been
directed to determinate disturbances and means for dealing

with them. The group is represented at its extreme by those who believe there is a necessary historical law which governs the course of events so that all that is needed is deliberate acting in accord with it. The law by which class conflict produces by its own dialectic its complete opposite becomes then the supreme and sole regulator for determining policies and methods of action.

That more adequate knowledge of human nature is demanded if the release of physical powers is to serve human ends is undeniable. But it is a mistake to suppose that this knowledge of itself enables us to control human energies as physical science has enabled us to control physical energies. It suffers from the fallacy into which those have fallen who have supposed that physical energies put at our disposal by science are sure to produce human progress and prosperity. A more adequate science of human nature might conceivably only multiply the agencies by which some human beings manipulate other human beings for their own advantage. Failure to take account of the moral phase of the problem, the question of values and ends, marks, although from the opposite pole, a relapse into the fallacy of the theorists of a century ago who assumed that "free"—that is to say, politically unrestrained—manifestation of human wants and impulses would tend to bring about social prosperity, progress, and harmony. It is a counterpart fallacy to the Marxist notion that there is an economic or "materialistic," dialectic of history by which a certain desirable (and in that sense moral) end will be brought about with no intervention of choice of values and effort to realize them. As I wrote some years ago, "the assimilation of human science to physical science represents only another form of absolutistic logic, a kind of physical absolutism."

Social events will continue, in any case, to be products of interaction of human nature with cultural conditions. Hence the primary and fundamental question will always be what sort of social results we supremely want. Improved science of human nature would put at our disposal means, now lacking, for defining the problem and working effectively for its solution. But save as it should reinforce respect for the morale of science, and thereby extend and deepen the incorporation of the attitudes which form the method of science into the disposition of individuals, it might add a complication similar to that introduced by improved physical science. Anything that obscures the fundamentally moral nature of the social problem is harmful, no matter whether it proceeds from the side of physical or of psychological theory. Any doctrine that eliminates or even obscures the function of choice of values and enlistment of desires and emotions in behalf of those chosen weakens personal responsibility for judgment and for action. It thus helps create the attitudes that welcome and support the totalitarian state.

I have stated in bare outline some of the outstanding phases of the problem of culture in the service of democratic freedom. Difficulties and obstacles have been emphasized. This emphasis is a result of the fact that a *problem* is presented. Emphasis upon the problem is due to belief that many weaknesses which events have disclosed are connected with failure to see the immensity of the task involved in setting mankind upon the democratic road. That with a background of millennia of non-democratic societies behind them, the earlier advocates of democracy tremendously simplified the issue is natural. For a time the simplification was an undoubted asset. Too long continued it became a liability.

Recognition of the scope and depth of the problem is neither depressing nor discouraging when the democratic movement is placed in historic perspective. The ideas by which it formulated itself have a long history behind them. We can trace their source in Hellenic humanism and in Christian beliefs; and we can also find recurrent efforts to realize this or that special aspect of these ideas in some special struggle against a particular form of oppression. By proper selection and arrangement, we can even make out a case for the idea that all past history has been a movement, at first unconscious and then conscious, to attain freedom. A more sober view of history discloses that it took a very fortunate conjunction of events to bring about the rapid spread and seemingly complete victory of democracy during the nineteenth century. The conclusion to be drawn is not the depressing one that it is now in danger of destruction because of an unfavorable conjunction of events. The conclusion is that what was won in a more or less external and accidental manner must now be achieved and sustained by deliberate and intelligent endeavor.

The contrast thus suggested calls attention to the fact that underlying persistent attitudes of human beings were formed by traditions, customs, institutions, which existed when there was no democracy—when in fact democratic ideas and aspirations tended to be strangled at birth. Persistence of these basic dispositions accounts, on one side, for the sudden attack upon democracy; it is a reversion to old emotional and intellectual habits; or rather it is not so much a reversion as it is a manifestation of attitudes that have been there all the time but have been more or less covered up. Their persistence also explains the depth and range of the present problem. The struggle for democracy has to be maintained on as many fronts as culture has aspects: political, economic, international, educational, scientific and artistic, religious. The fact that we now have to accomplish of set purpose what in an earlier period was more or less a gift of grace renders the problem a moral one to be worked out on moral grounds.

Part of the fortunate conjunction of circumstances with respect to us who live here in the United States consists, as has been indicated, of the fact that our forefathers found themselves in a new land. The shock of physical dislocation effected a very considerable modification of old attitudes. Habits of thought and feeling which were the products of long centuries of acculturation were loosened. Less entrenched dispositions dropped off. The task of forming new institutions was thereby rendered immensely easier. The readjustment thus effected has been a chief factor in creating a general attitude of adaptability that has enabled us, save for the Civil War, to meet change with a minimum of external conflict and, in spite of an heritage of violence, with good nature. It is because of such consequences that the geographical New World may become a New World in a human sense. But, all the more on this account, the situation is such that most of the things about which we have been complacent and self-congratulatory now have to be won by thought and effort, instead of being results of evolution of a manifest destiny.

In the present state of affairs, a conflict of the moral Old and New Worlds is the essence of the struggle for democracy. It is not a question for us of isolationism, although the physical factors which make possible physical isolation from the warring ambitions of Europe are a factor to be cherished in an emergency. The conflict is not one waged with arms, although the question whether we again take up arms on European battlefields for ends that are foreign to the ends to which this country is dedicated will have weight in deciding whether we win or lose our own battle on our own ground. It is possible to stay out for reasons that have nothing to do with the maintenance of democracy, and a good deal to do with pecuniary profit, just as it is possible to be deluded into participation in the name of fighting for democracy.

The conflict as it concerns the democracy to which our history commits us is *within* our own institutions and attitudes. It can be won only by extending the application of democratic methods, methods of consultation, persuasion, negotiation, communication, cooperative intelligence, in the task of making our own politics, industry, education, our culture generally, a servant and an evolving manifestation of democratic ideas. Resort to military force is a first sure sign that we are giving up the struggle for the democratic way of life, and that the Old World has conquered morally as well as geographically—succeeding in imposing upon us its ideals and methods.

If there is one conclusion to which human experience unmistakably points it is that democratic ends demand democratic methods for their realization. Authoritarian methods now offer themselves to us in new guises. They come to us claiming to serve the ultimate ends of freedom and equity in a classless society. Or they recommend adoption of a totalitarian regime in order to fight totalitarianism. In whatever form they offer themselves, they owe their seductive power to their claim to serve ideal ends. Our first defense is to realize that democracy can be served only by the slow day by day adoption and contagious diffusion in every phase of our common life of methods that are identical with the ends to be reached and that recourse to monistic, wholesale, absolutist procedures is a betrayal of human freedom no matter in what guise it presents itself. An American democracy can serve the world only as it demonstrates in the conduct of its own life the efficacy of plural, partial, and experimental methods in securing and maintaining an ever-increasing release of the powers of human nature, in service of a freedom which is cooperative and a cooperation which is voluntary.

We have no right to appeal to time to justify complacency about the ultimate result. We have every right to point to the long non-democratic and anti-democratic course of human history and to the recentness of democracy in order to enforce the immensity of the task confronting us. The very novelty of the experiment explains the impossibility of restricting the problem to any one element, aspect, or phase of our common everyday life. We have every right to appeal to the long and slow process of time to protect our- selves from the pessimism that comes from taking a short- span temporal view of events—under one condition. We must know that the dependence of ends upon means is such that the only *ultimate* result is the result that is attained today, tomorrow, the next day, and day after day, in the succession of years and generations. Only thus can we be sure that we face our problems in detail one by one as they arise, with all the resources provided by collective intelli- gence operating in cooperative action. At the end as at the beginning the democratic method is as fundamentally simple and as immensely difficult as is the energetic, un- flagging, unceasing creation of an ever-present new road upon which we can walk together.

VII ♦ The Religion of Shared Experience

I. Faith and Its Object*

The aims and ideals that move us are generated through imagination. But they are not made out of imaginary stuff. They are made out of the hard stuff of the world of physical and social experience. The locomotive did not exist before Stevenson, nor the telegraph before the time of Morse. But the conditions for their existence were there in physical material and energies and in human capacity. Imagination seized hold upon the idea of a rearrangement of existing things that would evolve new objects. The same thing is true of a painter, a musician, a poet, a philanthropist, a moral prophet. The new vision does not arise out of nothing, but emerges through seeing, in terms of possibilities, that is, of imagination, old things in new relations serving a new end which the new end aids in creating.

Moreover the process of creation is experimental and continuous. The artist, scientific man, or good citizen, depends upon what others have done before him and are doing around him. The sense of new values that become ends to be realized arises first in dim and uncertain form. As the values are dwelt upon and carried forward in action they grow in definiteness and coherence. Interaction between aim and existent conditions improves and tests the ideal; and condi-

---

* From *A Common Faith*. New Haven: Yale University Press, 1934. By permission of Yale University Press.

tions are at the same time modified. Ideals change as they are applied in existent conditions. The process endures and advances with the life of humanity. What one person and one group accomplish becomes the standing ground and starting point of those who succeed them. When the vital factors in this natural process are generally acknowledged in emotion, thought and action, the process will be both accelerated and purified through elimination of that irrelevant element that culminates in the idea of the supernatural. When the vital factors attain the religious force that has been drafted into supernatural religions, the resulting reinforcement will be incalculable.

These considerations may be applied to the idea of God, or, to avoid misleading conceptions, to the idea of the divine. This idea is, as I have said, one of ideal possibilities unified through imaginative realization and projection. But this idea of God, or of the divine, is also connected with all the natural forces and conditions—including man and human association—that promote the growth of the ideal and that further its realization. We are in the presence neither of ideals completely embodied in existence nor yet of ideals that are mere rootless ideals, fantasies, utopias. For there are forces in nature and society that generate and support the ideals. They are further unified by the action that gives them coherence and solidity. It is this *active* relation between ideal and actual to which I would give the name "God." I would not insist that the name *must* be given. There are those who hold that the associations of the term with the supernatural are so numerous and close that any use of the word "God" is sure to give rise to misconception and be taken as a concession to traditional ideas.

They may be correct in this view. But the facts to which I have referred are there, and they need to be brought out with all possible clearness and force. There exist concretely and experimentally goods—the values of art in all its forms, of knowedge, of effort and of rest after striving, of education and fellowship, of friendship and love, of growth in mind and body. These goods are there and yet they are relatively embryonic. Many persons are shut out from generous participation in them; there are forces at work that threaten and sap existent goods as well as prevent their expansion. A clear and intense conception of a union of ideal ends with actual conditions is capable of arousing steady emotion. It may be fed by every experience, no matter what its material.

In a distracted age, the need for such an idea is urgent. It can unify interests and energies now dispersed; it can direct action and generate the heat of emotion and the light of intelligence. Whether one gives the name "God" to this union, operative in thought and action, is a matter for individual decision. But the *function* of such a working union of the ideal and actual seems to me to be identical with the force that has in fact been attached to the conception of God in all the religions that have a spiritual content; and a clear idea of that function seems to me urgently needed at the present time.

The sense of this union may, with some persons, be furthered by mystical experiences, using the term "mystical" in its broadest sense. That result depends largely upon temperament. But there is a marked difference between the union associated with mysticism and the union which I had in mind. There is nothing mystical about the latter; it is natural and moral. Nor is there anything mystical about the perception or consciousness of such union. Imagination of ideal ends pertinent to actual conditions represents the fruition of a disciplined mind. There is, indeed, even danger that resort to mystical experiences will be an escape, and that its result will be the passive feeling that the union of actual and ideal is already accomplished. But in fact this union is active and practical; it is a *uniting*, not something given.

One reason why personally I think it fitting to use the word "God" to denote that uniting of the ideal and actual which has been spoken of, lies in the fact that aggressive atheism seems to me to have something in common with traditional supernaturalism. I do not mean merely that the former is mainly so negative that it fails to give positive direction to thought, though that fact is pertinent. What I have in mind especially is the exclusive preoccupation of both militant atheism and supernaturalism with man in isolation. For in spite of supernaturalism's reference to something beyond nature, it conceives of this earth as the moral center of the universe and of man as the apex of the whole scheme of things. It regards the drama of sin and redemption enacted within the isolated and lonely soul of man as the one thing of ultimate importance. Apart from man, nature is held either accursed or negligible. Militant atheism is also affected by lack of natural piety. The ties binding man to nature that poets have always celebrated are passed over lightly. The attitude taken is often that of man living in an indifferent and hostile world and issuing blasts of defiance. A religious attitude, however, needs the sense of a connection of man, in the way of both dependence and support, with the enveloping world that the imagination feels is a universe. Use of the words "God" or "divine" to convey the union of actual with ideal may protect man from a sense of isolation and from consequent despair or defiance.

II. THE HUMAN ABODE OF THE RELIGIOUS FUNCTION

The emphasis that has been put upon intelligence as a method should not mislead anyone. Intelligence, as distinct from the older conception of reason, is inherently involved in action. Moreover, there is no opposition between it and emotion. There is such a thing as passionate intelligence, as ardor in behalf of light shining into the murky places of social existence, and as zeal for its refreshing and purifying effect. The whole story of man shows that there are no objects that may not deeply stir engrossing emotion. One of the few experiments in the attachment of emotion to ends that mankind has not tried is that of devotion, so intense as to be religious, to intelligence as a force in social action.

But this is only part of the scene. No matter how much evidence may be piled up against social institutions as they exist, affection and passionate desire for justice and security are realities in human nature. So are the emotions that arise from living in conditions of inequity, oppression, and insecurity. Combination of the two kinds of emotion has more than once produced those changes that go by the name of revolution. To say that emotions which are not fused with intelligence are blind is tautology. Intense emotion may utter itself in action that destroys institutions. But the only assurance of birth of better ones is the marriage of emotion with intelligence.

Criticism of the commitment of religion to the supernatural is thus positive in import. All modes of human association are "affected with a public interest," and full realization of this interest is equivalent to a sense of a significance that is religious in its function. The objection to supernaturalism is that it stands in the way of an effective realization of the sweep and depth of the implications of natural human relations. It stands in the way of using the means that are in our power to make radical changes in these relations. It is certainly true that great material changes might be made with no corresponding improvement of a spiritual or ideal nature. But development in the latter direction cannot be introduced from without; it cannot be brought about by dressing up material and economic changes with decorations derived from the supernatural. It can come only from more intense realization of values that inhere in the actual connections of human beings with one another. The attempt to segregate the implicit public interest and social value of all institutions and social arrangements in a particular organization is a fatal diversion.

Were men and women actuated throughout the length and breadth of human relations with the faith and ardor that have at times marked historic religions the consequences would be incalculable. To achieve this faith and *élan* is no easy task. But religions have attempted something similar, directed moreover toward a less promising object—the supernatural. It does not become those who hold that faith may move mountains to deny in advance the possibility of its manifestation on the basis of verifiable realities. There already exists, though in a rudimentary form, the capacity to relate social conditions and events to their causes, and the ability will grow with exercise. There is the technical skill with which to initiate a campaign for social health and sanity analogous to that made in behalf of physical public health. Human beings have impulses toward affection, compassion and justice, equality and freedom. It remains to weld all these things together. It is of no use merely to assert that the intrenched foes of class interest and power in high places are hostile to the realization of such a union. As I have already said, if this enemy did not exist, there would be little sense in urging *any* policy of change. The point to be grasped is that, unless one gives up the whole struggle as hopeless, one has to choose between alternatives. One alternative is dependence upon the supernatural; the other, the use of natural agencies.

There is then no sense, logical or practical, in pointing out the difficulties that stand in the way of the latter course, until the question of the alternative is faced. If it is faced, it will also be realized that one factor in the choice is dependence upon enlisting only those committed to the supernatural and alliance with all men and women who feel the stir of social emotion, including the large number of those who, consciously or unconsciously, have turned their backs upon the supernatural. Those who face the alternatives will also have to choose between a continued and even more systematic *laissez faire* depreciation of intelligence and the resources of natural knowledge and understanding, and conscious and organized effort to turn the use of these means from narrow ends, personal and class, to larger human purposes. They will have to ask, as far as they nominally believe in the need for radical social change, whether what they accomplish when they point with one hand to the seriousness of present evils is not undone when the other hand points away from man and nature for their remedy.

The transfer of idealizing imagination, thought and emotion to natural human relations would not signify the destruction of churches that now exist. It would rather offer the means for a recovery of the vitality. The fund of human values that are prized and that need to be cherished, values that are satisfied and rectified by *all* human concerns and arrangements, could be celebrated and reinforced, in different ways and with differing symbols, by the churches. In that way the churches would indeed become catholic. The demand that churches show a more active interest in social affairs, that they take a definite stand upon such questions as war, economic injustice, political corruption, that they stimulate action for a divine kingdom on earth, is one of the signs of the times. But as long as social values are related to a supernatural for which the churches stand in some peculiar way, there is an inherent inconsistency between the demand and efforts to execute it. On the one hand, it is urged that the churches are going outside their special province when they involve themselves in economic and political issues. On the other hand, the very fact that they claim if not a monopoly of supreme values and motivating forces, yet a unique relation to them, makes it impossible for the churches to participate in promotion of social ends on a natural and equal human basis. The surrender of claims to an exclusive and authoritative position is a *sine qua non* for doing away with the dilemma in which churches now find themselves in respect to their sphere of social action.

At the outset, I referred to an outstanding historic fact. The coincidence of the realm of social interests and activities with a tribal or civic community has vanished. Secular interests and activities have grown up outside of organized religions and are independent of their authority. The hold of these interests upon the thoughts and desires of men has crowded the social importance of organized religions into a corner and the area of this corner is decreasing. This change either marks a terrible decline in everything that can justly be termed religious in value, in traditional religions, or it provides the opportunity for expansion of these qualities on a new basis and with a new outlook. It is impossible to ignore the fact that historic Christianity has been committed to a separation of sheep and goats; the saved and the lost; the elect and the mass. Spiritual aristocracy as well as *laissez faire* with respect to natural and human intervention, is deeply embedded in its traditions. Lip service—often more than lip service—has been given to the idea of the common brotherhood of all men. But those outside the fold of the church and those who do not rely upon belief in the supernatural have been regarded as only potential brothers, still requiring adoption into the family. I cannot understand how any realization of the democratic ideal as a vital moral and spiritual ideal in human affairs is possible without surrender of the conception of the basic division to which supernatural Christianity is committed. Whether or no we are, save in some metaphorical sense, all brothers, we are at least all in the same boat traversing the same turbulent ocean. The potential religious significance of this fact is infinite.

In the opening chapter I made a distinction between religion and the religious. I pointed out that religion—or religions—is charged with beliefs, practices and modes of organization that have accrued to and been loaded upon the religious element in experience by the state of culture in which religions have developed. I urged that conditions are now ripe for emancipation of the religious quality from accretions that have grown up about it and that limit the creditability and the influence of religion. In the second chapter, I developed this idea with respect to the faith in ideals that is immanent in the religious value of experience, and asserted that the power of this faith would be enhanced were belief freed from the conception that the significance and validity of the ideal are bound up with intellectual assent to the proposition that the ideal is already embodied in some supernatural or metaphysical sense in the very framework of existence.

The matter touched upon in the present chapter includes within itself all that has been previously set forth. It does so upon both its negative and positive sides. The community of causes and consequences in which we, together with those not born, are enmeshed is the widest and deepest symbol of the mysterious totality of being the imagination calls the universe. It is the embodiment for sense and thought of that encompassing scope of existence the intellect cannot grasp. It is the matrix within which our ideal aspirations are born and bred. It is the source of the values that the moral imagination projects as directive criteria and as shaping purposes.

The continuing life of this comprehensive community of beings includes all the significant achievement of men in science and art and all the kindly offices of intercourse and communication. It holds within its content all the material that gives verifiable intellectual support to our ideal faiths. A "creed" founded on this material will change and grow, but it cannot be shaken. What it surrenders it gives up gladly because of new light and not as a reluctant concession. What it adds, it adds because new knowledge gives further insight into the conditions that bear upon the formation and execution of our life purposes. A one-sided psychology, a reflex of eighteenth-century "individualism," treated knowledge as an accomplishment of a lonely mind.

We should now be aware that it is a product of the cooperative and communicative operations of human beings living together. Its communal origin is an indication of its rightful communal use. The unification of what is known at any given time, not upon an impossible eternal and abstract basis but upon that of its bearing upon the unification of human desire and purpose, furnishes a sufficient creed for human acceptance, one that would provide a religious release and reinforcement of knowledge.

"Agnosticism" is a shadow cast by the eclipse of the supernatural. Of course, acknowledgment that we do not know what we do not know is a necessity of all intellectual integrity. But generalized agnosticism is only a halfway elimination of the supernatural. Its meaning departs when the intellectual outlook is directed wholly to the natural world. When it is so directed, there are plenty of particular matters regarding which we must say we do not know; we only inquire and form hypotheses which future inquiry will confirm or reject. But such doubts are an incident of faith in the method of intelligence. They are signs of faith, not of a pale and impotent skepticism. We doubt in order that we may find out, not because some inaccessible supernatural lurks behind whatever *we* can know. The substantial background of practical faith in ideal ends is positive and outreaching.

The considerations put forward in the present chapter may be summed up in what they imply. The ideal ends to which we attach our faith are not shadowy and wavering. They assume concrete form in our understanding of our relations to one another and the values contained in these relations. We who now live are parts of a humanity that extends into the remote past, a humanity that has interacted with nature. The things in civilization we most prize are not of ourselves. They exist by grace of the doings and sufferings of the continuous human community in which we are a link. Ours is the responsibility of conserving, transmitting, rectifying and expanding the heritage of values we have received that those who come after us may receive it more solid and secure, more widely accessible and more generously shared than we have received it. Here are all the elements for a religious faith that shall not be confined to sect, class, or race. Such a faith has always been implicitly the common faith of mankind. It remains to make it explicit and militant.

VIII ⬥ Democracy as a Moral Ideal

I. CREATIVE DEMOCRACY—THE TASK BEFORE US*

UNDER present circumstances I cannot hope to conceal the fact that I have managed to exist eighty years. Mention of the fact may suggest to you a more important fact—namely, that events of the utmost significance for the destiny of this country have taken place during the past four-fifths of a century, a period that covers more than half of its national life in its present form. For obvious reasons I shall not attempt a summary of even the more important of these events. I refer here to them because of their bearing upon the issue to which this country committed itself when the nation took shape—the creation of democracy, an issue which is now as urgent as it was a hundred and fifty years ago when the most experienced and wisest men of the country gathered to take stock of conditions and to create the political structure of a self-governing society.

For the net import of the changes that have taken place in these later years is that ways of life and institutions which were once the natural, almost the inevitable, product of fortunate conditions have now to be won by conscious and resolute effort. Not all the country was in a pioneer state eighty years ago. But it was still, save perhaps in a few

* An address delivered by Dewey at a celebration of his eightieth birthday. Printed in *The Philosopher of the Common Man*. New York: G. P. Putnam's Sons, 1940. By permission of G. P. Putnam's Sons.

large cities, so close to the pioneer stage of American life that the traditions of the pioneer, indeed of the frontier, were active agencies in forming the thoughts and shaping the beliefs of those who were born into its life. In imagination at least the country was still having an open frontier, one of unused and unappropriated resources. It was a country of physical opportunity and invitation. Even so, there was more than a marvelous conjuction of physical circumstances involved in bringing to birth this new nation. There was in existence a group of men who were capable of readapting older institutions and ideas to meet the situations provided by new physical conditions—a group of men extraordinarily gifted in political inventiveness.

At the present time, the frontier is moral, not physical. The period of free lands that seemed boundless in extent has vanished. Unused resources are now human rather than material. They are found in the waste of grown men and women who are without the chance to work, and in the young men and young women who find doors closed where there was once opportunity. The crisis that one hundred and fifty years ago called out social and political inventiveness is with us in a form which puts a heavier demand on human creativeness.

At all events this is what I mean when I say that we now have to re-create by deliberate and determined endeavor the kind of democracy which in its origin one hundred and fifty years ago was largely the product of a fortunate combination of men and circumstances. We have lived for a long time upon the heritage that came to us from the happy conjunction of men and events in an earlier day. The present state of the world is more than a reminder that we have now to put forth every energy of our own to prove worthy of our heritage. It is a challenge to do for the critical and complex conditions of today what the men of an earlier day did for simpler conditions.

If I emphasize that the task can be accomplished only by

inventive effort and creative activity, it is in part because the
depth of the present crisis is due in considerable part to the
fact that for a long period we acted as if our democracy
were something that perpetuated itself automatically; as if
our ancestors had succeeded in setting up a machine that
solved the problem of perpetual motion in politics. We acted
as if democracy were something that took place mainly at
Washington and Albany—or some other state capital—
under the impetus of what happened when men and women
went to the polls once a year or so—which is a somewhat
extreme way of saying that we have had the habit of thinking of democracy as a kind of political mechanism that will
work as long as citizens were reasonably faithful in performing political duties.

Of late years we have heard more and more frequently
that this is not enough; that democracy is a way of life. This
saying gets down to hard pan. But I am not sure that something of the externality of the old idea does not cling to the
new and better statement. In any case we can escape from
this external way of thinking only as we realize in thought
and act that democracy is a *personal* way of individual life;
that it signifies the possession and continual use of certain
attitudes, forming personal character and determining desire and purpose in all the relations of life. Instead of thinking of our own dispositions and habits as accommodated to
certain institutions we have to learn to think of the latter
as expressions, projections, and extensions of habitually
dominant personal attitudes.

Democracy as a personal, an individual, way of life involves nothing fundamentally new. But when applied it puts
a new practical meaning in old ideas. Put into effect it signifies that powerful present enemies of democracy can be
successfully met only by the creation of personal attitudes
in individual human beings; that we must get over our tendency to think that its defense can be found in any external
means whatever, whether military or civil, if they are sepa-

rated from individual attitudes so deep-seated as to constitute personal character.

Democracy is a way of life controlled by a working faith in the possibilities of human nature. Belief in the Common Man is a familiar article in the democratic creed. That belief is without basis and significance save as it means faith in the potentialities of human nature as that nature is exhibited in every human being irrespective of race, color, sex, birth, and family, of material or cultural wealth. This faith may be enacted in statutes, but it is only on paper unless it is put in force in the attitudes which human beings display to one another in all the incidents and relations of daily life. To denounce Naziism for intolerance, cruelty and stimulation of hatred amounts to fostering insincerity if, in our personal relations to other persons, if, in our daily walk and conversation, we are moved by racial, color, or other class prejudice; indeed, by anything save a generous belief in their possibilities as human beings, a belief which brings with it the need for providing conditions which will enable these capacities to reach fulfillment. The democratic faith in human equality is belief that every human being, independent of the quantity or range of his personal endowment, has the right to equal opportunity with every other person for development of whatever gifts he has. The democratic belief in the principle of leadership is a generous one. It is universal. It is belief in the capacity of every person to lead his own life free from coercion and imposition by others provided right conditions are supplied.

Democracy is a way of personal life controlled not merely by faith in human nature in general but by faith in the capacity of human beings for intelligent judgement and action if proper conditions are furnished. I have been accused more than once and from opposed quarters of an undue, a utopian, faith in the possibilities of intelligence and in education as a correlate of intelligence. At all events, I did not invent this faith. I acquired it from my surroundings as far as those surroundings were animated by the democratic spirit. For what is the faith of democracy in the rôle of consultation, of conference, of persuasion, of discussion, in formation of public opinion, which in the long run is self-corrective, except faith in the capacity of the intelligence of the common man to respond with common sense to the free play of facts and ideas which are secured by effective guarantees of free inquiry, free assembly, and free communication? I am willing to leave to upholders of totalitarian states of the right and the left the view that faith in the capacities of intelligence is utopian. For the faith is so deeply embedded in the methods which are intrinsic to democracy that when a professed democrat denies the faith he convicts himself of treachery to his profession.

When I think of the conditions under which men and women are living in many foreign countries today, fear of espionage, with danger hanging over the meeting of friends for friendly conversation in private gatherings, I am inclined to believe that the heart and final guarantee of democracy is in free gatherings of neighbors on the street corner to discuss back and forth what is read in uncensored news of the day, and in gatherings of friends in the living rooms of houses and apartments to converse freely with one another. Intolerance, abuse, calling of names because of differences of opinion about religion or politics or business, as well as because of differences of race, color, wealth, or degree of culture, are treason to the democratic way of life. For everything which bars freedom and fullness of communication sets up barriers that divide human beings into sets and cliques, into antagonistic sects and factions, and thereby undermines the democratic way of life. Merely legal guarantees of the civil liberties of free belief, free expression, free assembly are of little avail if in daily life freedom of communication, the give and take of ideas, facts, experiences, is choked by mutual suspicion, by abuse, by fear and hatred.

These things destroy the essential condition of the democratic way of living even more effectually than open coercion, which—as the example of totalitarian states proves—is effective only when it succeeds in breeding hate, suspicion, intolerance in the minds of individual human beings.

Finally, given the two conditions just mentioned, democracy as a way of life is controlled by personal faith in personal day-by-day working together with others. Democracy is the belief that even when needs and ends or consequences are different for each individual, the habit of amicable cooperation—which may include, as in sport, rivalry and competition—is itself a priceless addition to life. To take as far as possible every conflict which arises—and they are bound to arise—out of the atmosphere and medium of force, of violence as a means of settlement, into that of discussion and of intelligence, is to treat those who disagree—even profoundly—with us as those from whom we may learn, and in so far, as friends. A genuinely democratic faith in peace in the possibility of conducting disputes, controversies, and conflicts as cooperative undertakings in which both parties learn by giving the other a chance to express itself, instead of having one party conquer by forceful suppression of the other—a suppression which is none the less one of violence when it takes place by psychological means of ridicule, abuse, intimidation, instead of by overt imprisonment or in concentration camps. To cooperate by giving differences a chance to show themselves because of the belief that the expression of difference is not only a right of the other persons but is a means of enriching one's own life-experience, is inherent in the democratic personal way of life.

If what has been said is charged with being a set of moral commonplaces, my only reply is that that is just the point in saying them. For to get rid of the habit of thinking of democracy as something institutional and external and to acquire the habit of treating it as a way of personal life is to realize that democracy is a moral ideal and so far as it becomes a fact is a moral fact. It is to realize that democracy is a reality only as it is indeed a commonplace of living.

Since my adult years have been given to the pursuit of philosophy, I shall ask your indulgence if in concluding I state briefly the democratic faith in the formal terms of a philosophic position. So stated, democracy is belief in the ability of human experience to generate the aims and methods by which further experience will grow in ordered richness. Every other form of moral and social faith rests upon the idea that experience must be subjected at some point or other to some form of external control; to some "authority" alleged to exist outside the process of experience. Democracy is the faith that the process of experience is more important than any special result attained, so that special results achieved are of ultimate value only as they are used to enrich and order the ongoing process. Since the process of experience is capable of being educative, faith in democracy is all one with faith in experience and education. All ends and values that are cut off from the ongoing process become arrests, fixations. They strive to fixate what has been gained instead of using it to open the road and point the way to new and better experiences.

If one asks what is meant by experience in this connection, my reply is that it is that free interaction of individual human beings with surrounding conditions, especially the human surroundings, which develops and satisfies need and desire by increasing knowledge of things as they are. Knowledge of conditions as they are is the only solid ground for communication and sharing; all other communication means the subjection of some persons to the personal opinion of other persons. Need and desire—out of which grow purpose and direction of energy—go beyond what exists, and hence beyond knowledge, beyond science. They continually open the way into the unexplored and unattained future.

Democracy as compared with other ways of life is the sole way of living which believes wholeheartedly in the process of experience as end and as means; as that which is capable of generating the science which is the sole dependable authority for the direction of further experience and which releases emotions, needs, and desires so as to call into being the things that have not existed in the past. For every way of life that fails in its democracy limits the contacts, the exchanges, the communications, the interactions by which experience is steadied while it is also enlarged and enriched. The task of this release and enrichment is one that has to be carried on day by day. Since it is one that can have no end till experience itself comes to an end, the task of democracy is forever that of creation of a freer and more humane experience in which all share and to which all contribute.

INDEX

INDEX

A

Adams, John, 240
Aims in education, 159
Aristotle, 45, 48, 56, 248
Arts, and democracy, 243-244

B

Bacon, Francis, 57, 65
Barnes, Albert C., 25
Bentham, Jeremy, 72
Bergson, Henri, 32
Blanshard, Brand, 25
Blanshard, Paul, 25

C

Christianity, 304
Civil war, the, 294
Common man, democratic belief in, 311
Common School system, 271
Comte, Auguste, 42
Condillac, Etienne, Bonnot de, 57
Culture, 160; and problem of freedom and democracy, 241-255; attempts to find one determinate factor of, 249, 269; as the determining influence

Culture—*cont.*
on human nature, 251-255; and human nature, 256-277; *Kultur*, 261; the direction of inquiry into, 263-264; scientific information grasped prescientifically, 271-277

D

Darwin, Charles, 21, 250
Declaration of Independence, 240, 278
Deism, 279
Democracy, 87; and America, 277-296; as a way of life, 308-311; as a moral ideal, 308-315; philosophic statement of the democratic faith, 314. *See also* Culture, Education
Dewey, Alice Freeman, 25
Dewey, John, life, 25; influence of, 22-28; visit to China, Japan, Russia, 26; theory of thinking as an instrumental activity, 28-31; leading ideas of: Inquiry, Experience, Education, 30-31; theory of Experience and Nature, 30-31; view of Change, 32; and liberalism, 33-34

319